THE CONCEPT OF COHERENCE IN ART

KARL ASCHENBRENNER

University of California, Berkeley

THE CONCEPT OF COHERENCE IN ART

D. REIDEL PUBLISHING COMPANY

A MEMBER OF THE KLUWER  ACADEMIC PUBLISHERS GROUP

DORDRECHT / BOSTON / LANCASTER / TOKYO

Library of Congress Cataloging-in-Publication Data

Aschenbrenner, Karl.
    The concept of coherence in art.

    Bibliography: p.
    Includes index.
    1. Form (Aesthetics) I. Title.
BH301.F6A83   1985   700′.1   85–19610
ISBN 90-277-1959-4

Published by D. Reidel Publishing Company,
P.O. Box 17, 3300 AA Dordrecht, Holland.

Sold and distributed in the U.S.A. and Canada
by Kluwer Academic Publishers,
190 Old Derby Street, Hingham, MA 02043, U.S.A.

In all other countries, sold and distributed
by Kluwer Academic Publishers Group,
P.O. Box 322, 3300 AH Dordrecht, Holland.

Printed The Netherlands

TABLE OF CONTENTS

PREFACE   ix

ACKNOWLEDGMENTS   xi

PART ONE: THE CONCEPT OF COHERENCE

Preamble   3
1. Introduction   5
2. The Aesthetic Complex and its Elements   9
3. The Ordination of Elements (1: First Relation of Elements)   17
4. The Magnitude of Figures (2)   21
5. Elements and Intervals (3)   27
6. Dimensions of Elements: Their Comparative Relations (4)   35
7. Contextual Relations of Elements (5)   45
8. Tendentive Powers of Elements (6)   51
9. Expression: "Instant Coherence" (7)   64
10. How is Art Possible? (1)   73
11. How is Art Possible? (2)   82
12. The Compositional Order of Art   89
13. Feelings, Forces and Form   103

PART TWO: THE INTERPRETATION OF FORM

Preamble   111
14. Coherence in Narrative Art   112
    (1) Robert Browning, 'The Confessional'   112
    (2) Thomas Hardy, 'The Sacrilege'   115
    (3) James Dickey, 'The Shark's Parlor'   123
15. Coherence in Visual Art   128
    (1) Elgin Marbles, 'Horse of Selene'   132
    (2) 'Temple of Neptune', Paestum   132
    (3) Donatello, 'Gattamelata'   133
    (4) Map of Paris   133
    (5) Twin Rocks, Oregon   133
    (6) Raphael, 'The School of Athens'   134
    (7) Velazquez, 'Infanta Margareta Theresa'   134
    (8) Giorgione, 'Adoration of the Shepherds'   135
    (9) Perugino, 'The Crucifixion'   135
    (10) Albrecht Dürer, 'The Apostles'   136
    (11) Marc Haeger, 'Stilt Race'   136

(12) Marcel Duchamp, 'Nude Descending a Staircase, No. 2'
(13) Willem de Kooning, Lithograph
(14) Jackson Pollock
16. Coherence in Music
16.1 Song
(1) The Ordinary of the Mass
(2) 'Dies Irae'
(3) Schubert: 'Der Leiermann', *Die Winterreise*
(4) Hugo Wolf: 'Zur Ruh', zur Ruh'!' *Lieder nach verschiedenen Dichtern*, Nr. 18.
16.2 Instrumental Music
(1) J. S. Bach: Suite 1 in G Major for Violoncello Solo, Courante
(2) Beethoven: Sonata for Piano in D Major, Op. 28, First Movement
(3) Beethoven: Piano Concerto in E♭ Major, Op. 73 (The "Emperor"), Third Movement
(4) Schoenberg: Klavierstück, Op. 33a
17. Conclusion: The Uses of Form

APPENDIX

BIBLIOGRAPHY

INDEX

for our children
Lisbeth, Peter, John

PREFACE

This book concerns a single topic, coherence in the several arts, which is vague to begin with, but becomes progressively more precise as we proceed. While the book is not a formalist theory of art it aims to take steps toward clearing up the concept of form, which is of central interest in art, either by its observance or by deliberate defiance.

While our interest is thus in one concept, it is as a matter of fact complex and covers some seven subordinate topics. Each of these important subjects is covered in separate chapters: the *number* of principal parts of artworks, their *extent*, size or magnitude, the *intervallic relation* between them, and their *dimensional, contextual, tendentive*, and *connotational* relations, all of which will be explained as we proceed. There are ample analyses or critiques devoted to particular artworks which appear in Part Two.

While the book keeps to a fairly narrow range of subjects, breadth is there too, and the implication for all the arts is manifest. The examples cover mainly music, but there is a broad selection of architecture, sculpture, painting, both abstract and figural, and a brief selection from the field of narrative poetic art. Many more types of the arts had to be excluded to make the book of manageable size.

The origin of the book goes back some years to the late fifties. With the award of a Guggenheim Fellowship I set to work on it in earnest, but thereafter could work on it only intermittently because of many professorial commitments and other duties. Because of the research on three works devoted to the language of characterization, and one on Kant (which since then have been published), I was able to revise and complete it only recently. I am grateful that the book has at length been published. It served as one of the texts for courses in aesthetics given previous to my retirement.

I wish especially to express my thanks to the Guggenheim Foundation for the award of the Fellowship. I wish also to thank John Emerson of the University of California, Berkeley, Music Department for expert and friendly advice in preparing part of the text of 'The Ordinary of the Mass' and the 'Dies Irae'; Soli Pierce, who did the fine drawings for the figures appearing on pp. 22 and 23; and John Aschenbrenner, who produced the analytical diagrams for the Schoenberg *Klavierstück*, op. 33a.

Berkeley 1985

ACKNOWLEDGMENTS

Die Winterreise, 'Der Leiermann', by Franz Schubert edited by Sergius Kagen, used by permission of International Music Company.

Karlheinz Stockhausen, *Klavierstücke* I–IV, number III, © 1954 by Universal Edition (London) Ltd., London. Copyright renewed. All rights reserved. Used by permission of European American Music Distributors Corporation, sole U.S. agent for Universal Edition.

'The Shark's Parlor,' copyright © 1965 by James Dickey. Reprinted from *Poems* 1957–1967 by permission of Wesleyan University Press. This poem first appeared in *The New Yorker*.

Les perles ne font pas le collier:
c'est le fil.

— Flaubert

PART ONE

THE CONCEPT OF COHERENCE

PREAMBLE

Coherence, unity, form and their negations are notions that are commonly used in an evaluative manner when they appear in talk about artworks. They deserve study for the simple reason that although they are sooner or later on everyone's tongue, it is by no means obvious what they mean to say. If we can throw some light on these ideas we may also along the way learn why they are used to separate the aesthetically worthwhile from the worthless. We shall see that artistic procedures which make for coherence, where this can be specified in some definite manner, are important because they help maintain the very existence of objects as artworks.

I do not maintain that coherence alone is what is valuable in art nor have I surveyed the whole field to find out what is, and whether there are other criteria besides this. The aim is analytical, hoping to develop a useful exposition of *one* of the key notions in aesthetic discourse. The result is not really a comprehensive "aesthetic theory," whatever use that sort of thing may be to anyone. And since *the* value of artworks has not been identified with coherence or anything else, it will be a mistake, however tempting, to think of what follows as a "formalist theory of aesthetics," though it may contribute something to our understanding of aesthetic form.

The question about form or coherence is not so much about whether it has some relevance to the value of artworks but rather how much, and what in fact it is in each art. It is not difficult to turn up apparently successful works which violate the demands of coherence which we are likely to make of such things; we may also find coherent works which seem failures on the whole. But the importance of coherence is shown by the fact that works of the first sort succeed despite their want of coherence, not because of it, while those of the second are at least no worse for their inner order and may owe it a saving grace. It think Professor Meyer has stated the question about coherence very concisely:

A good piece of music must have consistency of style: That is, it must employ a unified system of expectations and probabilities; it should possess clarity of basic intent; it should have variety, unity, and all the other categories which are so easy to find after the fact. But these are, I think, only necessary causes. And while they may enable us to distinguish a good or satisfactory piece from a downright bad one, they will not help us very much when we try to discriminate between a pretty good work and a very good one, let alone distinguish the charactetistics of greatness.[1]

Professor Meyer is conceding that coherence (or his equivalent for this) is in general a "better-making" and want of coherence a "worse-making" property in artworks. But one can go further than this if one can show that form is not only better-making but also life-giving. This we hope to demonstrate here. But nothing is so apt to be interpreted in too narrow a fashion as the notion of form in the arts: perhaps a broader view of it than Professor Meyer is according it here will take us a large step closer toward comprehending greatness by revealing it to be not only a better-making but indeed a life-giving property.

Part One proceeds in the conviction that the notions of form, unity, or coherence are essentially one in all the arts and I am happy to controvert the claims of those who find so many differences among the arts that they apologize for our rash use of one term for the varied series of enterprises that go by the name 'art.' Lofty charges of "Platonizing" against those who take the term 'art' seriously are not worth refuting. But I refrain from going into an extended discussion of this that would only involve us in the familiar polemic of philosophers that does not really advance the matter in hand.

I shall have to divide attention unevenly among the arts. Visual art is given comparatively brief attention, yet in a sense our account of coherence is mainly oriented in that direction. Since I am reluctant to discuss artworks that are not accessible to the reader under the same cover I have confined my attention to literary works to brief narrative poems. Even the quotation of these works cannot of course insure their accessibility to the reader unless he is properly prepared. Music occupies the most prominent place in the exposition particularly because of the manner in which it illustrates the tendentive power of aesthetic elements, as will be explained. Since it is impossible to expound any aspect to music without the use of the musician's technical vocabulary, I have not hesitated to use it. I have, however, made an effort to help readers who are unfamiliar with it. For some, the exposition for one or another of the arts will appear too elementary, while it will inevitably baffle others. There is virtually no remedy for this. What one really needs to know to expound or to understand a subject such as this transcends almost every individual's capacity (certainly the present writer's), since one ought to be at once creator, connoisseur and critic; artist, musician and poet; and philosopher, psychologist, and art historian to boot. One ought to welcome any hand that can do any part of it better than he can himself.

NOTE

[1] Leonard B. Meyer: 1959, 'Some Remarks on Value and Greatness in Music', *Journal of Aesthetics and Art Criticism* 17, 487.

CHAPTER 1

INTRODUCTION

Clamor for the overturn of the prevailing order is scarcely anything new. What characterizes our own turmoil is the loud, frequent, and insistent demand from some quarters *for* disorder, or for unorder for its own sake, and not just for a new order to replace the old. But one could scarcely heed or comply with such a demand, even if one were minded to do so, unless one first determined what was being asked for and whether it was actually, even logically, possible. 'Unorder' may be but a dramatic way of saying something quite other than what it appears to say, an overreaction to an old order that may only be budged by opposing it with what is ostensibly its full antithesis. In present circumstances this may be the most plausible interpretation of what we may, in brief, call the demand for *antiform*.

But this is only one shape which the demand may have. Since it wishes to divert the target of interest, that is to say art, into a new direction with extremist measures, a kind of political purpose may possibly be served by this. So far as this is what is afoot, one should evaluate the result by political criteria, but one must also ask whether indeed larger, moral interests are well served by such a nonuse, if not misuse, of art and the artist – even if it is the artist who is using himself in this manner.

Assuming that some and perhaps even most crusaders for antiform are really aesthetically motivated, we may find that extremism is often undertaken to advance to new forms, and perhaps for good reasons. Form is always in danger of being identified with some particular "form of form," that is, with particular manifestations and exemplifications of form, perhaps of the present or the immediately past or passing age. Such an identification is a pathetic error when it is committed by the established order, but it is tragic when it is affirmed by the ascendant generation. What the latter needs to learn is that form is nobody's property: there are many, even infinite forms of form. And since there are, new generations will flounder painfully until they discover this, learn how to forgive the "fathers" for their overinclusiveness and possessiveness about form as they saw it, and learn how to work out new visions of it.

This is not to say that there is an aboriginal form of form, an *Urform*, for this is no doubt a mirage. Yet there are some fairly specifiable types of moves, gambits, stratagems, or procedures that artists can pursue in an endless variety of ways and on a limitless variety of materials. If we are determined to explore this far enough we may come to see that there are certain things that artists in any and all of the arts can and indeed must do because it is the materials themselves in perception and imagination, in space and in time, that dictate it – not the hated "father" or Establishment. This is what we are here seeking to uncover, pursuing the matter so far as possible from the artist's standpoint, and asking ourselves, as he does, first, what is the available material and its foreseeable, and perhaps even unforeseeable, properties, and second, what can be done with it.

The first of these is modified by the second. What someone as an artist does with the material will reveal what it has in it to reveal, or some selection of it at least. Equally obviously the latter is determined by the former. These two and their interworkings are the subject matters we are concerned with here and have deliberately treated on a level of very considerable generality. The reason, even though this commonly escapes the practical man and often the practicing artist, is that the thorough comprehension of generality, here as everywhere, yields power, a maxim that Aristotle's *Organon* first taught the ancient world, with some success, and Bacon's *New Organon* the modern world, with fantastic results. Our purpose is to observe the unity of art by discriminating the common method that underlies the arts. But we must learn this from the arts themselves. Only an artist in the end knows what the materials of art are and what they can do.

The materials of art have dimensions and other intrinsic powers and properties that the artist appropriates to his purposes. In an important, essentially metaphysical sense they are beyond his creativity: he can only choose to reveal or to conceal them in the materials. No artist, nor any other finite being, can create a quality, except, of course, in a familiar "manner of speaking." The first part, but not necessarily, of course, the earliest part, of an artist's education is to learn what he is working with, in a spirit of creative receptivity.[1] Only if he knows this, but again not necessarily after he knows it, is he in a position to exercise intelligent choice in the manner. There two determinants, the material and formal causes of the process, so to speak, we may call the *intrinsic order* and the *compositional order*.

The *intrinsic order* derives from the fact that the artist's usable material is, in degree, a matter of parts or elements in relation to one another. Necessarily the elements *number* so many (no matter how many) and are of a certain *magnitude* (no matter of what magnitude). Each of these already helps to determine the perceptibility or imaginability of the materials and therefore their aesthetic potentiality. But this is obviously even more strictly affected by the intrinsic *dimensions* of the elements, for example, the physical dimensions of tones (or clangs or noises) and colors. Even this is not all, for the elements the artist works with vary in the degree to which they are affected causally or *contextually* in one another's presence and the manner in which they move and *tend toward* or repel one another. The elements may further gain other properties simply by being part of a world of meaningful and useful things, properties which are *connotational* and expressive. The latter are in degree dispensable, but artists have more often than not used and exploited them rather than dispensed with them. They lie on the border between the intrinsic and extrinsic properties of elements.

The artist invariably gains a knowledge of all of this by doing something with the material, that is to say, by resort to the *compositional order*. He will only be able to learn what red does to blue (or with it) by painting a red and a blue of determined size, shape and shade. "What it does" is essential and intrinsic to red and to blue and to red-blue. What then has he, not it, done? The answer is he has taken those steps that are necessary to reveal relationships among the elements. Assuming that what he produces is of a finite size in time or space or in some manner in the imagination, his creative activity, as against creative receptivity, consists in including, excluding and ordering elements. All of *his* efforts are comprised under these.

In the compositional order, a limited variety of artistic procedures can be distinguished: first, the *closure*, isolation or centralization of the work and its more prominent figuring; second, the *repetition* and recurrence of elements within it; and third, the *development* along numerous lines of continuity toward culminating points or areas in it. These are sometimes employed separately, sometimes in concert with one another, and they apply to and can have an unobscure interpretation for every art.

Having employed one or more of these procedures, the artist imparts the conviction that the elements he has chosen *belong* in it and that they artistically *justify* the place they occupy relative to one another. Even if he resorts to what are called aleatory, or chance, techniques, he conveys the same message. Our question now is, what is meant by 'belonging' and 'justifying' in these contexts? It is in order to try to reduce some of the mystery of this that we have undertaken to explore *coherence*, for this term means for us *the unique way in which elements belong to the artwork and justify their place in it*. We shall not, in the end, have reduced this mystery to zero if this means to give an exhaustive "discursive explanation," for if this could be done the artwork would itself be virtually superfluous. "Wenn man Musik mit Worten schildern könnte würde ich keine Noten mehr setzen," said Felix Mendelssohn, an educated man, not only in music, and handy with words. We can, however, hope to remove some obstacles so that we can have a better vision of what we are seeing. Obviously, only to glance at a painting is not to see it. But what *is* there to be seen? What *is* there to be heard in music? An effort to understand what an artist *does* with just these means is our only hope for enlightening ourselves on this matter.

'Coherence,' then, is here not confined to what is neat, orderly, symmetrical, smooth, and balanced although these terms do readily characterize the coherent in many instances. An art or a scheme of art criticism that looked *only* for consonance, mellifluousness, sweetness and light would not be fit even for infants. Art is life. It is the sublime as well as the beautiful, difficult as well as easy beauty.

If we must guard against interpreting the notions of *form, coherence* or *justifying* too narrowly, in terms of what is generally praised as "harmony" and "balance," we must equally avoid interpreting them so broadly that everything whatever is "formful" simply because it has parts in relation to one another. Any scribble will be altogether orderly in the sense that we can find one or more algebraic functions to describe it with some accuracy, if we can find any reason for taking the time and trouble. Similarly, a singularly useless notion of artistic form arises if we identify it with merely having elements in relation to one another. But our problem is not merely one of finding some middle ground between overinclusive and overlimited notions of form. Rather, we are trying to get at uniquely artistic reasons for ordering and excluding elements. Symmetry or accommodation, we shall find, is one of these, but so is conflict.

If we now ask what end these and other orderings may serve, what fundamental satisfaction they may afford, the answer we suggest is the perfection of our modes of apprehension themselves, this is to say, the perfection of vision itself, audition itself. It is to this end that the procedures of the compositional order are directed. Vision is not a condition for art so much as art is the necessary condition for vision. Vision, but vision indeed, is for the visual artist its own reward. It is in this direction that we must look for reasons in art.

SUMMARY

The call for unform or antiform, if it is aesthetically motivated, is likely to be an extremist measure that hopes to propel art into a new direction, or, if it is not, tends to employ or misemploy art for nonaesthetic ends. We need first to understand clearly what is being promoted as an alternative to form or order.

When form is under attack, it is often merely the form which form has assumed for a past or passing generation. But form is an intrinsic, indefeasible aspect of all art: either the sum of the relations which can be revealed in the materials of art, or the sum of those into which they can be placed by the thought and effort of the artist.

The first of these comprises the *intrinsic order* of the materials of art, exemplified especially in the dimensions of the elements of artworks, and their contextual and tendentive properties, as explained below.

The second comprises the *compositional order*, that is, the procedures of composition open to the artist.

In his finished work, the artist conveys the thought that what he has placed in the artwork belongs in it, that the place each element occupies is justified in relation to the others – 'belonging' and 'justifying' having here a unique sense appropriate to art, and not, for example, the sense appropriate to morals or scientific explanation. This constitutes the essence of the notion of coherence in art that is here to be discussed.

Our exposition of coherence is primarily directed toward the understanding of this idea rather than the development of a standard of aesthetic evaluation. Neither the compositional devices that lead to coherence nor coherence itself are to be thought of as ultimate ends in art. They serve to advance the aesthetic goal of the realization, that is, the perfect seeability and hearability of the object, an object so constituted that it facilitates a perfect perception of itself.

NOTE

[1] Karl Aschenbrenner: 1963, 'Creative Receptivity', *Journal of Aesthetics and Art Criticism* **22**, 149–151.

CHAPTER 2

THE AESTHETIC COMPLEX AND ITS ELEMENTS

We may draw attention to the field we are examining by saying that that which stirs aesthetic interest or response is found in the *phenomenal* domain of the senses and the imagination. It is sometimes said that there are also other objects of aesthetic interest, for example, pure objects of thought, such as numbers and theories about them. But the aesthetic attributes these have are conceivable only in relation to a perceptible symbolism, a phenomenal or imaginal vehicle to present the thought. The aesthetic appeal of such a vehicle is severely limited since considerations of its truth override all aesthetic considerations. It can scarcely sustain even the mathematician's aesthetic interest if he knows that the thought it conveys is logically false or confused. But a map of the fictitious lost continent of Atlantis may retain its aesthetic value, if it has any, forever.

We must first take note of what appears to be an altogether obvious fact about such objects, namely, that they are constituted of *parts*. To perceive any datum at all, in vision, audition, or the other senses, is to be able to discern in some measure, its parts, its inner differences, its extent. The datum stretches from here to there, or it begins and ends in time, and it has an intervening career, however short. The smaller its extent, or the less complex it is, the more its nature must be defined in terms of its difference from what lies outside it. The more extended and complex, the more its character is to be defined by its inner differences.

Sometimes at least, the parts of such objects are discerned in the same act of awareness by which the object as a whole is discerned. That is to say, the whole object counts as one object. Many ancient philosophical puzzles turn about matters such as these, how anything can be one and yet many. Likewise, the most elementary questions about perception involve this notion. With it we are immediately in the midst of our subject.

That some given perceived thing is one phenomenon is of great importance for art and the theory of art. Since the world of phenomena appears to run on without limit and is scarcely to be comprised in one glimpse or grasp, what we count as one phenomenon or object of aesthetic attention must first of all be delimited or circumscribed. We speak of this picture on the wall as one thing and then proceed to the wall as another single phenomenon and to its parts in turn. Suppose that we wish to consider where to hang a picture: so far from this wall, so far from the other, in relation to other things which occupy space in the room or on or along the wall. Of course, there is variation between persons in their opinion as to where the picture ought to be placed. We need to observe of this only that we have to do with parts in a whole phenomenon and that we demand that the phenomenon have some kind of internal coherence. We do not commonly treat the-picture-and-the-window as one thing and move that peculiar complex about the wall, although with sufficient labor we could so so. But we are always concerned with parts in variable relation to one another. These we shall call *elements*. A picture and the rest of the wall, the area of the wall which the picture does not occupy can be taken as two elements. The window becomes a third element, its panes of glass and what they reveal outdoors are still other elements. There are elements within elements. An element is

9

marked by a significant difference in a complex, and differences may range from least discernible differences to a limiting pair of greatest differences in the complex which we shall later analyze as *first order figure and ground.*

We must immediately differentiate the meaning of 'element' in the theory of art from its meaning in other contexts, such as geometry or chemistry for example. What we accept as an aesthetic element is not arbitrary. To illustrate, let us suppose someone lays out a grid mesh of one inch squares over a wall or a painting in the way that geographers, in effect, lay out meridians and parallels of latitude on "the earth." Such a grid might be appropriate in the transcription of a small picture onto a large wall, but it could scarcely serve any aesthetic purpose. From the artist's standpoint, only those divisions are elements that reflect perceptual differences and emphases in the complex, the several fairly distinct masses in it together with their lesser detail. Since what is regarded as an element should exhibit a pervasive and distinctive character for any given context, it will be literally irrelevant to say, "But after all your element is not elemental, for when you look closely you see that it is very complex." To withdraw it from context, to "look more closely at it" is to change the context, and possibly even to change the element or to *ex*change it for another. It would also be irrelevant to take as "more elemental" what a microscope would reveal on a canvas, unless we were concerned with the mechanical or chemical structure of the paint, for this would be merely to change the subject, to substitute a new and different object in place of the ordinary object for aesthetic consideration. In deciding what are to be taken as the elements for any given aesthetic complex we are free to set a certain limit or level of perception. The critical consideration is that the perception be indeed perceptible, that its elements truly appear.

It is not necessary to restrict the notion of element to what is internally uniform. As we have said, there may be elements within elements. All that is necessary is that the eye or ear, and not only reason, should comprehend them, that is, literally hold, hear, or see them together.

An aesthetic complex thus shows perceptible external and internal discontinuities. It begins and ends. It is white here and black there. It is a note of high pitch here, a low-pitched noise there. Without discontinuities of this sort our perceptions might eventually approach a state of "blindness." If we performed an experiment here by having a subject stare at a blank uniform expanse such as the clear northern daylight sky in summer, he would at first see it as blue. But if the experiment continued indefinitely and if the subject could see no part whatever of his body to afford contrast, or if he were just an eyeball suspended in space, would he see anything after a few days or weeks?[1] (Let the experiment exclude changes of night and day.) Perhaps no one knows the answer to this question. But it is likely that he would see nothing, nothing blue, after a period. Obviously it is difficult to imagine any such state of "blindness." For a sighted person, darkness is seen as a kind of black. To him darkness is black if anything is black. The eventual state of our experimental subject is not like this, for we believe that eventually he sees nothing. His "blindness" has become blindness in the ordinary sense, blindness of the blind. This is imaginable for sighted persons only as the kind of state all of us are in respecting infra-red and ultra-violet "light." A uniform borderless expanse of color would be literally nothing.

It should now be evident that elements define themselves only through negation. There are always borders and emergent qualities in our sense fields, and they emerge by their difference. We do not so much know what colors "really are" as know a whole galaxy of contrasts. What is this green before me? It is the color which contrasts with this white *so*, with this red *so*, etc. The pairs define themselves in just these contrasts, and the "so" is simply the experience had. I find that this green is just such and such a green when I find that it is *not different* from it. We have then, as we say, *identified* the color. There is no way in which we can say what any color is, except by reciting a whole list of items which it is not, or by saying of some item that it is not different from it. The life of the artwork is in its internal differentiations, and the sum of these contribute whatever "essence" it has. The task of the artist is the skilful exploitation of difference.

In speaking of aesthetic elements we must therefore guard against the notion that they are like atoms or standard items like tins of peas and beans at a grocer's. The artist does not construct complexes out of such standard, atomic items, the same everywhere. Nor are the analyses of Platonistic philosophers of any relevance. When we ask about the character of any element, it is idle to be referred to some transcendent essence which it is said to "resemble" or in which it "participates." The artist's definition of his elements can be nothing but contextual and is determined by a system of differentiations.

It is now apparent that elements in aesthetic contexts are very different from ordinary "objects" which are thought to retain a fixed nature that is independent of their context. Such objects undergo alteration from inner or outer causes, as when a hot object warms adjacent bodies through radiation. But there is no such thing as a detectable "aesthetic radiation:" transactions between aesthetic elements are not causal in this sense at all. They become something other than themselves (there is no alternative to this rather paradoxical form of speech) merely by being brought near enough to one another to form a context; the latter is partly a result of their own "doing" and partly of a decision we ourselves make.

But if elements alter in one another's presence we must not suppose that the "real character" of an element is its character when it is wholly withdrawn from a context. For if it is withdrawn, it has nothing in reference to which it can define itself and accordingly it simply ceases to be. Moreover, any philosophical question of the reality of the element or of its character is never of any aesthetic concern to us. Locke may be right in thinking that in some sense colors are not real. Real or not, it is colors that we are interested in. It is best to avoid altogether the metaphysician's language of appearance and reality when speaking of aesthetic elements. We do not speak accurately when we say that they are "not real" nor when we say that they or their apparent effects are "only apparent." Since, however, the phenomenon of contextual alteration is so much a part of the "behavior" of aesthetic elements it may be well to pursue this matter somewhat further.

It is an old contention of a whole tradition of thought, philosophical *idealism* being its most recent representative, that things can change their very essence by getting into different situations, by changing their relations to other things, and that a whole may be something other than the sum of its parts. While this point of view may be wholly untenable respecting "things" in the universe, nevertheless it has a perfect application, and perhaps its only significant application in perception and thus in aesthetics. For the elements of aesthetic objects such as streaks or patches of color in any ordinary object or in the detail of a painting most certainly do change their character as we separate out an element, or change its contrasting ground, or move it from one place to another. Any house painter knows this. The idealistic philosopher may be speaking in riddles. The painter is speaking of plain facts.

But we must proceed with caution since our language tends to be treacherous here. For if we say that the character of some phenomenon depends upon the context in which it is exhibited we must ask what *it* is? This leads to a kind of paradox, for when we change contexts an element must either *become* something else or be *replaced by* something else. Neither of these is a welcome result. For if we say *x* becomes non-*x* we seem to violate good sense; or if in such a situation we suppose *x* vanishes and is suddenly replaced by *y*, we must wonder why we thought there was a sameness or identity.

The source of our difficulty is that we separate out elements, e.g. colors, from objects and yet retain the style of speech appropriate only to objects. We speak of yellow as if it were an object like this pencil. We are surprised to find that something which we would never tend to believe of objects is nevertheless true of yellow. No ordinary unphilosophical person thinks that this pencil's "nature" (whatever that may be) is contextual, that the pencil becomes a different pencil when we move it about, that its nature depends upon the relations into which it enters, unless there was actually a causal change. But the yellow of the pencil is indeed contextual, depends upon its surroundings, the light upon it, the comparative extent of it, and so forth. This is surprising only because we tend to think of yellow as a kind of object.

What we have just observed of patches or shades of colors is typical of anything that can turn up as an element in an aesthetic complex. Aesthetic data are wholes whose character is more than or other than can be anticipated from the parts. As we have said, this is emphatically not true of physical quantities. It is just as little true of mathematical quantities, for these are conditioned by their components, not by their contexts. This shows how profoundly these domains differ from the aesthetic. But the difference can hardly be construed as any incompatibility between them.

Despite the dangers of language and of metaphysics, and indeed because of them, must insure the meaningfulness of certain ways of speaking which cannot be avoided. In speaking of *elements themselves* we must not think of them as outside all context, for as we have seen, to do so is to reduce them to voids altogether. Nor can we seek to define them with finality, for this would be to place them in a limitless array of contexts. The only solution is to think of the character of elements in either a *focal* or a *nonfocal* direction. In principle, we can always specify a given character decisively because we are free to proceed in either direction. This means that for certain purposes we shall speak of the character of an element as simply whatever it reveals as we make it *focal* and *remove* more and more of its contextual conditions, and for certain others, whatever it reveals as we make it *nonfocal* and *add* more and more conditions and think of it in relation to them. Fortunately, our interest will always be limited to apprehending what elements are in certain definite contexts. A picture that I here and now have before me has a limited number of determinants of each patch of color in it, namely all the other patches in it — we are obliged to "define" each patch by reference only to these, not to the limitless number of possible hues and values. In this respect, each aesthetic complex is a limited world of its own. If the complex seems worth the trouble, we wish to grasp all of it nonfocally and also each and every part of it focally. To do both, and both at once, is no doubt an ideal that is rarely reached. In all of this our aim is a certain kind of aesthetic apprehension of aesthetic wholes rather than an intellectual or cognitive "definition" of each of their elements or an exhaustive "account" of all their parts.

What now transpires in this transaction between ourselves and the aesthetic complex depends both upon it and upon ourselves. It is always easy to lose oneself in the details at the expense of the whole. No art complex with whatever devices of emphasis and contrast it has can wholly prevent this, but it is certainly one of the first duties of an artist to avoid being himself responsible for our erring and loitering in details at the expense of the whole. Details, may, as it were, get out of his control. He cannot prevent this altogether, for we all bring to the work different gifts and psychic constitutions, and different demands and readinesses; nor need he seek to prevent it wholly, for if there is no varied participation in the display of detail there can be little interest in the whole.

Different arts may seem to have different problems here. Do not the spatial arts with the compresence of all elements have the advantage over temporal ones? This is an illusion. Grasp of totalities is dependent entirely upon the gifts of the participant. It is true that although we grasp whole stretches of space, or rather, things in space, compresently, we seem always at any given instant to be hovering on only one note or chord of a temporal complex such as a musical composition. But a musical intelligence such as almost any of those named in concert programs can grasp vast aggregations of musical notes as easily as the ordinary person grasps a simple tune. He holds it together in the same way in which a grammatical sentence is held together by him who thoughtfully utters it. Mozart, the classical example, asserted that he heard in one flash a whole movement in this way. Since we are dealing with what is a matter of degree of difference of musical ability, there is no need to doubt his word: even if we have only the modest ability to hum a whole tune, or in some sense to "think" it when it "comes to mind," we have a basic synoptic ability, and we can progressively improve it with effort. Nevertheless, it must be admitted that the difficulties for extending the grasp of a multiplicity of elements for most persons are greater in "temporal arts" than in "spatial" ones. As a temporal complex progresses, the temporal conditions force us in a sense to tear every element out of its context and to discern its focal character, only to lose it altogether a moment afterward if we are not musically gifted, at least as auditors.

If we think of our response only in a momentary, non-synoptic sense, the *moment aigu* of the present, we lose sight of nearly everything that gives temporal complexes their "sense" or "meaning." We must contrast the *sentence* as it is uttered with its *meaning*. We are, to be sure, in *uttering* the sentence, "Roses are red and violets blue," temporally at some point finishing 'are' and proceeding to 'red,' and so forth, but the *thought* or *meaning* of the sentence has little to do with time, if indeed anything; we grasp it all at once. In arguing or demonstrating a point in a paragraph, the point itself is timeless, and that point, and not a momentary word that may be uttered, is the focus of the whole logical complex. Or again, we may recall that the strategy of solving a problem of geometry or logic comes to us "all at once," and such a proof may, in fact, involve a dozen or a score or more of "steps." In a "flash" we have the conviction that we "know know to" solve the problem or we "see our way to" solving it. This phenomenon can be explained only in a holistic manner, only as a Gestalt. The layman should try to use this model in trying to grasp how the composer thinks. For most of us the notion of a synthesis of temporally successive elements is more difficult and thus a more awesome feat than synthesis of spatial elements. We tend to think of the complex as a great multitude of bits and pieces. For the artist, on the other hand, *forms* emerge, and this is why he can lay hold of it. If we may speculate a bit about Mozart's "vision," perhaps not every element in it was focal in character, but rather assumed the importance he would attach to it in a performance. Even the ideal artistic intelligence, and indeed this one above all, grasps the complex as a tissue of relative emphases. But it is meaningless to speak of emphasis where every thing is equally emphasized.

We come, thus, to a new factor in the complexes we are treating. We have found that they contain more than one element and that they contain relative degrees of internal *contrast*. Now we see that they must have varying degrees of emphasis. Without inner contrast perception itself, and thus also any aesthetic complex, comes to an end. But contrast must also facilitate something more, since it is only the first step. For example, almost any woven textile of what would be called a uniform color would reveal tiny squares, the intersections of warp and woof. There is contrast here that enables us to see it at close range, but contrast in this degree is not enough to sustain perception at a more customary distance: the uniformity soon renders it virtually a perceptual void except for external contrast. But even if we enlarge the degree of contrast with a regular print discriminable at ordinary range, we still look for something "more" to happen. This expectation is only fulfilled when either some part of the complex acquires a uniqueness, an emphasis, or when the complex as a whole (for example as a garment clothing a body) gains the center of our attention. If a perceptual, but particularly an aesthetic complex, is to "survive," something must *happen*, must take place in it. This introduces a new phenomenon: *emergence and recedence*, figure and ground.

Complete equality or equipollence of emphasis among elements prevents the realization of emphasis itself. Emphasis by its nature involves something of greater potency or intensity in some one place or some few places. For this there must be an implicit *scale* which enables us to perceive the *degree* of difference: higher, lower, longer, shorter, louder, softer, together with possible combinations of these and a possible ordering of elements toward maxima or minima.

As such elements are ordered, we immediately discern the possibility of more than one emphasis, of an emphasis among emphases: the possibility of a *hierarchy* arises. If there is but one emphatic emergent, it appears within a complex with its appropriate recedent. (Multiple cases will be considered as we proceed.) This emergent is of course itself an element of a complex, but not necessarily a simple or undifferentiated element. The emergent that so emerges in whatever is the purported whole complex may be called a *first-order emergent*. Then, if we can satisfy ourselves as to the precise bounds of this emergent, we may find within it other emergents until we exhaust the perceptible detail. For every first-order emergent, there is necessarily one and only one *first-order recedent*. This element also may have further details. There can thus be subordinate emergents and recedents within either first-order emergents or first-order recedents. The first division is the most important for the aesthetic complex, and for it we can formulate a generalization to the effect that in every *individual* aesthetic complex there is at least one basic scheme of contrast which exhaustively divides the complex into two first-order elements, the first-order emergent and the first-order recedent.

We see, then, that we cannot understand emergence only in terms of contrast. Contrast is a relation between pairs of elements and this relation can prevail even if we find it impossible to say which of the constituent elements is more emphatic. In order to say that there is emergence something must incline the balance toward some element, showing it to be more intense or higher in some scalar sense. The painter learns by practice what arrangements generally further emergence: differences of size, of color or dimensions of color, of geometrical shape (for example, an isolated or centralized color mass) may all be put to use. In music the soprano voice tends to emerge because it provides the upper profile of the tonal mass; but the effect can also be gained by an increase in dyanmics of a lower voice, or by a distinctive timbre as with woodwinds or brass. In literature devices are enormously varied: not only the heroism or the notoriety of a figure will make him emphatic, but even the sheer amount of attention he demands, such as the number of lines he is given to speak in a drama. All of the dimensions of emergent figures may be employed or exploited. (Questions about the magnitude of the emergent will occupy us very particularly in Chapter 4 below.)

A question about emergents that has already arisen concerns their number: whether there can be two or more emergents, or only one. We shall in the next section consider this "unicity" of the emergent in detail. We have presented the emergent and recedent as necessary to one another and forming a kind of unity. If we insist on this complementarity it is not to lay down a norm or law to the effect that anything with more than one emergent is not a work of art but only that it may not be *one* work of art. The larger question we must now attend to is the effect in our experience of multiple artworks that pretend to some kind of unity when they are really multiple and the sources of this effect in their structure.

We have in a general way sought to present the artwork as a relatively bounded entity within a sense modality, consisting of parts or elements that are both differentiated among themselves and capable of relevance to one another. We shall first examine the effects in terms of emergence and recedence that elements can have on one another from their number and their size. We proceed to their more complex relations: their qualitative dimensions, contextual or causal powers, attractions and affinities, and yet others. We shall then be able to see virtually all the creative moves that are open to artists in the several media of the arts.

SUMMARY

Objects of aesthetic attention are phenomenal.

The internal variegation, contrast, discontinuity, and emphasis in aesthetic complexes reveal their elements. These are never abstract or intellectual and must not be confused with what are elements in other senses of the term.

As aesthetic attention changes its scope, what is treated as element will likewise differ.

An aesthetic element that was wholly undifferentiated internally and occupied the whole attention would be destructive of all aesthetic and even perceptual functioning.

The character of the elements in a complex is determined first of all by the relations of the elements to one another, particularly their qualitative contrasts.

The character of an element in itself or apart from its appearance in a context (so far as this is possible) is designated its elemental character. Its character as determined by other elements in its context is designated its formal character. Corresponding to these, an element may have one appeal purely as an element, its elemental appeal, and another in its context, its formal appeal.

Neither the focal nor the nonfocal, the element or the non-elemental, character of an element is its "real" character. The notion of a real character is largely dispensable in aesthetic contexts.

The emphasis which must prevail in some part of the total complex for an element to be realized involves not only the differentiation of elements from one another but also the emergence of some elements over others that are by comparison recedent. These emergents or figures arise to dominate recedents or grounds by some greater scalar intensity that is inherent in the elements themselves.

NOTE

1 Immanuel Kant: "No one can definitely think a negation unless he bases it upon the opposing affirmation. The person born blind cannot have the remotest conception of darkness since he has none of light. The savage has no conception of poverty since he has none of wealth, nor the ignorant of his want of knowledge since he has none of knowledge itself." *Critique of Pure Reason* (A575/B603).

CHAPTER 3

THE ORDINATION OF ELEMENTS

(1: *First Relation of Elements*)

If all art complexes are internally multiple and if, as we have shown, emergents must appear in them, there will tend to be either several coordinate-coordinate (C–C) emergents coequal in magnitude and character or a dominant emergent, a superordinate element with several more or less related subordinate elements (S–S). Any unity or coherence a complex has will depend upon the relation that elements have to one another in these orders. We shall now address ourselves to these relations. Altogether *seven* classes of them will be considered: the *number* of ordinates, their *size*, extent, magnitude, the *intervallic relation* between them, and their *dimensional, contextual, tendentive*, and *connotative* relations. Since the simplest way in which ordinates may be related to one another, any may therefore, with others, determine the unity of the aesthetic complex, is their *number*, we shall consider this first.

Aesthetic complexes in C–C order include first of all those which contain two or more emergents that are virtually identical in extent, shape and character and also others in which emergents may pretend to equality in more complex ways, for example, characters in narrative literature. It is not always easy to draw a line between C–C and S–S orders or to produce pure examples of them, especially of the former. Are the pyramids of Gizeh comprehended in vision as one or as the other? What of the spires of Gothic cathedrals, such as Cologne or Amiens?

There are first some very loose *collocations* that readily come to mind but cannot be considered very seriously as coordinates, even though they may make a pretense in this direction. Contrasting but related pictures are frequently hung in complementing relation to one another. Musical compositions are arranged to form programs. Part of the charm of such collocations is the way in which they tease us into thinking out the implicit connections or relations between the members. The movements of a sonata, on the other hand, are internally organized more toward S–S order, and of course as movements of a whole are most often deliberately composed to "fit" together some strategy of *development*. Actual repetition in music, as we shall see, is for special reasons generally not to be thought of as an example of coordinate order.

Another kind of connected order is found in the *polyptych* where explicit lines and motifs carry over from one member to another. This again tends toward S–S order: we are led from one panel to some event in another, and perhaps back again. By their nature, they are not meant to be thought apart from one another. (Cf. the Perugino Crucifixion, illustrated below, Chapter 15(9).) A superb example of virtually equally dominant figures in painting is afforded by Albrecht Dürer's Four Apostles in the Munich Pinokothek (see below, Chapter 15(10)).

We can easily construct an artificial model for a bimodal C–C complex in which two identical "monoliths" appear, for example two red disks of identical size side by side on a white or black ground. Such a complex is almost instantly felt to be not very interesting. It will be characterized as rigid, frigid, stiff, stark, and so on. The fact that few examples in art of this kind of bi-modalism are actually to be found is, of course, instructive.

Obviously, a much more "interesting" kind of bimodalism is to be found in such complexes as symmetrical west façades of many cathedrals, notably Notre Dame in Paris, or in the Zodiacal symbol of Gemini, the Twins. What is now immediately striking about this sort of bimodalism, in contrast to Dürer's Apostles, is that the architectural figures together tend to form a *unitary* figure. But it is thereby immediately lifted out of C–C order.

If we may call monolithic disks a case of rigid bimodalism or multi-modalism, another may be called *accommodating* multi-modalism, where the elements may be said to accommodate one another. In the former, the emergents being of equal power seek to dominate one another but are unable to do so, and their overwhelming "self-assertiveness" toward each other makes us virtually forget their relationship to any ground or recedent. In the second, a unitary figure develops: it is this figure which is emergent and thus dominates whatever is present as a recedent.

Rigid multi-modalism can, of course, be extended to more than two figures. Possibly as many as a limit of eight similar figures may be perceptually comprehended, according to psychologists. The power or effectiveness of monoliths diminishes with increasing numbers, beginning even with two. With three equally spaced monoliths the outer members may begins to appear peripheral, distracting or derivative, and so also perhaps with five or seven members. We cannot fail to see that the power aimed at in multi-modalism breaks down almost as soon as it is "asserted."

We must, however, confine the generalizations just made to emergent elements. Multi-modalism is more or less inherently unsuccessful when an ostentatiously emergent and dominant *figure* is repeated, although as we have seen accommodation may succeed in redeeming such a feature. There is also another way of employing multi-modalism effectively in complexes and that is to remove it to the *ground*, to a recedent position. The most prominent form of this is the repeated figure of a rhythm, for example in the accompaniment to homophonic music where a single emergent voice such as the soprano is concerted above other voices that sound a monotonous accompanying figure, or in a repetitious border or some other subordinate visual figuration as in wallpaper. All repetitious uses of coordination are immensely powerful devices of unification, so potent that their tendency toward monotony must always be reckoned with. If the C–C order is confined to something other than the prime emergent, it can occur as a *tolerable monotony* in a ground. When tolerable monotonies become highly numerous they become mere *textures*. We can proceed through plaids, for example, down to the pattern of warp and woof in textiles.

The exploitation of all these devices in practice will be gone into at some length in Chapter 12.

Although in general figural multi-modalism is aesthetically indefensible, a defense may still be offered of one particular use of equally dominant figures or emergents, namely, the *conflict* of the figures. No one could wish to exclude this as a theme for treatment. But if the artist manages to present conflict deliberately as his theme he has thereby established a kind of "community" for the "parties to the conflict" and not in a merely paradoxical sense. In conflict, protagonists exert force of nearly equivalent magnitude and direct it toward one another. Here mutually repelling forces themselves create a context in which figures emerge, and they lend them vitality. To say of two things that they are in conflict is to say that they are not in equilibrium, that they alternate at attack and defense: otherwise conflict comes to an end.

When conflict is presented in phenomenal or aesthetic contexts, both spatial and dynamic, we see now this, now that motif in an attitude of emergence. Unless a community of conflict is established among multi-modal members, or, unless there is some way in which they prove to accommodate one another, they inevitably fall apart. This outcome is increasingly likely as we add more members. And without accommodation rigidly mutli-modal complexes tend to break up into *distinct* spaceworks or timeworks in each of which a figure emerges: they dominate, but cannot dominate one another. They can be thought of as single complexes only in the sense that they are limiting cases.

There is nothing in all of this to prevent us from preferring or promoting nonaccommodating multi-modal complexes. There might be several motives for employing such devices. Artists may say that they are by no means bound to pursue harmony or order as an older aesthetic demanded. They may defy established norms even when they concede them to have been successful. As already noted above (in Chapter 1), many defiant gestures and desperate remedies are resorted to for "aesthetic-political" purposes.

Although the physical work of visual art may not be in motion, our experience of it is. Observation is a ceaseless exploration, like William James' "flights and perches." Our alternation in sensing the strength of each party to the conflict, our weighing of the effect of one on the other, goes on in time. And at any given time we are either perched on one emergent or the other or thrust out of the nest and in flight toward the other. In the same manner, one or another figure in a conflicting context is at any given time dominant within it.

But with that, we see how we are again led back from C–C to S–S order. Even if elements are in conflict they are relevant to one another. Thus, as we have said, C–C order is at best but a limiting case; for if it were to be fully in effect the components of the complex would immediately fall apart altogether.

We can now offer a first and somewhat tentative generalization about devices of coherence in artworks. (Others will come to light as we proceed.) When emergents are of perfectly equal force and stature and perhaps of literally identical shape we have coordinated forms (C–C). If these do not accommodate one another in a larger more comprehensive form they tend to come into conflict and to break into separate units. If, however, conflict *is* convincingly presented as the theme, they again develop a context of mutual relevance, possibly one of alternate emergence. If not, and if the coordinates still appear to be intended as relevant, we must not for that reason regard the complex as necessarily less valuable as art: but we must raise the question whether they constitute *one* artwork. If it divides into several, each work must now also exhibit C–C or S–S order, and so on. Thus the basic condition for coherence is that of a single prime emergent. We shall speak of this as the numerical oneness or the *unicity* of the prime emergent. This probably underlies all other order. We must now, however, identify unity itself with a single central figure which provides coherence by means of simple *closure*. As we shall see, different arts have different problems and different solutions to the problem of coherence.

These are some of the essential numerical factors that bear upon the coherence of elements regardless of the particular nature of the medium. We are, of course, presuming certain bounds or limits of relevance in which elements function. The artist commonly provides for this by allowing the picture to be placed in a frame, by asking that the tonework be heard alone and not simultaneously with other sounds. When he does so he spells out a *context of relevance*, the principle of which is that *everything beyond the picture or tonework is strictly irrelevant and* that *what is relevant is within the work and nowhere else.* There is a moderate presumption or pretense to unity in any one work, simply by its being enclosed or framed. But the artist cannot be compelled to say that all that is contained in the work is relevant, from part to part. The point is of great importance: whatever is relevant is contained in the work; but as to the converse of this, that all that is contained in the work is strictly relevant, all we can do is to point out the danger of violating it. The possible irrelevancies run from minor competitive detail at one extreme, through competing prime emergents, to utter chaos at the other, one form of which is a surfeit of prime emergents of equal force.

SUMMARY

The unity of complexes is affected by the number of their component elements and their ordinating relations (C–C or S–S) to one another: coordinate-coordinate, superordinate-subordinate.

Coordinating complexes are inherently difficult to maintain except when coordinates accommodate one another in larger unities, or when employed as part of grounds as rhythms, textures, and other "tolerable monotonies," or when dominant emergents conflict but maintain a kind of mutual "community of conflict."

Stress must be laid upon the bounds of the complex within which elements are counted as being relevant to one another as emergents and recedents. Such a context of relevance rests on the implicit principle that what is relevant is present in the complex and what is not present is irrelevant.

CHAPTER 4

THE MAGNITUDE OF FIGURES

(2: *Second Relation of Elements*)

The present section will consider the question of figural emergence and its extent largely from the standpoint of vision. The application of questions of the magnitude of figures or emergents in other media will be taken up in due course in other sections.

We have arrived very early at the conclusion that the artwork contains at least two elements (these may contain subordinate elements). These are most effective in S–S form. As such we attribute an intensive or emphatic magnitude to one of them. The more emphatic of two or more constituent elements is designated as the *emergent* (E), the less emphatic as the *recedent* (R). In speaking of emphasis in the emergent we have as yet said little of the devices which secure this property. Let us consider the size of the emergent and the effects which it determines. Purely speculatively the facts may be approximately indicated in the Graph 1:

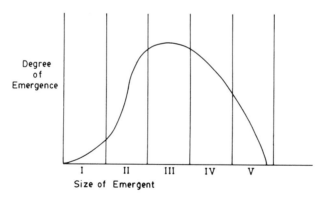

Graph 1

Here we may suppose that a very tiny emergent element on an otherwise neutral ground is unemphatic or unemergent (I). But as we increase its size its emphatic value shoots up rapidly (II). Increasing this factor soon leads (III) to a plateau where little emphasis is gained by expanding the size of the emergent. In IV diminishing returns set in, and every more rapidly. As the size of the emergent approaches that of the total area, the emphatic value of the emergent quickly decreases and the curve cuts the horizontal axis sharply (V).

It should be noted that as projected here the maximum degree of emergence is thought to occur in the region where the emergent occupies less than half of the total area. We may give the following further designations for these areas:

      I Subdominance
  II–III–IV Predominance
       V Superdominance

21

The map of Paris, reproduced in Chapter 15(4), should be classified in the superdominant region. There is so little of the recedent (the environs of the city) left in the map that it has been nearly, but not quite, overwhelmed.

In order to raise these matters above the level of mere surmise and speculation, we may create a series of simple aesthetic paradigms. Consider Figures 0–5.

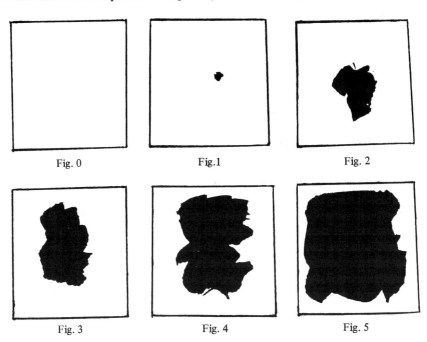

Fig. 0   Fig.1   Fig. 2

Fig. 3   Fig. 4   Fig. 5

There is no question here of a "better" figure. We note merely the degree of dominance in each. In Fig. 5 (corresponding to V above) the size of E approaches the total area of the set and there is little left to the recedent area. It is not an especially appealing figure, and its rather elephantine bulk renders it almost grotesque in this area. Its dominating emphatic power is weak, despite its size, because dominance becomes pointless when there is little left to dominate. In Fig. 4 we have more and in Fig. 3 still more emergent, dominant power as E shrinks in size. In Fig. 4, as compared with Fig. 3, we may sense a waste and superfluity of this power because the eventless background still offers so little resistance. In Fig. 3, on the other hand, the power of R is well displayed. E by its compact character succeeds in holding its own very ably against the nothingness of R. It is like a well-trained regiment that overcomes a huge, but untrained horde. In Fig. 2, E still has great dominating power. But the huge size of R by comparison begins to puzzle us. The essential power of E is now given its severest test. E must be really interesting and appealing to justify such an egotistic display, where everything is cleared away from its vicinity. If E were of extraordinary elemental interest the whole set could still succeed, even under these disproportionate conditions. But a diminution of E to its size in Fig. 1 and its diminution beyond that bring us to the point where E seems only a blemish or even a jest. We are left with little more than the nothingness of R. Obviously E has done less than nothing to overcome this, because it only displays the immense scope of R. It is like a blank canvas which has barely received a blotch of paint, or like the hush that precedes the beginning of the overture – but without the overture.

We have begun with a comparatively complex figure, and the observer may have noted that even in Fig. 2 the figure retains some force. But suppose that the size of E approaches that of the frame (and thus the *surround*, as we may call it). Then the weakness of superdominant figures becomes apparent. Here we move from Fig. 6 to Fig. 7.

Fig. 6   Fig. 7

We must characterize subdominance and superdominance as *underdominance* and *overdominance* when they approach their extreme ends; short of these they may have important uses. In Fig. 6, we have a comparatively potent E, but in Fig. 7 we have real nothingness in E. We expect something to happen in it, and if the dark area in it is declared to be E, we are forced to regard the whole thing as a practical joke. But let this area now receive a figure, thus:

Fig. 8

and something has been gained. In Fig. 8 the shaded figure now replaces the black as E and the remainder is obviously R. What was R at the preceding stage is now a white border. It sinks into the status of a *surround* or frame.

We must now venture into more complex applications of this. The use of superdominance in portraits is sometimes resorted to, but as a kind of defiance of the principles we have explored. Anyone who has ever cut out a head from an ordinary photograph and placed it into a child's locket has an example of superdominance, if an R of only slight extent is left in the total cut. No matter how small the total cut, the effect somewhat strains the observer. As we proceed toward the removal of even the outlines of the head, we find that the details of the face, such as the eye or the nose, are now brought into a relative prominence. This changes the entire character of the complex. Instead of an organized face we now have, for example, an eye as a figure against cheeks. Such a form as the eye is, of course, a rather rare though quite fit subject of aesthetic treatment. But an eye alone is not a face, and in an area where a face is highly overdominant in some R, the eye of necessity begins to compete as the E in the total set with the face itself. The result is a confusion of interests on the observer's part. The face becomes superdominant, the eye subdominant, but nothing is properly predominant.

It is true that many examples would have to be examined to confirm all this. Careful attention will, I think, show that artists in appearing to defy these generalizations actually use subtle means to comply with them. Where they do not one should remember that our interests in artworks are so varied that extra-aesthetic interests may sustain the work for many observers (consider the example of portraits), even if they are strictly deficient aesthetically.

One may test what is being said here by taking inexpensive reproductions of artworks and cutting off R until some E is superdominant. One quickly notices how the artist has proportioned the areas to each. What he has intended as detail or texture in the whole complex now emerges as figure, but its resonance, its echoes and reverberations in other areas are lost. The practice of making such cuts ("details") in descriptive books on painting, is instructive. Their composition is determined by the editor, and the artist. The use of the device, when purely heuristic, that is, to enable us to discover something new in the painting is, of course, entirely harmless if we again go back to the painting and allow this new-found detail to merge into the total work and enrich it.

There are conceivable occasions on which such an "editor" may be a better artist then the artist himself, and many a painting has been cut in this manner. Popular taste may itself edit a work and select out a portion of a larger work and devote itself entirely to this. These are not matters that any theory such as ours need show much concern about. No important principle is threatened if the figure of Plato is detached (in reproduction) from a vast fresco like Raphael's The School of Athens (see Chapter 15(6)). Nor is it a serious matter that only an isolated aria is sung from an otherwise uninspired opera. Matters become aesthetically serious only when the excision actually mutilates a work, and this also would be thought to be a morally serious matter. In general, the penalties of unjustifiable aberration toward superdominance and subdominance are easily felt and reckoned with.

These are some of the few generalizations we can make about the comparative size of emergents and recedents. They concern principally the spatial arts, but one can also apply them to musical art. In music, the occurrence of a theme twice or more times is something quite different from the appearance of several more or less identical masses in one visual complex. *Its effect, in music, is to drive home the one heard figure.* It may, therefore, become superdominant and thus overdominant by an insufficiency of contrasting thought. This is different from monotonous repetition in vision where the several masses each occupy a distinct relative position in a total complex. In spatial symmetry of the order ABA, B is generally the dominant figure from its central position. In music it is A because it has received the greater emphasis.

The value of generalizations such as these is often underestimated, since they are evidently not precise. The sceptic will ask, how large is too large (superdominant, overdominant)? or too small? But the issue must rather be put in the form in which the artist puts it to himself. The eye alone has the answers but he must also know how to interrogate it: is this part too large, too small, and so on? What the unskilled artist's work shows is precisely that he has never asked himself the relevant questions and doesn't know what they are. The greater part of aesthetic education, that which *can* be taught in the arts, is comprised in asking such questions. The artist who allows his figure or emergent to approach the condition typified in Fig. 1 or Fig. 7 or even Fig. 5 has *usually* not asked himself what he expects of the aesthetic observer or participant when he presents him with the virtual void in either of the two directions typified by these paradigms. He has, for example, not asked himself about Fig. 7, is this the figure I mean to permit to emerge in this complex? Or, now that I have this field, what do I intend shall happen in it? If a superdominant *is* meant to succeed as a figure and not just as a ground for a figure, it is the artist's responsibility to convince the observer. Nothing prevents him from offering a subtle, ironic, and sophisticated figure in somewhat this form any more than the comedian is forbidden to tell a joke whose point is that is has no point.

The classic statement of the issue of the magnitude of the emergent in the artwork is given by Aristotle. It comprises nearly the whole of the seventh chapter of the *Poetics* and should be quoted in its entirety.

A tragedy is an imitation of an action that is complete in itself, as a whole of some magnitude; for a whole may be of no magnitude to speak of. Now a whole is that which has beginning, middle, and end. A beginning is that which is not itself necessarily after anything else, and which has naturally something else after it; an end is that which is naturally after something itself, either as its necessary or usual consequent, and with nothing else after it; and a middle, that which is by nature after one thing and has also another after it. A well-constructed plot, therefore, cannot either begin or end at any point one likes; beginning and end in it must be of the forms just described. Again: to be beautiful, a living creature, and every whole made up of parts, must not only present a certain order in its arrangement of parts, but also be of a certain definite magnitude. Beauty is a matter of size and order, and therefore impossible (1) in a very minute creature, since our perception becomes indistinct as it approaches instantaneity; of (2) in a creature of vast size − one, say, 1,000 miles long − as in that case, instead of the object being seen all at once, the unity and wholeness of it is lost to the beholder. Just in the same way, then, as a beautiful whole made up of parts, or a beautiful living creature, must be of some size, but a size to be taken in by the eye, so a story or plot must be of some length, but of a length to be taken in by the memory. As for the limit of its length, so far as that is relative to public performances and spectators, it does not fall within the theory of poetry. If they had to perform a hundred tragedies, they would be timed by water-clocks, as they are said to have been at one period. The limit, however, set by the actual nature of the thing is this: the longer the story, consistently with its being comprehensible as a whole, the finer it is by reason of its magnitude. As a rough general formula, 'a length which allows of the hero passing by a series of probably or necessary stages from misfortune to happiness, or from happiness to misfortune,' may suffice as a limit for the magnitude of the story.[1]

It is often made to appear as if aesthetic theses such as these of Aristotle are valueless, because they do not answer questions such as "How large?" or, "When is an aggregation a whole," and so forth. The sufficient answer to this is that one cannot expect of a principle that it both be a principle and also apply itself. The points which Aristotle raises are deliberately general and are inherent in the very fact that the artist has submitted to us a complex object occupying a discrete stretch of time or space that is intended to be "used" in a certain way. What we call *judgment* is needed to interpret these general considerations and apply them to particular media and particular works just as judgment of a certain sort is called for in the engineer's technological application of scientific knowledge.

When an artist has presented us with an object that is distinct in time or space or both he has in effect answered (even if he has not asked) questions such as Aristotle's: do I regard this as one or as more than or less than one artwork? Have I supplied everything that is relevant to this theme or do I rely also on the observer supplying content of his own in order to complete it? Is the observer in a position of encompassing the artwork or

is he, as it were, placed within it and how is his observation affected by this? Has anything distinctive or significant occurred in the artwork? Do all its parts lead or point
toward this and receive from it their reason for being? Does the complex fail to maintain
interest at beginning, middle, or end, or sustain it throughout? What can reasonably be
expected of an observer, or optimally or minimally expected, perception being what it is,
when he is confronted by a deliberately organized and controlled phenomenal area,
such as an artwork? Can the artist expect even momentary interest to be taken in a blank
expanse? Can more than one major center of interest be maintained in one grasp? And
so on.

Every artwork in effect propounds some kind of answer to these questions even if they
have not been asked. The purpose of art criticism and of the artist's own reflection is to
address them distinctly to each work. It is evident that considerations about the extent
and internal organization of artworks in their spatial or temporal extent cannot fail to
arise.

SUMMARY

The emergent can be subdominant, dominant, or superdominant with respect to the recedent in a
given complex.

Both subdominance and superdominance tend toward underdomination and overdomination, and
both of these tend to turn the complex into nothing, for at their extremes the emergent ceases to
exist: but if there is no emergent neither is there a recedent, and if neither of these, then no complex.

Without venturing to formulate specific norms for magnitude, we can nevertheless formulate a
number of relevant questions with which the artist and critic should address themselves to the work.

Numerous attempts at normative statements proposed in the past may profitably be reformulated
as relevant questions to be asked about artworks. Our aesthetic experience is not so much in the position of being incapable of deciding normative questions as of not having had answerable questions
addressed to it.

NOTE

[1] Aristotle: 'Poetics', tr. by Ingram Bywater, 1450^b 20–1451^a 15.

CHAPTER 5

ELEMENTS AND INTERVALS

(3: *Third Relation of Elements*)

Considerations about the ordering of elements in terms of their number and their extent are necessarily very general. We must now turn to relations that affect or involve elements in a much more material manner. The first of these, a direct result of the compresence of elements, is a remarkable phenomenon that without doubt holds within itself the key to the superiority of visual and auditory data as materials of the arts.

In order to explain what this is we may look to a kind of context in which there is a small number of clear and distinct elements, figures, or emergents, in interaction with one another. Counterpoint in music affords an example of this, and we could also employ certain modes of visual art to make the same point.

In counterpoint there is a simultaneous flow of several voices, each in a distinct "register" or level. The page of an organ fugue by a pupil of Bach quoted here will serve as an illustration. There are three strata or "voices." A distinct voice first sounds a motif or theme in the bass line; a second voice then enunciates the same at another level in the seventh bar; the soprano repeats it once more beginning in the sixteenth bar. Each voice, once it has sounded the same theme or motif at different levels, then contributes other musical thoughts as the fugue proceeds. It usually subordinates itself politely, once it has spoken, to the other voices during the time they are sounding the motif. Here we have a distinctly shaped and sounded figure, the motif, as the emergent and one or more "supporting" or "conflicting" voices as recedents. The relation between them is fairly plainly S–S, but the locale of the emergent constantly shifts as now one and now another voice, high or low, comes into prominence by sounding the motif. Sometimes fugues employ more than one motif. Such motifs must in turn be related to one another in S–S or C–C manner. The conflicts and the solutions will be analogous to these we have already explored.

The composer may expect or demand various responses to the employment of counterpoint. He may expect the observer at a given time to take one voice as emergent and the others as recedent or to hear two or more voices together to form a new emergent. He has to reckon with the conditions and limitations of his medium and the musical comprehension of his auditor. As already noted, the soprano or highest voice is naturally emergent, forming the profile of a tonal mass. If the artist wishes to produce an equal effect of two voices simultaneously where both are strong thematically (perhaps by earlier iteration) he must offset the natural emergence of the highest voice by some device such as increased dynamics in the lower one, or other devices. The result may be the situation of conflict we have already described, and the auditor may be fascinated and stimulated by the phenomenon, and possibly overwhelmed by it. He may be in a better position to comprehend it towards the end of a fugal or contrapuntal tonework after the force of each conflicting theme or motif has been driven home. The composer must always take note of the auditor's possible fatigue from following the complexities of the development (though not necessarily that of the average or mediocre auditor).

27

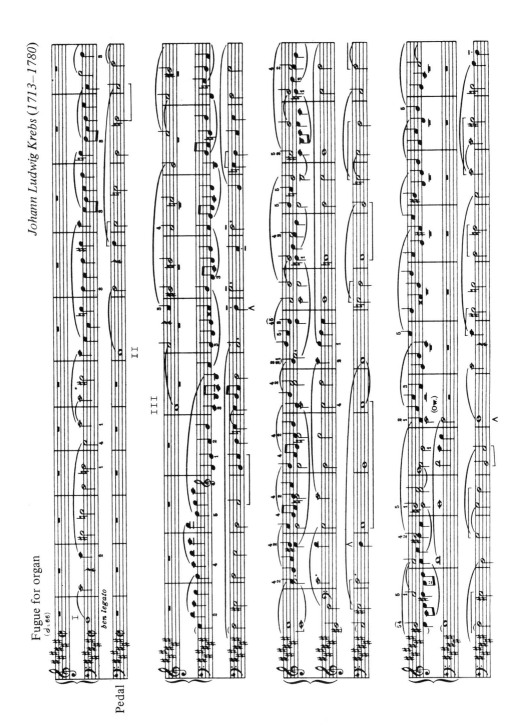

So far we have attended more to the fact that in counterpoint we seem to have two or more voices that seem to go severally their own way. Yet although they may *appear* to do so, their very difference introduces a novelty, a new reality which makes music as we know it possible, and not only music, but other arts too. This is the phenomenon of the *interval* which in dividing elements unites them and in uniting them reveals their difference.

In the second chapter we saw how colors and tones "define" themselves by standing in contrast with other colors and tones. They also appear to effect changes in one another according to the context in which they appear. (These effects will be considered at greater length in Chapter 7.) The present phenomenon is somewhat different from this. It is rather a kind of *tertium quid* that elements bring into being together or between them, as it were. It is illustrated best in the musical interval and chord and in the joint product of two or more adjacent or neighboring lines or masses. The quality of the interval is something which cannot be deduced or predicted from the nature of the component intervals themselves. It is no mere intellectual relation but something as real as the elements themselves.

The contrast of color areas, leaving geometrical aspects aside so far as possible, does not produce as noticeable an effect of a "third thing" as contrasts of tones and masses do, in my opinion. The effect of color contrast is largely confined to *contextual interaction* (v. Chapter 7). But the line between interval and interaction is perhaps only somewhat more difficult to draw here. The phenomenon of interaction is apparently felt by the visual artist with extraordinary power. The resources for the artist that vision does afford, even if not so strongly intervallic as in music, are almost endless. He commands not only color, line, mass, and volume but the seen and felt differences of color against color, line against line, mass against mass, volume against volume. Besides this, we shall also see that each of these is qualified by a number of other dimensions and that each discriminable area is determinate and variable in each such dimension.

Spatial areas taken by themselves behave somewhat differently from both color and tones: spatial figures and grounds are absolutely exclusive of one another, whereas intervals and chords in music can be heard simultaneously with the component tones. Yet even with figured areas both are at work even if we are not consciously aware of both. Would the colonnade of a Greek or Roman temple or a balustrade be the same if the ground intervals were greater or smaller, or if in other ways they were to be altered? Certainly not. One may concentrate alternately on the balusters and then on the generally unnoticed but elegant intervallic area or ground between them in the figure. Both of them, it should be remembered, are recorded on the retina and are equally at work as parts of both the visible and the "hidden order of art." [1]

There is nothing comparable to the interval in sense-modalities other than vision and audition. To savor an olive and an orange at the same time is simply to have two savors, or perhaps a *blend*. But a tonal, spatial or color *interval* is in no sense a blend. Whatever possibility other modalities have for fostering arts depends upon the degree of dimensionality and of intervallic quality there is in their elements. For these above all give them aesthetic intelligibility. *The interval even more than the elements themselves is the true structural unit, particularly of musical art.* Together with the dimensional structure of all visual and auditory elements it helps to account for the easy ascendancy of the arts in these modalities above all others.

The very difference of elements or figures that presents itself in the interval has the remarkable result of providing a bond between them. Whether the figures find themselves in C–C or in S–S order, they cannot but interact through the very fact of their difference and "distance" from one another. Relevance is in part defined by intervallic bonds. None of this, it should be noted, is "our doing:" it is inherent in the materials themselves, part of the *intrinsic order*.

Since music affords an emphatic example of the foregoing, we may in conclusion observe it more closely. It is apparent that if we restrict ourselves, as the piano does, to twelve tones in an octave there will also be twelve intervals. For example, if we begin on middle C we have twelve intervals in one octave. The distance is reckoned in semitones, the distance from one note to the very next (black or white). Of course, we can also begin on any note other than C and obtain the same intervals by counting the corresponding number of semitones.

We may regard C♯ is identical with D♭, E♭ with D♯, and so on. It is little short of astounding to find that, with this (the so-called enharmonic) convention (C♯ = D♭, etc.), all the music that has ever been written in Europe, with almost trifling exceptions, has been written with just these intervals: nothing on any page of Plainsong, Palestrina, Bach, Beethoven, or Schoenberg is expressed in anything other than these intervals. Only in our time have significant departures set in, the extent and permanence of which cannot yet be gauged. Intervals have proved to be far more important in musical structures than the component tones.

There are, of course, still larger intervals as we extend the range into two or more octaves. Those that lie in the first octave and a half exhibit the intervallic auditory phenomenon best. It is not confined to the intervals noted but appears in some strength anywhere in the audible range. But with very low notes, the results are somewhat muddied; with very high ones they are not as keenly heard and felt; with tones that are widely spaced (at the top and bottom of a keyboard instrument or even in a range of two or three octaves) there is also a weaker intervallic effect. In general, an interval always sounds the same wherever we play it, except in the extreme registers. Thus, counting nine semitones from C up to A, or E up to C♯, and so on, we obtain

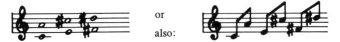

These are three major sixths, and they all exhibit the same effect; we may allow for the fact that if they are played soon after one another the second interval will, of course, differ from the first in pitch. Since it is the intervals that are really distinctive, it is *they, not the tones, that are the true elements, in our sense, in music*. The intervals *C A* sounded yesterday and *E C♯* sounded today will be recognized as exactly the same (or we can learn to recognize them), whereas two tones, C sounded yesterday and D today, for anyone who does not command the unique and comparatively rare power of "absolute pitch," will evoke no recognition of an interval whatever. The composer, unless he is working with sounds other than *tones*, works mainly with such intervals, and these will define the identity of his composition. So, for example, a song may be written in the key of C for the soprano voice, but some particular singer may prefer to sing it slightly higher in the key of C♯. Here the song has been "transposed:" every interval remains exactly the same, but every tone is different. With this convention it is said that the *same song* has been sung in two keys.

In certain respects intervals retain their character even when they are noticeably different through wider spacing. For example, the intervals in each bar here are harmonically either the same or have a certain close kinship:

They may be spaced still more by moving them another octave or more, up or down. But the musical effect may be very different as we may see from an example. Let us look at one of the Nr. 2 Klavierstücke of Karlheinz Stockhausen published in 1954. One may here note in what sense an interval such as a major second both resembles and differs from the major ninth with which it is for many purposes harmonically identical; notice bar (ii) above.

Thus we might rewrite the first line of Klavierstück III (page 32) in order to bring everything into the compass of one octave, and then compare the result with the original.

Of course this forfeits the "pointillist" character of the original. Whatever musical quality the rewritten line has, it is evident that everything in the original is now somehow transformed. The composer's purpose was to use the huge resources of the keyboard but to do so with a tight economy. He asked us to catch difficult relationships at great range which might be too obvious if he had presented them as we have rewritten them. The broad spacing also makes possible a real composition. At close range the notes seem to form merely a single melodic voice instead.

It should be noted that in spite of the very "advanced" character of this composition its novelty and its essence must reside in the musical nature of just these intervals arranged in just this order. The same must be said of every other composition.

When we now add a third note to an interval we get a *chord*, for example,

Chords, like intervals, are the direct but unpredictable result of combining tones into intervals. The first of these chords contains C, A, and C, and also the intervals *CA, AC,*

Karlheinz Stockhausen, Nr. 2 Klavierstücke

III

CC; the second, C, F, and A, and the intervals *CF, FA*, and *CA* and all of these can be distinctly heard. The result is not just more tones or intervals, but a new thing, the chord. Robert Browning's Abt Vogler, "extemporizing upon the musical instrument of his invention," was thinking of just this in the lines:

> But here is the finger of God, a flash of the will that can,
> Existent behind all laws, that made them and, lo, they are!
> And I know not if, save in this, such gift be allowed to man,
> That out of three sounds he frame, not a fourth sound, but a star.
> Consider it well: each tone of our scale in itself is naught:
> It is everywhere in the world — loud, soft, and all is said:
> Give it to me to use! I mix it with two in my thought:
> And there! Ye have heard and seen: consider and bow the head![2]

There is scarcely a more astounding process of "emergent evolution" than joining three sounds, each in themselves "naught" and getting as the transcendent result a chord!

To return now to counterpoint (see p. 28), we see that when a second voice enters we get not just a second distinct entity in "competition" with the first. We get the remarkable result of the interval; and when we add a third voice we get a real or implicit chord and thereby, harmony. Thus, in the portion of the *fugue* we have quoted, we have the motif first in the bass voice for six full measures. Then it reappears in the pedal voice beginning in the seventh bar and finally in the soprano voice beginning in the sixteenth bar. At the seventh bar we have not just a second voice coming in: we have the intervals $C\#C\#$, an octave, $C\#G\#$, a perfect fifth, $C\#E\#$, a major third; in the next measure, $F\#A\#$, a major third, $F\#G\#$, a major second. In the sixteenth measure we have the interval-chord, $E\natural C\#F\#$, $D\#BF\#$, and so on. Some of these intervals are not actually struck, but are implicit in the suspensions (e.g. $C\#{}^{\prime}G\#$ in the seventh bar).

The remarkable thing is that the plurality of voices running horizontally in the counterpoint does not result in the conflict of two or more heterogeneous figures (in our sense of 'figure'), but rather in novel phenomena, intervals and chords — Browning's stars — that provide a new unity and relation between the voices. Yet this unity is only possible through the diversity of the tones and through the fact that their compresence has produced the phenomenon of the interval.

It should be noted that in contrapuntal music, especially in the fugue, there are two "forces" at work: the vertical pull of intervals and chords and thus toward a "reconciling" of the components in something new, and horizontal pull of the figures or motifs, driven by the underlying rhythm. The interval phenomenon is not always as strongly felt between elements along the horizontal dimension. We shall explore both of these at length below.

We see, then, that even on the minature scale of the interval and the chord there are ways in which there can be conflict and relevance between elements in aesthetic complexes. Even minimal elements united in one context stand in an S–S or C–C order. The first of these fits them, other things being equal, for a continuant mutual status since each supplies a kind of need of the other. The second generally issues either in an accommodation where the two form together another a bimodal figure, or in rhythmic configuration, or in conflict. But whether they unite, or accommodate, or conflict they always yield a more or less unpredictable result when they are present together in a context. We have no way of *knowing*, of producing a deductive proof, that two gases, hydrogen and oxygen, will form a *liquid* when combined and will produce the sensation of wetness. Neither can we say what unique character of intervals, chords, colors, or geometric shapes will emerge when aesthetic elements are combined. Often natural affinities come to light; for this the synthesizing sight and hearing of the artist is necessary. If the artist is successful, his larger stratagems of organization have the strength of the affinities he discovers among elements. He is indeed fortunate if on the larger scale his work achieves the unity or coherence of parts, the inner magnetism, that tonal elements can have in a single chord.

It is difficult to overestimate the potency of the resources of unity that we have sketched out in this section; what has been treated in a very general fashion here will be considered in application to more examples later on when we have explored all the bonds of relation and relevance among elements and have gone into the devices of organization and composition that are open to the artist.

SUMMARY

The intervallic effect that emerges from the compresence of elements is found in music and to a certain extent in geometric and color contrast. It both differentiates elements and unites them by bonds that lie "between" them.

Intervallic phenomena render the differences of elements in musical and spatial art orderly and intelligible in a manner that contrasts with the mere difference of elements in extra-aesthetic or sub-aesthetic media.

The connections of elements which have been introduced here, and are explored further below, must be reckoned with by the artist in his own ordering of aesthetic materials.

NOTES

[1] The phrase is of course that of the excellent study by the late Anton Ehrenzweig: 1967, *The Hidden Order of Art*, University of California Press, Berkeley and Los Angeles.

[2] Quoted by Robert M. Ogden: 1938, *The Psychology of Art*, Scribner's, New York, p. 42.

CHAPTER 6

DIMENSIONS OF ELEMENTS: THEIR COMPARATIVE RELATIONS

(4: *Fourth Relation of Elements*)

A figure may emerge or dominate because it is simply spatially larger, or occupies more of our time and attention. It can also dominate in other ways that may enhance, offset, or even nullify spatial or temporal dominance; for example, through greater brightness or saturation of color, higher level of pitch, greater loudness or intensity, unusual (for the context) timbre, and so on. The emergence we have suggested in Chapter 4, through expanse in space and duration in time, is certainly of the first importance, but other magnitudes than those of size are equally arresting and, as often as not, more so.

What we have in spatial and temporal dominance is simply a comparative variance in spatial size and temporal extent. These provide an introduction to the *dimensions* of the elements. Dimensions are usually *scalar* systems of relation. A is related to B by the fact that A is, let us say, four times the size of B. Thus B's size forms a module by which we can attend to the size of A: four B's make an A. It is not necessary, and in aesthetic contexts it is rarely of any consequence, that the module be repeated in the larger element *precisely* so many times. But although it may be of no consequence in conscious attention, theories have sought to show that proportions are subtly at work even if beneath the threshold of awareness. The ancient doctrine of the *Golden Section* is one of the earliest efforts to achieve precision in questions of spatial aesthetic magnitudes. It was, however, less concerned with the comparative proportions of discrete figures, and more with the relation of the height to the breadth of a building.

Size or expanse, then, is one of the dimensions which help to determine dominance. We have very keen and subtle powers of discrimination in this dimension. We detect even minute differences of size or distance; nearly anyone can tell whether a picture is hung in a perfect horizontal position. Size is in a sense a somewhat "brutal" dimensions. One can always manage, up to a point, to make an emergent dominant simply by enlarging it in the time or space of the whole it occupies to the point where it overwhelms it. Just because of its immense power, such a dimension should be treated with restraint. For, as we have seen, a dominant emergent eventually destroys itself literally as it becomes more and more superdominant and at last coincides with the whole — it leaves a sheer void, or what after a time becomes a void in our attention. There are no principles, and little more than rules of thumb, to follow as to where such danger points are reached, that is, where either an emergent or a recedent, a figure or a ground, comes not only to super-dominate (for this has its uses) but to overdominate its complex. This is equally true of works in space or in time. How long may one expose a figure in time, how long may one extend a pause or silence? One can only advise alertness to the effects of overextension, either of spatial or musical-temporal figures, or of spatial voids or musical-temporal silences. (The experiments of avant-garde composers with silence provide interesting examples.)

Dimensions of elements enable us to say *what* the element is: it is a large, bright and highly saturated hexagon of Prussian blue over a white ground of the relative size of a hand; it is a loud, keen, intense middle C on an oboe, occupying a relative duration of about five seconds. Here some dimensions, or systems of scalar dimension, are called upon to specify *what* these elements are. In fact, every predicate we add cites a dimension if it is possible to specify it in a scalar manner.

But not every predicate will *describe* or specify an element: Some of them will *characterize* it. A characterization, roughly speaking, indicates the effect of something on us, perhaps its "emotional" effect. This involves what we spoke of earlier as the *appeal* of the element. Characterization is the substance of criticism and presents a distinctive vocabulary that, unlike description, either credits or discredits the subject. We may say of tones that they are brassy, doleful, droning, leaden, raucous, screeching, or wailing; of light or color that it is vivid, flashy, garish, gaudy, lurid, drab or dull. These are the kinds of terms likely to turn up in criticism. Are they *descriptive* of tones or colors? Should they be treated as dimensions? Are they scalar as true dimensions are? These predicates should not be regarded as descriptive nor as specifying or anything scalar dimensional. Unlike descriptive terms, they are not neutral or objective but are used to credit or discredit.[1]

Let us consider the warmth and coolness of colors, and perhaps of musical tones as well. Of course, the temperature of physical bodies is scalar. As soon as we remind ourselves of that, we may be prepared to abandon the notion that the warmth of colors is scalar. Are we saying *what* some yellow or some blue is, are we describing or specifying the dimensions of colors when we say that they are warm or cool, or are we offering only a word about our emotional response to them, to which we would not demand the agreement of others as we would to saying that they are yellow or blue or have the shape of hexagons? Professor Pepper regards the terms as something more than merely emotive: they are dimensional even though not scalar.[2] Warmth and coolness he regards as the *apparent temperature* of colors, and as 'secondary characteristics" of color. (For characteristics, I think we may say 'dimensions.') He regards them as having "emotional connotations" and yet as more objective than mere emotional responses to color. Another such dimension he mentions is *apparent distance*; thus white appears to retreat from us and dark colors advance towards us, at least relatively. A still further secondary characteristic or dimension is that of *color quality*, a trait that he correlates with musical timbre (e.g., the quality that distinguishes middle C on an oboe, a violin, and any other instrument). Despite their weak scalarity, I am inclined to agree with Professor Pepper's view about these characteristics (this is not to be confused with what we have referred to as "characterizations").

Provided we keep the number of dimensions to a comparatively small number and do not permit them to range over the limitless number of interesting predicates we may use in speaking of colors and tones, dimensions help us to set forth what the color and the tone are. For colors we shall have *hue, brightness* (or value, the degree of lightness and darkness), *saturation* (amount of gray in a color), and other dimensions such as quality, apparent temperature, and apparent distance. These presuppose the further dimension of the *expanse* or geometrical extension of the color. For tones we shall have *pitch, intensity* (loudness), *timbre*, and of course *duration*. In addition, one may mention secondary dimensions such as *extensity* (breadth of tone), *vocality* (vowel quality; for example, the "oo" or "augh" of a deep organ pipe, the "ee" or "eye" of a note of high pitch), and certain others. Some of these may vary direction with pitch and thus be actually part of pitch rather than separate dimensions.

What now is the purpose or point of distinguishing these aspects of visual or auditory data? For the artist, for the builder of instruments and the color chemist or technician, the differences cannot be overestimated. By varying dimensions in such suitable ways as he chooses, the artist creates a figure, makes it or lets it appear: it dominates because its size or hue or intensity of color, or its duration or timbre or pitch or loudness is of just such a magnitude as to dominate the complex. This is how appearances appear, how perceptions become real for us, and since by such devices the dominant or figure or emergent becomes real we can say that they set forth its *nature*. We may now consider one of these dimensions in greater detail, namely, pitch, the pre-eminent dimension of music.

In music we find a rich dimensionality of the elements. All of its dimensions are scalar, but pitch is particularly interesting in this respect since its scalarity is not only continuous but *cyclic*. Let us see how our music came to make its choice of tones, thus determining the harmonic system and so the character of our music itself, in whole or part.

All of the factors underlying tone, their dimensions, may nowadays be varied by electronic means in such a way that an ever-increasing range of them is available for purposes of music. We can produce "tones" too high and too low to be heard, and we can produce a far greater number of timbres or qualities than are afforded, for example, by the instruments of the symphony orchestra. This expanded range is gradually being explored to see of what use it will be as music. The electric organ already produces an enormous range of new possibilities.

The scalarity of the dimensions is easily seen in the fact that tones are, as we say, higher-lower, louder-softer, longer-shorter, and of a huge range of tone qualities. The last factor is also scalar but of limitless complexity — almost too much to be of use to us in its full range. Of the several dimensions, pitch is by far the most important for music.

Everyone knows that an instrument such as a trombone can produce a limitless number of pitches when the player moves the slide through all or part of its range. A sound not unlike a fire siren is produced. The same result can be produced on a stringed instrument if we draw the bow across a string at the same time we "stop" the string with a finger moving from one end to the other. The possible range of pitches is literally infinite both in its whole audible extent (from about 16 to 16,000 cycles) and in any shorter stretch. This is a limitless wealth from which all the music ever heard has been drawn.

When we look at a piano we find, however, that there are only a few of these tones available to us from this limitless store, eighty-eight to be exact. Why do we limit ourselves so severely? This is, as one says, a good question. Part of the reason is that an infinite number of tones is also a confusion, too much for the mind to grasp or to make use of. At the same time it should be noted that we do use many more than eighty-eight day in and day out. Voices ranging from high to low are different; probably no two persons pronounce the vowel in the word 'knife' at *exactly* the same pitch, although all voices will stay within a definite range. We also hear and recognize bells, gongs, sirens, drums and many other noise makers that produce a large number of tones, often in an indiscriminate mixture.

The question we should now try to answer at least in part, is how we came to settle on some seven dozen tones for our music. Without doubt the key to the answer lies in a marvellous cyclic phenomenon that underlies all scalarity of tones and that every child can recognize instantly, namely the *octave*. As we sing or play our way up or down the "gamut" of pitches we learn to recognize a certain familiar tone that appears at what prove to be regular intervals. This tone appears to be the same tone we sounded a few moments ago, but this time it seems to lie "higher," and it recurs again and again. It is well known to most of us that the phenomenon depends on the fact that the number of vibrations has been doubled each time we reach this tone starting upwards from a given tone, or better, we hear the octave every time we double the vibrations. We can also produce this effect by increasing the tension or by halving the length of the sounding string. This phenomenon exists in no medium except tone. Light or color shows no such effect when we double or halve the wave length or frequency, nor does any other kind of dataum for which we have sense organs.

The octave enables us to find our bearings among the myriad tones: a recognizable "mile post" is planted every so often. Although our auditory environment is already "organized" for us by society from birth on, it is possible nevertheless that we would even independently of it tend to limit ourselves to a very small selection from the many possible tones, particularly if we somehow learned to *sing* without the benefit of an organized environment. As soon as we try to make a selection of a comparatively small number of tones within each octave we see that the way from one octave to the next can proceed by what appear to be contiguous *steps*.

We also seem to be able to distinguish *steps* from *skips*. Let us try to keep our selection of intra-octave tones to where they seem to proceed stepwise, without skips, and see what happens. (It should be noted that literally everything depends upon the precise tones that we select and the number of them, just as we determine our motions by deciding to make the steps of a staircase 4, 6, 7, or any fixed number of inches high. In music, what is so determined is the system of tonal relations, or harmony.) Supposing that we know that the (upper) octave of a given tone has double the number of vibrations, we can then proceed to divide the octave up once, twice, three times and so on and see what we get. Middle C has 256 vibrations per second; so its octave has 512. Halfway between the two tones lies some note or other (X) with 384. When we sing these notes, C–X–C, the result seems like a huge skip. Let us therefore divide the octave into three parts. This time we have C–Y–Z–C: the tones have approximately the vibration numbers 256, 341, 437, 512. Again huge skips appear.

Let us now use the piano to simplify matters for ourselves, since there are already 12 tones in each octave that happen to be about equally spaced as follows:

1	2	3	4	5	6	7	8	9	10	11	12	13	– – –	Semitone series
C	C♯	D	E♭	E	F	F♯	G	A♭	A	B♭	B	C		number

We can now produce several of our divisions by using these 12. If we make a division into six we have:

1	3	5	7	9	11	1
C	D	E	F♯	A♭	B♭	C

This certainly sounds as if it rose stepwise, but it is somehow odd to our ears. It is the whole tone scale. If we make a division into four we have:

1	4	7	10	1
C	E♭	F♯	A	C

This no longer sounds like a stepwise progression but a succession of skips. It happens to be a familiar chord, the so-called dimensioned seventh. Division into three will give us even greater skips.

$$1 \quad 5 \quad 9 \qquad 1$$
$$C \quad E \quad \begin{pmatrix} A\flat \\ G\sharp \end{pmatrix} \quad C$$

This is really a familiar chord. It is known as the augmented triad.

Our best candidate so far is the one with sixth divisions which definitely sounds like a step progression and thus seems to take us from one tone to the *very next one*. But when we sing this "scale," as we may call it, we find we can sing another tone between each of the existing six. Hence we get twelve. This is the chromatic scale, that is, our previous 1, 2, 3, . . . , 12. We need not stop at this point, if only to try to see where we *can* go.

We have now heard the following divisions: into 2, 3, 4, 6, and 12 parts. What about 5, 7, 8, 9, 10, and 11? We should first observe that now we must abandon the piano. It divides the octave into 12 and any factor of 12, such as 2, 3, 4, and 6, but permits no other.

At this point anthropology comes to our aid and informs us that a Javanese scale has five equal divisions of the octave, and a Siamese scale has seven equal divisions.[3] Neither of these will sound, when sung or played on instruments devised by these peoples, like our own scales, although both of them have tones that come fairly close to what we call F and G within an octave from C to C.

This leaves the possibilities: 8, 9, 10, and 11. Division into eight will give a curious result. Half of the tones will appear on the piano, half will not. Thus we have the series:

$$1 \quad 2\tfrac{1}{2} \quad 4 \quad 5\tfrac{1}{2} \quad 7 \quad 8\tfrac{1}{2} \quad 10 \quad 11\tfrac{1}{2} \quad 1$$
$$C \quad C\sharp\uparrow \quad E\flat \quad E\uparrow \quad F\sharp \quad G\uparrow \quad A \quad B\flat\uparrow \quad C$$

We will have four tones that lie halfway between C♯ and D, E and F, G and A♭, and B♭ and B. So far as I know, no people have sung or played this scale. Division into nine, ten, and eleven tones seems even more remote.

The result, then, is this. To have a stepwise progression we seem to need at least six divisions (although the Javanese ear seems content with five). The choice seems to come down to six and twelve.

But assuming that we have completely "unpreoccupied" hearing (impossible for any one who can read this, and many more persons who cannot) the result is still not very satisfactory. We hear the 12 tones as steps (they are called *semitones*) but they seem somehow to be too close for comfortable singing. The six-tone scale seems to move at a more normal pace. Shall we therefore settle for it? The answer that Western man, and also the Chinese and certain others, gave to this was an emphatic No. They seemed instead to make a quite irregular selection *from among the twelve*. As it turned out, East and West made virtually opposite selections. The pentatonic scale of the Chinese comprised tones numbered 2, 4, 7, 9, 11 (or 1, 3, 6, 8, 10). The Greeks (or whoever) chose among a total of a dozen scales, one that had tones 1, 3, 5, 6, 8, 10, 12. This turns out to be C, D, E, F, G, A, B, and of course C again at the end: our own major scale. (We shall explain the choice in chapter 8.0.)

This no doubt is a curiously unhistorical way in which to expound the pitch series. But it is deliberately unhistorical and also instructive to proceed in this way, since we can see that in principle we had to make a selection out of an infinity of tones or else be content simply to slide from one tone to another in an indeterminate fashion. The choice, then, came down to *steps* or *skips* among the tones. At this point the scalarity of tones, which *is* to say their stepwise character, carried the day. The ear, however, heard different things in different places, but all of them seemed to hear a stepwise scale tone, that is a tone ladder, *with no missing rungs*.

There is in fact no one scale even in western history. The middle ages made a selection like that of the twelve (or more) Greek scales. This is the so-called *modal* period of music: some twelve modes (or systems of choice of tones from among the twelve semitones) predominating. The early modern age (the sixteenth century) reduced the modes from twelve to two, now called major and minor. The early twentieth century saw a revolution in favor of a twelve tone scale (1 through 12 above), and though it was a somewhat abortive attempt, even twenty-four (with quarter tones) and more. Historically, the choice of the twelve chromatic tones was, of course, based upon the overtone series and its intervals rather than the arithmetical division we have expounded here.

The scale with its five or seven or twelve tones is one of mankind's greatest inventions or discoveries (or both). It is an inexhaustible well of musical potentiality.

Occupying one particular place on the scale (or key or mode) is largely what makes a tone what it is. Pitch relations are the source of all harmony and melody, and the advantage of the Western gamut of pitches is that it made a complex and interesting harmony possible. Only by an exhaustive study of harmony, or rather the many "harmonies" old and new and even "anti-harmony" as one may speak of it, can one hope to gain a knowledge of what individual tones are, for they are what they are in relation to one another. That is to say their essence is pervasively contextual. We may repeat what was said earlier, that we get a particular set of contextual or harmonic possibilities when we decide on such and such tones within the octave and exclude all others.

Pitch affords a particularly good example of how elements, in this instance musical elements, define themselves by being placed in, or we might say, finding themselves in, a scalar relation to other elements. We may now proceed to the exploration of the dimensions of elements in some of the other sense-modalities.

Colors in respect of the dimension of *hue* arrange themselves in the spectrum in a band running from violet to red, and this may be folded back upon itself to form a circle: violet, indigo, blue, green, yellow, orange, red, and thence with the addition of purple it begins again. Hues may be represented around the "waist" of a double cone, the so-called color cone. Of course this is not a scalar order in the sense of the pitch series. It is irrelevant to point to the seriality of the numbers of the Ångstrom units or the frequencies for color from short wave radiation (violet) to long wave (red) since, of course, these numbers cannot be even remotely suspected or divined from visible colors themselves. Colors are more like families whose interrelations of consanguinity we learn by immersing ourselves in their genealogies. We can always find our way by a step-by-step process even if this is not to be "quantified" in a familiar sense.

We are in scarcely any better position to quantify the dimension of the saturation of colors, that is, the relation of a given hue to a given point on the achromatic series from white through gray to black. But this too can be set forth schematically on a color cone.

Saturation can be represented by circular disks that cut the cone transversely and degrees of saturation by the distance from the axis of the double cone.

The value, or light and dark aspects, of colors is represented by the "distance" of a hue of a given saturation from perfect white or perfect black at the two apexes of the double cone. But even this is scalar only in the sense that the production of such colors is made possible by physical determinants of definite scalar character.

Distinctions in apparent distance and apparent temperature are, like those of the major dimensions, susceptible of a very definite more-or-less without being mathematically scalar. It is this more-or-less conviction that is in all these matters decisive.

There are ways in which contrasts and thereby perceptibility are facilitated in the visible world. The skilled artist learns how to employ these scalar variants effectively. Visual works of art wish above all to attract attention to themselves: "look upon me, behold how fair, you dare not ignore me." But no one beholds unless he is made to do so. That is where the artist's work begins. It must not be supposed that these are all the devices available to him, even though some artists confine themselves to color and space to the exclusion of everything else, if that is possible. As we have remarked earlier, each dimension has a certain range of power and effectiveness, others being equal.

One of these others has powers ·for revelation that must never be underestimated. This is what we shall investigate further on as *connotation*, that is, the respect in which natural objects are never purely or exclusively "arrangements" in color and space, but also have some kind of meaning. Everything we see is *a something or other* even if we find difficulty in naming or describing it. The artist is never free to choose whether he shall employ extension, hue, saturation, brightness or other dimensions of color, for every patch of color necessarily possesses each and all of them — although he may vary them and virtually set some of them at nought. But he can very nearly choose to ignore connotations altogether, at least in the *naive* sense of suggesting a house or hat or fish. He cannot avoid suggesting the more categorial characters of spatial things such as their linearity or extendedness or massiveness.[4]

The point now is that although connotations may be avoided altogether, except in the *categorial* sense, they are powerful even if the merest hints of them are permitted to appear. Wherever they appear they can overcome the power of the purely visual dimensions with an ease that is sometimes altogether fatal to a picture. For example, the artist may compose something which exploits only the purely visual dimensions, so far as this is possible, then in a capricious mood add a comparatively tiny but potent connotative detail or suggestion to it: a pretty child, a nude, a face, a house, a mutilated body, a bird, or what not. Human attention being what it is, pictures cannot help but draw us toward whatever we find meaningful, interesting, gripping, absorbing, moving. It is irrelevant that such a picture may in particular (though, of course, not necessarily) be condemned as bad art: we are now interested only in the fact that this is an effective way in which elements may become visible, may succeed in exhibiting themselves. There is no single piece of "representational" art in existence that does not exemplify the problems and pitfalls of our somewhat extreme example. The artist may need to remind himself that his art is first of all something *visible* and hence has something of every visual dimension, possibly even the connotative. We are permitted to presume that he has them all under his command.

As we saw in earlier chapters, size or extent or sheer prominence is one of the basic dimensions of aesthetic elements, and it is of course a prime illustration of scalarity. We may now turn to another art to see how this dimension is exemplified where we may not readily have thought of it. Let us consider the appearance of fictional figures in drama.

Dramatic art, the novel, epic, and ballad would seem to be far too complex to be accommodated to any view of art such as we have developed so far in looking toward visual art and music. Yet these forms also involve elements in relation like the others, only we dare not oversimplify them since they are exemplified by personalities in *causal* and *motivational interaction* with one another, with all the infinite complexities we know personalities to have. Since we shall later apply some of our procedures more fully to narrative art, we may at this point concentrate on the respect in which the literary artist, like others, is engaged in imaginally visualizing and realizing the elements of his work and in this instance in a virtually measurable manner. It will be a literary application of the topic considered in Chapter 4, the magnitude of figures.

When we think of Shakespeare's figures and heroines, a crowd of recollections helps to determine the personalities we know as Hamlet or Macbeth or Henry V. The plays present themselves as tableaux, panoramas, canvasses, even cinemas, in which figures appear as major and minor and of every intermediate degree. The artist exposes characters for varying lengths of time, thus employing the dimension of *temporal extension*. It is not surprising that we find the major figures of these plays occupying the stage for a greater length of time than the lesser ones, The number of lines spoken affords an index, among others of course, of the importance of each character. Thus the data in the table are easily gathered from scholarly works on the plays.

Play	Character	Number of lines spoken
Hamlet	Hamlet	1458
	Claudius	544
	Polonius	350
	Horatio	284
	Ophelia	158
	Queen	157
Julius Caesar	Brutus	720
	Cassius	529
	Antony	328
	Caesar	150
	Octavius	47
Othello	Othello	890
	Iago	899
	Desdemona	374
	Cassio	279
	Brabantio	139
Macbeth	Macbeth	710
	Lady Macbeth	255
	Malcolm	208
	Macduff	176
	Ross	134
	Banquo	111

Play	Character	Number of lines spoken
Henry V	Henry	1019
	Fluellen	267
	Canterbury	223
	Exeter	130
A Midsummer Night's Dream	Bottom the Weaver	242
	Theseus	235
	Helena	229
	Oberon	224
	Puck	206
	Lysander	100–200
	Demetrius	"
	Hermia	"
	Quince	"
	Titania	"

These figures are instructive principally in hindsight toward what we already know is significant in the plays. Prominence inherently tends to lend or affirm significance. We are not surprised that Hamlet speaks nearly half the lines of the play, excluding the altogether minor characters. As a character, a vision, Shakespeare has certainly visualized and *realized* this figure: a large part of his impact is through sheer extension in time. Nor are we surprised at the King's great role, though perhaps we may have thought the Queen cut a larger figure. Of course, still another measure of extension here would be the proportion of time the characters appear on stage whether speaking or not.

What of the other figures? Is their importance, or want of it, truly proportional to their lines or their time on stage? Certainly not always. The great engine of action behind the play is in one sense the Ghost of the elder King Hamlet, yet he speaks only 95 lines. The point is, of course, that the playwright has provided this character with other sources of power than that of ceaseless presence on the stage. In other words, there are other dimensions than temporal extension, exactly as one ought to expect.

In *Julius Caesar* a similar result is obtained with the omnipotent figure of Caesar who speaks only 150 lines and dies at the beginning of the third act when the play is not yet even half finished. Certainly Caesar and Caesar's blood are the life of the play, even though Brutus is obviously the tragic hero. Except for Cassius, Brutus utters far more lines than any other character, over twice as many as Antony. Much attention must be given to these figures to enable them to be heard over the powerful voice of Caesar, whether alive or dead.

The distribution of lines in *Othello* and in *Macbeth* is not surprising. The murdered Duncan, a kind of counterpart of the elder Hamlet or of Caesar, plays a much less powerful subliminal role. He is certainly no Caesar. Our attention is riveted upon the good and evil in Macbeth's own soul and in Lady Macbeth's as this affects Macbeth himself.

The pomp and circumstance of *Henry V* culminates not surprisingly in the King himself who in terms of sheer extension overwhelms his companions. Our favorable impression of the King and the happy issue of the play serve to heighten the work's portraiture.

No character in *A Midsummer Night's Dream* utters more than 250 lines. The profusion of characters and their rather equal "extension" comports with the loose-joined movement or tumult of a dream. The memorability of the characters derives from their fantastic individuality. Puck darts in and out like a bee or a bird, keenly visualized and realized on every occasion. The immense contrasts of the company of nobles, the company of the fairies, and the company of the "rude mechanicals" (Quince, Snug, Bottom, Flute, Snout and Starveling) are augmented by the great differences of the characters among themselves so that there are further dominations, extensional and otherwise, in each of these companies. Thus the roaring, irresistible figure of Bottom clearly stands out among his fellows — he is their "leader."

For what it is that augments, diminishes, compensates and otherwise qualifies the extensional dimensions of each of these figures we must of course look to each of them: how they speak, think, and feel, how they look, stand, and walk, how they live and die. In all instances they are "comparable quantities," just as elements through their dimensions (e.g. tones by virtue of their pitch) are comparable among themselves. As human figures, their dimensions are rich and varied, but they are also all bound together: any respect in which they can be compared with one another on some degree or scale is one of the dimensions along which they are united.

We have sought to show how figures or emergents are realized, "made real" for us. The artist helps us to see *what* the element is by putting it into a context with other elements. We must observe its place in a scalar or ordinal system. I know something of what this tone *is* when I know where it stands relatively in the dimensions of pitch, intensity, timbre, and temporal extension, and any other schemata of comparison that may come to light. But this is only part of the story, for there are other aspects of its nature that are revealed not merely through comparison with other elements but through observation of its interaction with them. We also learn how elements hang together when we know what they are capable of doing to one another.

SUMMARY

Figures or emergents assert their place by differentiating themselves from other elements. They can do so insofar as they can be compared with them in terms of common aspects or dimensions.

The nature of elements is thus revealed through their dimensions, which are unique scalar properties.

Reference to and manipulation of dimensions enables the artist to differentiate elements and thus to bring figures and series of figures to realization.

Dimensions reveal only the comparative relations of elements. To learn what lends unity and cohesiveness to elements we must see how they interact.

NOTES

[1] Karl Aschenbrenner: 1974, *The Concepts of Criticism*, Reidel, §4.0.
[2] Stephen C. Pepper: 1938, *Principles of Art Appreciation*, Harcourt Brace, New York, pp. 162 ff.
[3] Robert M. Ogden: 1938, *The Psychology of Art*, Scribner's, New York, pp. 58ff.
[4] Karl Aschenbrenner: 1959, 'Aesthetic Theory: Conflict and Conciliation', *Journal of Aesthetics and Art Criticism* 18, 90–108.

CHAPTER 7

CONTEXTUAL RELATIONS OF ELEMENTS

(5: *Fifth Relation of Elements*)

So far, elements have been looked upon only in relation to one another by reference to scalar order, but we have not as yet suggested much about how they develop and affect one another. This is as if we had considered families of animals or persons only in respect to their resemblances to one another, their place on the animal family tree, but not their descent from one another, the effects of their proximity to one another, their friendly or hostile acts towards one another. It is not enough to know that this red and that green are complementary and equally saturated. We must also ask what effect they have on one another when they are of a given size and shape and stand at a given remove from one another. Hamlet and Horatio or Hamlet and Laertes, are, of course, interesting in a comparative or contrasting sense. But we also wish to know what effect Hamlet's presence or absence has on the King, the Queen, Ophelia, Laertes, Horatio, Polonius, and the rest, at such and such stages of the development of the tragic action.

We are continuing the topic broached in Chapter 2, the formal appeal of elements. What happens to them in interaction? Their character is in part determined by what they are taken by themselves, so far as one can think of them as having a character when they are entirely removed from context. The character they have when they interact is essentially unpredictable much as most types of chemical reactions or their outcomes are not predictable from what we know about the molecules that enter into them. One can therefore only wait to learn what the results are from experiment.

We should carefully distinguish contextual interaction from the kind of interaction which has already been explained as the intervallic phenomenon. The interval, it is true, is contextual in the sense that it exists only when elements are within some range of mutual effectiveness. But the outcome of this interaction is something in addition to each of the elements, which remain distinct from and essentially unaffected by one another, and yet are newly united by the interval they have "produced." In purely contextual relations change appears to be produced in each element that enters into the relation, and it may alter as often as the relations change.

The phenomenon of contextual alteration is shown in music and also in other media. Color is a frequent example, and literary examples are easy to find. In *Der Rosenkavalier* by Richard Strauss and poet Hugo von Hoffmannsthal we see young Octavian (this is a male role played by a woman) dallying with her lover, the Marschallin. The frequent exchange between male and female in opera has a unique effect in itself. But in this instance a further piquancy is added when the female-male Octavian must presently hide in a closet to escape from a threatened return of the Marschallin's husband and then return to the stage in the disguise of a female chambermaid. Here we have first a female pretending to be a male and then a female pretending to be a male pretending to be a female — this makes quite considerable demands on the dramatic abilities of the singer. In playing the chambermaid, the singer cannot simply revert to the natural stances and gestures of a woman. She must for example take the longer strides of a male, but

45

awkwardly, since these are not to be the strides generally characteristic of a woman walking but of a woman pretending to be a man pretending to be a woman walking. Even if man and woman here are not simple elements, as in cases of colors and tones, we can see that the same contextual effect is manifested when persons as elements assume different roles.

There are also much simpler examples of contextual change in literature. Almost any character in fiction finds himself in a variety of situations which reveal something about him. He is poor but finds himself suddenly among the rich, he is a young person thrown in with the elderly, he is modestly talented but suddenly finds himself among geniuses, and so on.

In music the contextual phenomenon is exemplified in enharmonic change. Thus chord 1 would commonly appear in the key of E♭ minor and chord 2 in B major. They would have an altogether different function, feeling and effect in these two keys. Yet as appearing in a piano composition, the

very same strings sound these two chords. In relation to other elements of the key of E♭ minor this same sounded elements is one thing, in relation to those of B major it is another, and its appearance in one context or the other has "produced" the result.

The same chord can illustrate the intervallic phenomenon. Suppose B♭ (or A♯) is sounded on Monday, E♭ (D♯) on Tuesday, and G♭ (F♯) on Wednesday. No one will hear the intervallic effect of these three, since at that remove from one another there is none. But sounded simultaneously, or a second apart, or even a bit longer, an E♭ triad (in second inversion) is heard, but also quite distinctly elements B♭, E♭, and G♭ (not to mention component intervals $B♭E♭$, $B♭G♭$, $E♭G♭$). The tones have both maintained their identity and jointly produced something new, the chord.

As already noted, the intervallic effect is not strictly the same as the contextual. It is perhaps an open question whether the following exemplifies the one or the other. Suppose we sound the following succession of fourths:

The succession of fourths, although permitted vocally in medieval music, where it was known as organum, was rather strictly avoided in the intervening centuries and finally forbidden in classical harmony. But suppose we add another line to the above, as Mendelssohn does in one of his *Songs Without Words* (No. 42):

In the resulting progression, the harsh open fourths seem to be transformed and softened by the sweeter thirds and sixths that now appear with the third line. Effects of this sort are really astonishing when we think about them; the effect seems to exceed so far the cause. Indeed, this is true. We would have no way of knowing in advance what effect was to ensue if we had never heard the components in any way but separately. Virtually any page of music as we now know it illustrates the contextual phenomenon profusely.

Turning to visual art, we see that the skilled artist takes the trouble to learn what the "reactions" of colors are to one another. An aesthetic psychologist writes:

When red is contrasted with yellow, the red becomes slightly bluish, and yellow greenish, but also less yellow because of the blue which the red induces upon it. If, as is usually the case, the red is much darker than the yellow, the contrast-effect of brightness will darken the red and brighten the yellow, thus decreasing the color of each. These are among the reasons why red is said to 'kill' the effect of the yellow.

There follows a discussion of the effect of yellow on green, green on blue, and blue on red. He concludes: "Contrasts of red or green with blue enhance the 'blue' . . . contrasts of red or green with yellow tend to kill the yellow." The author is confident that "with these principles in mind, contrasts of any two intermediate colors can be predicted."[1]

Predictability as between unions of colors or of tones, however, is of little consequence to the artist; he is bound to be an empiricist. It is of the nature of elements (of tone and color) to permit little more to be said of themselves than their names and their scales or dimensions. We see that these are comparatively few in the case of colors and tones. If there are vastly more than this in literary works we discover only how much more complex they are than other elements.

When we now speak of the interactions of elements we must be cautious to see that this is only a convenient way of speaking. Aesthetic elements do not interact in the manner of gravitating or radiant bodies where causal changes can ensue from contact or proximity. They do however appear to alter in character when they are placed in context with one another. We must remember that, unlikely physically interacting bodies, their apparent character is emphatically their real character. If they are removed some distance from one another we find that they have no contextual relations whatever. Or to put it another way, elements must be brought into one another's vicinity to have any contextual "effect" on one another.

We may ask what limits the range of the contextual effect of elements. The outer limits of this are restricted by certain conventions. We generally find a frame (using the term generally for all media), a limit of relevance that separates an aesthetic complex, a figure-ground, from the surround. Presumably nothing that occurs in the surround is relevant. It may, however, *intrude* itself: fire sirens in the street may be heard with and above the *tutti* of the orchestra, or bad lights or shadows or reflections intrude themselves upon pictures. These distractions are "intrusively relevant" and must be dealt with: the work is meant to live a kind of life of its own, but it nevertheless also inhabits a transaesthetic world and must come to terms with it.

The current movement toward the abolition or the diminishment of frames, stages, proscenium arches, museums (sometimes characterized as mausoleums) in favor of the involvement of the spectator in the work of art, of making him a participant, does not abolish surrounds: it merely revises their limits. More of life, it is said, must have an aesthetic dimension — in some important respects a beneficent trend.

Assuming that the inner limit of surrounds are drawn somewhere or other, we find important consequences for the aesthetic complex. If elements are relevant in any sense they affect the complex as a whole: they make or mar it. And the eye or ear instinctively "interrogates" the element as to whether it *belongs* or does not. We expunge the fire siren, we try to ignore it, we are relieved as soon as it passes. But what the artist has placed into the work, this we can neither ignore nor, in accord with conventions hitherto prevailing, can we remove or revise it. (One recalls the axe the Dadaists conveniently provided with some of their exhibits!)

There is now likely to follow some extended dialectic between the artist and the observer or participant. The artist will most likely turn a deaf ear if he hears we object to this or that (element) in his work. He is likely to think or say, "if thine eye offend thee, pluck it out:" the defect is not in what you are seeing but in your eyes. There is no real termination to such a controversy as there is over the location of a house or road or bridge, for these can in principle be re-located. Artworks are by convention "incorrigible," at least by the spectator.

But the omnipotence the artist appears to possess is an illusion. We have seen in this and preceding sections that the materials of the arts are not "docile:" they assert themselves and have effects which are not subject to the programs of the artist. No one will deny that the artist has a unique freedom: he is not an ant, bee, or beaver. But he subjects himself to the inherent nature of his materials when he undertakes to work with them. He stands at the intersection of the inner ways of such materials on the one hand, and his purposes on the other. He can, of course, decide in terms of sheer extent how to set the limits or bounds of his work. But within this framework his decisions as to where he places his elements must be guided by their inherent powers. In other words, the decisions must be *justified*.

This is a unique and completely unverbal kind of justification: no amount of talk can justify the inclusion or exclusion of a visual or auditory element if the eye or ear is not convinced. Yet persistent attempts are made. Artists often proffer ridiculous verbal programs of what their music or their pictures "express". But we must always presume that all such "librettos" and even the very titles of artworks will sooner or later be lost. What words could Michelangelo or Bach or Mozart possibly have added to "explain" their works? One greets their silence with relief. The justification of the choice, exclusion, and placement of parts or elements in their works is in the works themselves.

When we demand that parts of art works "justify" their presence we have to look both at the detailed connection or relation of individual parts with adjacent parts and at the placement of parts as demanded by the artist's conception. Both of these are potent determinants of the outcome of the work as a whole. In the first case, one sees that the choice of elements may be that of the artist and yet their effects and their affinities are their own doing: the artist cannot prevent such and such colors taken by themselves from having certain effects and affinities nor can a musician prevent a dominant chord by itself from pointing in a certain tonal direction. Here the artist must know what his materials can do. In the second case, it is apparent that the powers of elements can be manipulated by the choice of the larger directions of the work, for example, the primary figure and ground system.

It is evident that there is always a tension between the medium and the artist, that is to say, the artist's intention. He may say that only when we know this, can we judge whether the inclusion or exclusion or some other disposition of an element is necessitated. But how much of a reason can intention really afford? Either the intention is itself somehow present *in* the artwork, or it is not. If it is not, it is difficult to see how it can determine anything in it whatever. If it is, then we return to the original question as to how *it* justifies the presence or absence of something, how the presence or place of an element is justified by that of another. The artist, the master of the work, if anyone is, is in fact less powerful than he supposes. His work must speak for him, and it must not only be permitted to do so, but it emphatically does so no matter what he does: *the medium asserts itself*. It may say what it has in it to say regardless of what the artist is saying alongside it.

This raises the question of *expression* (considered at greater length in Chapter 9). For the present, we may observe that there are two fundamental directions for what is called expression to take: first, extrinsic or communicative *expression*, the use of a perceivable entity, even an artwork, to serve to convey thought or feeling (although the term 'convey' is here only metaphoric), either by somehow resembling it or by conventional association with it; second, intrinsic expression or *expressiveness*, the evocation of thought or feeling by whatever power the perceivable entity inherently has in it. Certainly, no one may wish to deny the artist the freedom to convey *his* thought or intention by means of his artworks commensurably with his powers. But it is even more important to discriminate the power of the artist's medium or material to convey *its* thought, as it were, and to distinguish this from the artist's intentions. The fateful consequence for the artwork is that the more the first of these predominates the more the work becomes a mere utile vehicle, a device for the transportation of thought or feeling: the artwork becomes calligraphic, iconographic, epigraphic, semantic: the artist becomes a spokesman and the vehicle is incidental to the message. When the other form of expression dominates, the artist soon divines that he is in fact revealing what the medium has in it to reveal, or he helps it to *reveal itself* as much as he *expresses himself*. In this sense the artist's powers are shown in the depth to which he takes us into the inner reaches of the medium.

The artist's creativity is too often thought of as some godlike power to bring something into being out of nothing, like the Creator. But one need only ask himself, what has Beethoven "said" with the tones, intervals, chords, cadences, timbres, and tonal masses of his symphonies or sonatas that they do not inherently have in them to say? It is time to bring down the romantic cult of the artist-as-genius who transcends all this. No true genius has anything but humble respect for the potentialities of his instrument and medium as things greater than himself. Considering Beethoven's personality, one may say that the one thing he would be certain to be humble about is music itself: the "*holde Kunst*" celebrated by Schubert.

While we must thus obviously be prepared to see artists employing artworks to convey their thoughts and feelings, depth of intention can never be accepted as an excuse for running counter to what materials or media have it in them to express. Intentions all too quickly vanish and works then freely express whatever they have the power to express.

There are programs for music which composers themselves have developed as integral *parts* of their work. The listener is expected to read the program and to keep it more or less in mind while listening, to the end that his visual and synaesthetic imagination may be stimulated. The program becomes a kind of libretto. It is evident that some line must be drawn between this altogether valid procedure and one whether one senses that the artist must explain what his work expresses because in fact the work has failed to do so itself.

We see, then, that the artwork is determined both by its inherent contextual powers and by the choice of the elements themselves. We shall now consider the equally potent *tendentive* powers. This will place in better perspective the power which the artist's own effort at *expression* exercises (Chapter 9).

SUMMARY

The nature of elements is determined not only by the character they prove to have when dimensionally compared with each other but also by the reciprocal actions they appear to have on one another. We thus distinguish between the comparative and the contextual relations of elements.

The range of effectiveness of elements is the work itself as terminating at its surround. Determination of this extensive range is largely a matter of the artist's decision. The effectiveness of elements is, however, inherent in them alone.

Once decision about range is made, the observer is permitted to infer that what is relevant lies within the range, and whatever lies beyond it is irrelevant. Materials can be said to be relevant if their relation to one another is justifiable. This must be sought either in the materials themselves or, failing that, in the artist's purpose.

The nature of the artwork is affected by the tension between the inherent nature and powers of the materials, such as the contextual, and the intent of the artist.

Titles, comments, "librettos," programs are in general external to artworks unless they are deliberately integrated with the work. They often betray the fact that the work has failed to express some intent or other by itself. Each element must justify its presence in the company of just these other elements.

NOTE

[1] Robert M. Ogden: 1938, The *Psychology of Art*, Scribner's, New York, pp. 161, 162.

CHAPTER 8

TENDENTIVE POWERS OF ELEMENTS

(6: *Sixth Relation of Elements*)

If the artist's expressional intention cannot in the end alone justify the choice and disposition of elements, it is equally evident that the artwork cannot be explained solely through the inherent expressional or expressive powers of the elements. Artworks are done by deliberate intent; they do not grow like cells, although the analogy has occasionally some power to illuminate the process. Elements do indeed have powers that they exert on one another, but in art as we have known it heretofore at least, composition intervenes. Clearly both composition and the inherent powers of elements are at work. The structure of the work depends upon both of these.

In its plainest terms the question to which we must now more and more address ourselves to is, *what makes works of art hang together*? What makes them cohere, when they do, and what is there of proneness, bent, inclination or propensity in them or their parts to unite, that is absent or that has been injured when they fail to cohere? We have considered the contextual effects of elements on one another and have alluded briefly to the artist's effort to express himself. Both of these have confronted us directly with the coherence question. We must now take a further step and inquire after the powers that are or appear to be inherent in elements to unite with or repel one another, to lead toward or away from one another. We shall speak of this as their *tendentive* character, or as tendence, appropriating a term that is rare or disused enough to be able to bear an extension of its significance to the aesthetic context.

We must immediately come to terms with the somewhat, shall we say, animistic or vitalistic connotations of the notion of tendence. Surely, it will be said, if patches of blue or diminished fifths are elements, then affinities can be atrributed to them only by courtesy; for there is no objectively detectable magnetism or gravitational force that unites or sustains them; it is rather *we* who simply feel drawn this way or that, conditioned as we are by familiarity or association; we are likely to fall into such a familiar anthropomorphism, in thinking about the arts, another instance of the *pathetic fallacy*, in which we attribute falsely our own attitudes to objects of the environment.

Of course, one ought to accord a full hearing to this viewpoint if it is to be refuted. In fact, however, this is unnecessary. We grant the whole case. The leadings of elements from or to one another may indeed be as "subjective" as alleged. All that is necessary is that once such elements are brought to attention, they are *seen as* or *heard as* leading. Objectivity is here of no consequence in any strict or "scientific" sense. Music is by definition a matter of hearing: if leading tones are *heard to* lead, this trait will serve every purpose of objectivity. Peoples of Southeastern Asia did not happen to discover independently the Pythagorean system of tones. But this fact is an irrelevance to what the Western ear has heard in this system for some 3,000 years. What is alone relevant is whether Southeastern Asians come to hear what we hear when they are presented with this system. It is obvious that they do, so much so that they unfortunately soon lose interest in their own distinctive and interesting heritage.

More than this can be said in contrasting the data accepted by science with traits such as these, but it is really unnecessary. Since the arts are inherently concerned with sense and sensibilia, appearance is as good as reality. The artist can exploit anything he wishes if his audience or his observers can be brought to hear or see it, whether it be innate or acquired. That it may need to be acquired is irrelevant, since genetic questions are inherently extra-aesthetic.

Since we have alluded to the Pythagorean tonal system we may use the diatonic chord system that developed out of it to illustrate the tendentive power of elements. We must go into this in considerable detail. The so-called "technicalities" of music are here simply unavoidable.

Everyone has heard cadences many thousands of times, the most prominent being the authentic cadence, for example, the progression from a chord on the fifth to one on the first degree of the scale.[1] For example,

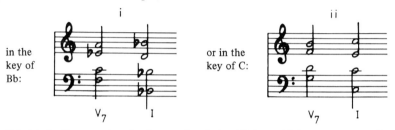

We hear this kind of succession in the music of the 17th to 19th centuries, and it is by no means extinct in our own. We are habituated to the succession of these two chords so that the ear tends to "expect" the second chord whenever under suitable circumstances it hears the first. At this point in our history it is not easy to shake off this habit to see whether in fact, if we had never heard the succession before and we now heard it for the first time, we would hear it with the same powerful effect. We may wish to attribute the "pull" of V toward I entirely to habit: in fact a stronger case than this for the connection can be made, but for the use we are making of the cadence, even attributing the power of the sequence to habit is by itself sufficient.

The habit, then, is one of hearing an, as it were, magnetic connection between these two in the order V–I. If we reverse the order, I–V, the ear demands I again, so that we have the full cadence I–V–I. Why? Not the least part of the reason lies in the intensely "dissonant" interval in V, that is, the interval from Eb to A, an augmented fourth, or tritone. This is generally considered the most dissonant of the intervals that are possible in a single octave. Its "feel" is variously characterized as a slight pain, grit between one's teeth, or a pebble or two in one's shoe. Relief is demanded, and chord I is precisely what furnishes it.

Here the element E – A *tends* toward (and for this reason we speak of *tendence* and the *tendentive*), toward – what? Is there only one way to "resolve" (to use the musician's technical term) this "painful" interval? In fact there are two ways, and the use of them is a convenient device whereby the composer can surprise us by resolving it in one way when we had been "expecting" the other. That is, assuming that the harmony preceding V–I to have established the key of Bb in the ear, what we may expect (or have been habituated to expect) is the sequence V–I. But there is another way resolve V. For example, We can have either iii (the treble of i above) or iv:

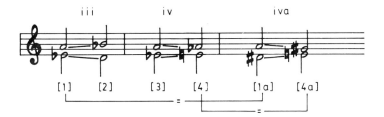

At the keyboard we see that E♭A resolves either by "expanding" to DB♭ or by "contracting" to EA♭. But EA♭ is identical with EG♯ which is normally a part of a totally different key from that of the preceding interval E♭A, which is B♭. It is a "normal" part of such keys as A major, E major, and B major, all of which are remote from B♭. Thus, if the composer, having established himself in the key of B♭, now moves from E♭A to EA♭, that is sequence iv, we are rather agreeably surprised rather than disappointed. Instead of sequence iii (or i), which we are prepared to hear and which leaves us in the key of B♭ major, we now find ourselves in quite a different setting: if the identical tones of iv are rewritten as iv a, this new setting or outcome, E major, is explicit. [1a] is identical with [1], [4a] with [4] on keyboard instruments. This is just as "convincing" to the ear, provided, of course, that other conditions of moving into this key are convincingly met.

Now the point of this is not that the first chord "hungers for" either of the two succeeding chords but that *if* we go to either of these from the first, we experience a certain satisfaction, a certain achievement of rest; we feel that some lack or want has been "made good." And in general we may say that no other of the numerous other possible succeeding chords with have quite so satisfying an effect.

Our other hungers are just like this. If somehow we were born as full-fledged adults, and if we then awoke to find ourselves having hungers or thirsts just like the ones we now feel, we could not identify these desires as being "for food" or "for water," since we assume we were never aware of eating or drinking before. We would simply be able to identify the feelings of desire by some mark or other, perhaps the semantic marks, 'hunger' and 'thirst.' These terms would, however, mean a good deal more to us after our first meal and our first glass of water, for things like these are what we *blindly* sought for before – they *do* satisfy us. In the same way, the tritone or the dominant is "seeking satisfaction," but we cannot say from knowing them alone just what will satisfy us until we encounter it, namely, a resolving interval or chord.

The cadence is the most powerful *tendentive* element in the diatonic system (there are several forms of the cadence). It is a kind of musical "magnetism" or "gravity" and exerts the strongest possible "pull." We hear it with extraordinary power in the music of Handel, but also in the work of all other composers down to be twentieth century.

We may observe the powerful "leading" or tendentive interval E♭A (or in general the interval of the tritone, six semitones, of which this is but one example) also in other chords, for example the so-called diminished seventh chord. In an earlier example in the key of B♭, page 52, we used a *dominant seventh* chord, that is, for example (transferring or transposing all the components into one octave), the chord:

[5]

If we now diminish or "narrow" this chord by a single half step, raising F to F♯ we get the *diminished seventh* chord:

[6]

The interesting thing about this chord is that it contains *two* tritones. Since this is, as already noted, the most tense and dissonant interval of all, it is not surprising that this chord is uniquely the chord to express tension and to put the ear in a state of heightened "uneasiness" and "expectation." The chord is pre-eminently used for this purpose by Beethoven, more perhaps than any other composer, although it is very common also in Wagner's operas. Because of the additional tritones, the number of ways in which it can be "resolved" is twice that of the single tritone in the dominant seventh chord. In our previous example, we moved either from [1] to [2], or [3] (that is [1] or [1a]) to [4] (or [4a]). Since we have two tritones in the diminished seventh chord 6, and

[7]   [8]

each tritone can resolve two ways, we have four ways to "ease the tension" that is compressed into this chord. Resolving [7] in each of two ways in the manner of iv and iii above (contraction or expansion by a semitone up and down), we get the first two:

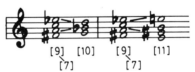

[9] [10]   [9]   [11]
[7]   [7]

(We must also make further adjustments in the other voices.) From this chord we can make a satisfying resolution of the tense and tendentive chord [9], which is our previous [6], to either [10] or [11].

But this is only half the story. When we resolve the other tritone, [8], in the chord, two more results are possible:

[9]   [12]   [9]   [13]
[8]   [8]

(Here we again make an adjustment in the other voices, but this is not relevant to the resolutions we are pointing out.)

These examples present a powerful harmonic device illustrating what I mean by 'tendentive' in the classical harmonic system. Underlying most of the music of Western Europe is the audentic cadence especially when (as in V_7–I in i above) it includes the dominant seventh. (A cadence, as the derivation of the term shows, is a falling, and that is what occurs here, just as we more from an unstable to a stable position when we physically fall down.) The power of the cadence has scarcely diminished in the twentieth century — there are merely many additional devices employed to "hold music together." Popular music is still dependent upon it, even if somewhat less than formerly. The diminished seventh chord, though it is used much less now than in the nineteenth century and is now regarded as somewhat trite, has lost little of its inherent power.

Let us go a little further into the foundations of the attracting "magnetism" exercised by the tonic toward the dominant and indeed, in one degree or another, directly or indirectly, toward all the other chords of the key. In the diatonic system the "chords of the key" are those built on thirds, this is, every other tone. Thus in the key of C we have these:

I   II   III   IV   V   VI   VII   I

Chord V, we have said, tends to move, to be followed by I, or rather, *when* it is followed by I, the music appears to move from a tense or unstable condition to one of rest. Obviously V and I do not always stand in this relation, or the music would never move at all. Music is vital, and like all living things it moves now in the direction of rest (or relative rest) and now toward motion (or relative motion).

Our account of the selection of the tones of a key which we explored to some extent in Chapter 6 must now be somewhat extended. The major scale, we found, contains the following selection among the twelves tones in one octave of the chromatic scale (the agreed upon total store of available tones in this system):

1	3	5	6	8	10	12	1	— — — — — — — — —	Semitone
C	D	E	F	G	A	B	C		series number

The choice of these tones may be accounted for as follows. Any *single* tone of, let us say, a plucked string is really a plurality. When we pluck the lowest string on a cello we hear this,

but not only this. A good ear can hear at least the three or four lowest of the following tones at the same time, and we can amplify all of them electronically:

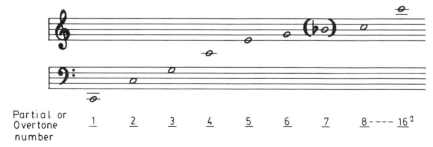

Partial or
Overtone   1   2   3   4   5   6   7   8 - - - - 16²
number

This is the so-called overtone series, and it continues indefinitely upwards. We notice that each member of the series *1, 2, 4, 8, 16,* . . . is a C. Similarly, each member of the series *3, 6, 12,* . . . is a G. And so on. There is a series like this for any fundamental tone such as may be sounded by a plucked string.

We see that the series already contains several members of our scale, that is, if we translate it downward or upward into the span of a single octave, we have

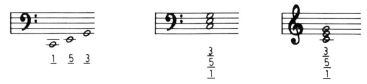

These, in fact, make up the basic or tonic chord of the key. Next we should observe that there are not only *tones* in this series but that there are just as noticeably the even more important constituents of music, the *intervals*. Notice the following intervals:

Between *1* and *2*, the octave
    "   *2* " *3*, the perfect with
    "   *3* " *4*, the perfect fourth
    "   *4* " *5*, the major third
    "   *5* " *6*, the minor third
    "   *3* " *5*, the major sixth
    "   *5* " *8*, the minor sixth

(These numbers are also the ratios of vibration frequencies in perfect intonation (e.g. *1 : 2* octave; *2 : 3* perfect fifth). It should be noted that because of the mathematical nature of the overtone series and the aesthetic and particularly harmonic demands of the ear, the construction of a usable pitch series of tones is a matter of considerable difficulty, which there is no need to go into here.) When we install these intervals within an octave we have almost all the components of our major scale:

The Roman numerals designate the degrees of the scale, the Arabic, the numbering of the semitones in the chromatic scale in one octave. (See the chromatic series, page 38.)

The derivation of this scale is as follows. We acquired I, III, and V from the overtones *1, 5,* and *3* (p. 112). Since we have established not just the several tones of the overtone series, but also the intervals between them, e.g. octave (*1–2*), fifth (*2–3*), fourth (*3–4*), third (*3–5*), etc., we are now justified in adding IV, because the interval of a fourth has appeared in the overtone series (*3–4*). IV is an interval of a perfect fourth above I. We may install VI because it is a major sixth (that is, *3–5* in the series) above I. We may install II, because it is a fifth below VI which we have just obtained. Finally we may install VII, because it is a fifth above III. Looking back we see that this gives us all the members of what is called the major mode: I, II, III, IV, V, VI, VII, or *1, 3, 5, 6, 8, 10, 12* (of the chromatic series) and the octave VIII which is again I, or 1.

There are several ways of arriving at the choice of the degrees of the scale. The fore-going illustrates one form of the derivation of the scale from the overtone series. Much depends upon what kind of scale we wish to construct and the uses to which it is to be put.

All of this, however, only provides us with the materials of music, and we can now compose a good many melodies. For example, the opening phrase of the Christmas carol, 'Joy to the World,' is simply the major scale in descending order. But many melodies need more tones than this, need, in fact, some of the remaining five members of the chromatic scale beyond the seven already given. These too can be derived from the overtone series. Moreover, all of the intervals we presented in Chapter 4 can be identified as relations among the present seven degrees. For example, the tritone is approximately the interval from IV to VII. The others are easily discovered.

The derivation of the scale reduces the infinite number of possible pitches to a manag-able few for the purposes of music and declares that these few have a unique connection and cohesion among themselves. This begins to answer the question we are concerned with in this section, how elements move toward and against one another.

Fundamentally, the answer has been sought in the overtone series, like the scale itself. As we see, the lower six members of the series themselves form a chord that is prominently heard whenever a single tone is struck. Moreover, these tones, most promi-nently the first, called the tonic, and in diminishing degrees the other tones in their order, exercise a kind of attraction toward others. Once the tonic has asserted itself, any motion away from it toward other tones will appear to be in the direction of insta-bility, and motion back to it even more powerfully toward stability. *This is the secret of the life and movement in music written in the classical harmonic system.* By judicious arrangement of tones exploiting this "gravitational force," the composer can maintain our interest in the sheer movement of tones even for long periods of time.

For any given tonic, then, tones will sound as if moving toward or away from a point of instability, or as maintaining a kind of equilibrium. Like gravitating bodies, some tones lie closer and others more distant, and the "force" is felt in proportion to this. This will help to define distant and related keys, for other tonics will be farther or closer to a given tonic. Movement back and forth so as to establish new or to dissolve old tonics is called modulation. In the classical system, conventions of composition were established in such a manner that the movement away from the tonic was always matched by a compensating return to the original tonic. With this, a sense of adventure and home-coming was conveyed — consciously for those who understood what was being done, and subconsciously, and almost equally effectively for those who did not. It is not surprising that music became the typical art of modern times.

To be as concrete as possible and yet also to keep matters as simple as we can, we may see how this "gravitational system" is thought to work on the simple level of individual tone sequences. These underlie all classical harmony, but they are immensely modified, or even virtually nullified, when we begin to work with intervals and chords. We shall leave these complexities to one side to look at the fundamentals.

What we are interested in is why tones move toward or against one another or stand neutrally. What musical psychology brings to light here is what is called the *tonic trend* or as we may speak of it in our terminology, *tonic tendence*, that is to say, the motion of a tone toward a tonic, or also, the power of a given tone to serve as a tonic in relation to certain other tones. It has been formulated about as follows: Sequences of two tones show an effect of finality or stability if the vibration frequency of the second in relation to the first reduces to the ratio-number 2 or a power of 2 (2, 4, 8, etc.).[2]

We see that the following applications of the principal governing tonic tendence are in order. (Middle C = 256 cycles/second)

	Ascending Motion toward Stability: (Reverse Motion toward Instability)					
Perfect Fourth	G → C	96:128	or	*3:4*	– –	$3:2^2$
Minor Sixth	E → C	80:128	"	*5:8*	– –	$5:2^3$
Semitone (Minor Second)	B → C	120:128	"	*15:16*	– –	$15:2^4$
Minor Seventh	D → C	72:128	"	*9:16*	– –	$9:2^4$
	Descending Motion toward Stability (Reverse Motion toward Instability)					
Perfect Fifth	C ← G	64:96	or	*2:3*	– –	$2^1:3$
Major Third	C ← E	64:80	"	*4:5*	– –	$2^2:5$
Whole Tone (Major Second)	C ← D	64:72	"	*8:9*	– –	$2^3:3$
Major Seventh	C ← B	64:120	"	*8:15*	– –	$2^3:15$
	Neutral Intervals (No power of 2 in the ratios)					
Major Sixth	C ⟷ A	64:106.66	or	*3:5*		
Minor Third	E ⟷ G	80:96	"	*5:6*		
	Special Cases					
Octave	C – C	64:128	or	*1:2*	– –	$2^0:2^1$
Tritone	F – B	85.33:120	"	$1:\sqrt{2}$	– –	$2^0:2^{\frac{1}{2}}$

These, of course, are not the only intervals in the octave, being confined to those that relate directly to the tonic (upper or lower C). The other instances of the intervals will show the same effect (for example, the ascending fourth E to A, the descending fifth A to D, and so on). But, of course, in these secondary instances the effect is modified if the overriding center of harmonic interest is C. As soon as there is modulation sufficiently convincing to establish, let us say, F as a new tonic, C will now function as the fifth degree of the new scale and not as its all-important first (or eighth). (The temporal scale which keyboard instruments must use to minimize certain mathematically inexorable difficulties of so-called pure intonation, on which the present figures are based, cannot be considered in this brief survey.)

The octave plays an exceptional role in apparent violation of the rule. Although its ratio (*1:2*) should be covered by the law of tonic tendence, it must actually be treated differently. An octave appears to re-present another tone *exactly*, except that it is higher or lower, whereas all the other intervals seem to present a real contrast to a given tone. In general, the octave can be reckoned among the neutral intervals. In Křenek's opinion, it "creates the impression of a complete standstill of the musical flow."[3]

The tritone is the devilish one. Lying in the center of the octave it is not so much neutral to the extremes as equally hostile to both. But it performs a necessary role. If it is said to be the most dissonant of intervals, this does not mean at all that it is to be avoided but rather that it is tense, abrasive, "thought-provoking," "anxious," unstable.[4] But all these qualities are absolutely necessary to make music move, like the spurs of a cavalryman. A characteristic use of the tritone that lies in the middle of the key structure (e.g. F♯ in the key of C) is to follow it by the fifth of the key, a semitone above it (moving up by a semitone as a characteristic trend).[5] Here is an example from the opening of Beethoven's Waldstein Sonata where F♯ quickly leads to a chord on G, the fifth of C:

Only moments later in the sixth bar the very same device is used to move from a new tonic in B♭ via E (a tritone above it) to an F chord. The rhythmic motion of the musical thought is here inherently rapid, but the tense tritones stimulate it even more.

The explanation of the trend may be left to physics and psychology. The important fact is that these sequences do show these trends provided they are heard either independent of context, or in the context of some key. this is another *ceteris paribus* condition such as we have encountered before.

Twelve-tone music may be thought to nullify and disprove the genuineness of these trends and affinities. On the contrary, it renders them all the more probable, since a large part of the harmonic strategy of this music has to be devoted to undoing and counteracting their power. Thus Křenek in discussing the construction of tone rows warns: "Avoid major or minor triads formed by a group of three consecutive tones, as for instance:

because the tonal implications emanating from a triad are incompatible with the principles of atonality."[6] The brackets map out four familiar triads.

We must remind ourselves that any sequence may be expected to occur sooner or later. There is no probability that motions of ascending or descending to a position of rest will occur oftener than those moving toward instability, nor is one of these to be preferred to the other. Since music must move, both of these are needed, as are the neutral or indifferent intervals.

It should also be pointed out that these generalizations about motion and rest apply principally to single tones. Harmonic progression is far more complex. And yet even with harmonic progression certain of these movements tend to hold. The composer employing the classical system will tend to close a movement with the tonic (I) and to approach it from the dominant (V). The bass voice is instructive to observe since it will generally move in accordance with the generalizations about the trend toward the tonic: at the final cadence the bass voice will either rise a fourth or descend a fifth. The soprano most often does likewise, or it ascends a semitone, or falls a whole tone towards the tonic. If we are looking for exceptions we may cite the "Amen Cadence" or "Plagal Cadence" which *descends* a fourth, instead of ascending, but only for a special effect and under conditions where the tonic has previously been very emphatically established.

The result, then, is that the tonic trend and the usual patterns of the classical harmony are very convincing to the ear, so much so, that if composers, such as Schoenberg and his school, wish to introduce an entirely new order, they must first undo the old: its strength is shown by the fact that it does not collapse of itself. It is not a mere set of conventions, but a kind of natural resource for music that nature provides us. We may, as we say, "take it or leave it," but taking it is by far the easier choice. None of this, of course, need discourage composers from attempting to found a *novus ordo rerum*, if they can.

We see from all this that there are tendentive connections for the artist to use that are illustrated by the tonic trend and the cadence. The vitality of the musical medium lies in the complex inner "magnetism" tones appear to be endowed with. Of course, the tendence represented by these features of classical harmony need not be employed any more than a painter must use complementary colors merely because nature affords them. There are also other life-giving powers such as rhythm and thematic continuity which the composer is at liberty to employ. There is, however, not the slightest doubt of the power of the devices we have here sketched out.

We began with the notion of elements and relations. Although this approach appears dangerously "atomistic" and is thus deservedly suspect in this kind of subject matter, it is really only a vocabulary for dealing with the arts. Artworks, we are always being told, are wholes, are organic, unified, one. But they are not undifferentiated wholes. Their interest lies precisely in the manner in which we can shift our attention from the whole to the parts, and back again. When we ask what the parts are, we find that parts have parts within parts. If any limits to this division can be found, these limits are what we may call elements in a strong sense of the term. As already explained in Chapters 2 and 3, we have no intention, in resorting to the vocabulary of elements and form, of imitating chemistry, or nuclear physics, or set theory, or structural psychology, or whatever other sciences employ the notion of elements. The point is solely that this vocabulary, suitably redefined for art, enables us to speak as precisely as we need to about the structure of artworks.

Our notion of element, or elemental character, was coupled with that of *elemental appeal*, and of form with *formal appeal*. As to the first of these, every element, or elemental quality, so far as it may be isolated (and in this we found some riddles which have never been solved), has some appeal, even if minimal. We must allow for this appeal and respect it as entirely autonomous except when the element is subjected to the influence of other elements. We allow the observer the completest freedom in his preferences. Your dislike of the timbre of the saxophone or the bassoon or the oboe, or Prussian blue or chrome yellow (these being as elemental as anything we encounter) is one which I may share, or pity, or deplore, but, in any event, I must accord it a kind of respect. There is no conceivable resolution of aesthetic differences and disputes wherever they are wholly of this sort.

The only kinds of disputes that are resolvable are those that concern the *formal appeal* of elements. And for this we must turn to the relations that obtain among the elements: the totality of the types of relations in a given complex constitutes the form of it. The relations of the last three types may now be summed up as follows:

(1) Two elements, x and y, have *comparative* relations with one another if, being concomitant in a context, they can be placed on some dimensional scale, for example, pitch, hue, size (extent or duration), etc. But they gain aesthetic significance only when they are *also* related in the following ways:

(2) x and y have a *contextual* relationship if in some context of relevance (e.g., the area enclosed by a frame) their concomitance mutually generates effects in them that they do not have in other contexts; and

(3) x and y have a *tendentive* relationship when, given that they differ and are concomitant, the tension or force in the one element is satisfied or fulfilled in the other, or one simply gravitates in some manner toward the other. Formal appeal, therefore, means that an element may justify its place in reference to others depending upon its relations to them in the foregoing manner.

Our three types of relations have a significance that is cumulative as we pass from the comparative relations, through the contextual to the tendentive. *First*, considering a previous example, if we merely take note of the fact that one element is, let us say, large and white, while some other is small and red, nothing of aesthetic significance, so far, follows; these are merely comparative relations. But *second*, when it is thought that there is some noticeable effect in one detail of given dimensions because of the presence of some other detail, serious consequences arise: we may call into question the competence of the artist in developing his materials in this manner, or in fact feel satisfaction in the result. *Third*, (and this is primarily a problem facing the artist, in view of the effect that elements may have on one another) the principal question arising about each element, from the greatest to the smallest, is what its inherent tendencies and affinities are and how these are or are not being satisfied in others in the work before us.

Pursuing the last point a little further we see that here the critic can at most be expected to point out what is wrong with the work, what demands have been frustrated, left unsatiated; it is an artistic, not a critical ability that is needed to devise better remedies. Although the artist in his work of composition is constantly confronted with questions in all of these three areas, he alone is *obliged to find answers* to them.

But artists and critics must also share one another's abilities, as it were. Clearly a critic who can only say of a work, "there's something wrong with it," is inferior to one who can say, "if the artist had done so and so the results would have been thus and so." We can also soon identify an "artist" who never works in a self-critical manner, who is apparently unconcerned or even unaware of the nature or character of the elements he is working with, their effect on and their affinities for one another. If he is not plagued by the desire to find "answers" to these questions in the medium he is working with, he is clearly not worth regarding as an artist. To deserve any esteem at all he must be concerned with such questions, both on the large scale, ordering prime emergents, and the small, reckoning the power of the least details. Looking at composition as a process in time we see that the first element chosen already limits the choice of the next and this in turn limits those that follow. Depth of interest and understanding and breadth of comprehension of all the ensuing complexities are necessary conditions of artistic creativity.

SUMMARY

Intention is by itself an inadequate justification for elements in relation to one another, since these also have inherent directions or affinities of their own which the artist must attend to. These inherent properties may be identified as the tendentive powers of elements, and are illustrated in all works of art.

The tendentive character of elements is a principal source of the inner relations of works of art and of what we have designated their formal character and formal appeal.

Artworks must be comprehended through the grasp of their form as articulated in these inner relations as well as through an understanding of the artistic strategies of composition, since form is essentially the response in one part of the artwork to the demands that are generated in another part.

NOTES

[1] In the key of C major, a chord built up on C is the tonic and numbered I. A chord built of the fifth degree (G) of the scale of C is called the dominant of that key and numbered V. (The sequence of chords in C major from I to VII is illustrated later in this chapter, page 55.) The sequence *V–I* is

called an authentic cadence in which the motion is felt as one toward rest. The reverse motion is felt as one of instability. Similarly, in the chord of Bb, the V is built on F yielding the chord (*F A C*) and the I on Bb yielding the chord (Bb D F). Chords in the classical system are built up in "thirds" (F to the next higher A is a third, and also A to C, and so on).

2 Robert M. Ogden: 1938, *The Psychology of Art*, Scribner, New York, p. 55ff. Max Schoen: 1940, *The Psychology of Music*, Ronald Press, New York, p. 26ff.

3 Ernst Křenek: 1940, *Studies in Counterpoint*, G. Schirmer, New York. p. 7.

4 The term 'dissonant' is not generally used in an appraisive sense by the musician and music theorist. What he is speaking of is the tense and somewhat clashing intervals as against those that seem smooth and accommodating. What we hear as consonant or dissonant has changed over the centuries. Medieval "organum" permitted simultaneous singing of two voices only at distances of the octave and the fourth or fifth. The latter when sounded successively came to be regarded as absolutely intolerable in the centuries in which tonalism prevailed. The intervals of the third and sixth, on the other hand, which seem smooth and sweet to us, were avoided in the early middle ages. It is said that Pope John XXII issued a bull forbidding their use. Of course, the bull was soon defied, and the third and sixth came to be cornerstones of diatonic harmony. It must not be thought that atonalism frowns upon the distinction consonant-dissonant. One may consult the discussion in Křenek (p. 7) to see how intervals are regarded in the system of atonalism.

5 Examples of tritones abound in virtually any page of music. A prominent example of the tritone resolving to a sixth is found in the treble at the opening chords of Hugo Wolf's 'Anacreons Grab' (with additional notes in the tenor).

The same reappears (on higher degrees) later in the same song.

6 Ernst Křenek: 1940, *Studies in Counterpoint*, G. Schirmer, New York, p. 1.

CHAPTER 9

EXPRESSION: "INSTANT COHERENCE"

(7: *Seventh Relation of Elements*)

We have been asking ourselves, what makes works of art hang together? The artist, being an artist, must ask himself this question fairly constantly, since he does not act from instinct like the bee building a hive or the beaver a dam. Even if he denies any concern about coherence, the chances are very great that he has merely decided to abandon the use of unifying devices handed down from an earlier generation, such as the employment of recognizable figures in painting or sculpture, or tonality in music, and resorted to others. He will almost certainly be asking himself about unity and coherence if he undertakes to employ only "abstract" devices. Even if he trusts to aleatory techniques, to chance, the form or coherence question is certain to arise again. For he is very unlikely to accept *every* "poem-shaped" object that chance or a computer turns up: he will accept some things and delete others. Among the untold billions of things that chance may turn up may also be all the sentimental ditties or picture post-card paintings a serious artist may heartily despise. Choice and guidance are thus in any event a compelling necessity.

The point now is that reproducing or representing nature or objects in the environment is *one* way in which an aesthetic complex can come to be united, since in fact they are already united simply by being there. Thus, representation may be resorted to for what we may call, inventing, or adapting a phrase from the current vernacular, "instance coherence."

As we have been using terms, parts or elements in the finished work cohere with one another when they can justify their presence or position. As already noted, this is not to be thought of as an argument, a verbal justification. Even the artist who is asked why this element is here and another over there and answers no more than, because it seems right to me, has offered a kind of justification.

If it is now objected that merely "being there" is not enough to produce any kind of coherence, and if all other representational or expressional devices are repudiated, we are thrown back on those resources for order already considered that are native to the dimensions and figures that constitute the object (comparative, contextual, tendentive and other relations). The matter of fact order in nature or in any environment where no effort has been made to control the shape of it from an aesthetic standpoint we may call 'concomitance.' The choice is then clear: either the desire for order is satisfied with one of the infinite number of concomitant situations in nature or it is not. If not, order must be sought somewhere else, that is, the artist makes of the object or complex an artefact and proceeds to organize or reorganize it according to other "canons of art" than nature has resorted to in simply putting things where they are and shaping them as they are. Interestingly enough, part of what will have to be attributed to nature is all those effects that artefacts have gained when *not* deliberately planned. Thus not only the view of Mt. Shasta or Mt. Hood (both of them post card favorites) but the man-made but unintentional view of Manhattan from Staten Island will be equally natural, for the sheer outline of these things was never planned to be what it is.

In passing, we may observe that the resort to "aleatory creativity" is the way in which nature has recently seemed almost to force its way back into the arts, for the laws of chance are as much a part of nature as any representable object or any physical law or truth.

Traditional representational arts were usually content with what seemed generally or usually to be the case. Any generalization about nature can be considered a law and this in no merely metaphorical sense. The exact measurements of the spatial dimension of a hand or head, yours or mine, may never apply perfectly to any other hand or head. But it is a zoological or anatomical law that a human hand has four fingers and a thumb, that two hands on one body are more or less perfectly inversely symmetrical, that a human head has two ears, two nostrils, one mouth, etc., etc. At the same time, depending on what our view of such inductive laws is, we see that things *might* have been different. This means that the concomitances in human bodies, for example, are only highly probable, and we must be prepared to find rare occasional exceptions.

One way, then, to unify a picture or other aesthetic complex, in addition to all the other ways we have already explored is, for example, to display a system of concomitance, such as a human body, clothed or unclothed, in whole or part. The inevitable result is that if the observer thinks he discerns a head, he can be relied upon to look for eyes and ears, and if these, then a mouth and nose, and if these then a neck and shoulders, and so on until he reaches either the outlines of a body or the edge of the picture.

Since these "visual inferences" are made with virtually instantaneous rapidity, we can see that the figure will cohere as soon as the observer *sees it as* an X, where X is some kind of body, scene, or situation with which some viewers at least will be familiar. Hence, "instant coherence."

As we look back over the centuries of painting, do we not find some paintings at least that are of undoubtedly poor design, or weak in tendentive connection from point to point, or disoriented from want of a definite or magnetic figure, and all of this apparently compensated for, or thought to be, by the legend, plot, scene, person, place, or thing depicted? Or on the other hand, have we not seen many works with apparently trivial subject matter (e.g., still lifes) admirably organized in every painterly aspect? In observing and listening to many painters of our century one finds an extraordinary determination to expunge every conceivable representational suggestion. There is more than one reason for this, but certainly the determination to be self-dependent and not to lean on "suggestive" subject matter to gain coherence has been the most prominent. The result has been a veritable detonation whose echoes will be heard for even more years to come. Burn your librettos, your other literary "ponies," they say: the work of art is here, on the canvas, not on the moors of Scotland, or the canals of Venice, or the overfamiliar contours of the human body.

It is evident that the artist may now easily lose sight of other values which painting and sculpture have in the past served to celebrate, and that he himself may thereby contribute to his alienation from a world which he inherently must address himself to no matter how eremitic the seclusion he seeks.

The subject matter we have been considering is what in the literature of aesthetics and criticism has been called "expression." What is expression and how may it or does it contribute to the way in which the picture or any other artwork "hangs together?" Since the term has been used in such a variety of ways we may now ask what they are.[1]

Expression is a notoriously difficult notion, but one that is fairly indispensable in talking about the arts. We are adverting to it for a quite special reason, the role it plays in ordering the artist's materials; we shall at most only be able to sketch in certain essentials. We may treat expression under several heads: as *intention* or as *symptom*, and as *vehicle* or *embodiment*. These are only some of the most prominent examples of the term.

(a) Under *intention* we shall place those devices or techniques which are not only available to the artist to express himself but themselves also express something. Obviously, sometimes these two will not be congruent, as we have noted before: the artist may intend one thing and yet the product may be read by the observer as "saying" something quite different. If the artist's expression is to be successful he must bring these two into line with each other. What, then, are the specific materials available to the artist other than those already considered?

The materials of expression derive their efficaciousness from the fact that they are already concomitant, either by nature or convention. They can make their power felt in a number of ways.

We may begin with the familiar device of attaching a *name* to the artwork. This instantly channels the observer's expectations in a certain direction, supposing, of course, that the name means something to him. The observer is immediately set to work "decoding," and as he does, things fall into place. Since the name may be that of a legend or situation as well as person, place or thing, it will obviously be far more effective than one might expect from the few words that constitute it. But the power of such a device is often so great that the artist will not only resist the use of it but find himself in competition with it for the observer's attention. He usually wants this to be centered upon the materials of the work itself; a name may conjure up images the observer brings to it and not those the artist wants to create. Since the rise of surrealism and expressionism, particularly German, artists have frequently adopted titles for their works that are completely incongruent with them or have even attached mere numbers to them, in the manner of composers of music. This illustrates as nothing else can the power which a name or title frequently exercises over a work and the experience of it. It tends to get between the observer and the work and may fail to perform the hermeneutic purpose it is meant to have. We must remember that titles are often the coinage of persons other than the artist. The title, then, is one prominent way to promote expression and thus to lend coherence to a work, or pretend to.

We turn next to the *paraphrase* which is frequently resorted to convey what the work is said to mean or express. Paraphrases are usually not the work of the artist himself. Most often they are the painfully worked out efforts of critics or interpreters of difficult works. Joyce's *Ulysses* and *Finnegans Wake* have evoked such paraphrases or interpretations.

To quote a fairly simple example which will serve our purpose, we may turn to a poem of Emerson with a paraphrase proposed by a fellow New England Brahmin, Oliver Wendell Holmes, the elder.[2]

Days

Daughters of Time, the hypocritic Days,
Muffled and dumb like barefoot dervishes,

> And marching single in an endless file,
> Bring diadems and fagots in their hands.
> To each they offer gifts after his will,
> Bread, kingdoms, stars, and sky that holds them all.
> I, in my pleachèd garden, watched the pomp,
> Forgot my morning wishes, hastily
> Took a few herbs and apples, and the Day
> Turned and departed silent. I, too late,
> Under her solemn fillet saw the scorn.

The paraphrase Dr. Holmes offered is:

The days were ever divine, as to the first Aryans. They come and go like muffled and veiled figures, sent from a distant friendly party; but they say nothing and if we do not use the gifts they bring, they carry them as silently away.

It is almost instantly evident that the paraphrase, while it certainly throws light on the poem, is not altogether accurate, or it omits what may seem to the reader of the poem important. For example, Holmes might, with a single word, have taken note of the fact that the departure of the days is not only taken in silence but with *scorn* at our not making full use of the time our lives occupy. What is even more significant is the way Holmes then goes on to characterize the difference between the poem and the paraphrase:

Now see this thought in full dress, and then ask what is the difference between the prose and poetry . . . Cinderella at the fireside, and Cinderella at the prince's ball! The full dress version of the thought is glittering with new images . . . . That one word pleachèd . . . gives to the noble sonnet an antique dignity and charm like the effect of an ancestral jewel.

(The term "sonnet' is, of course, used in a loose sense by Holmes.) The paraphrase, then, was to Holmes that which the poem expresses. And if we ask what the relation of the one to the other is we receive the answer that the poem is simply the paraphrasable content, plus decoration, this being the poetic form, in this case a rather free pentameter, and a certain grace and elegance in phraesology. I shall not take issue with this fairly standard notion of expression. The point is that if we ask what the poem expresses we may receive in answer the paraphrase, this one or some other. It is intended to help us gather what may be confused and straying thoughts on first reading into a *coherent* whole, the poem itself. As a matter of fact this poem of Emerson inspires rather varied interpretations, as we can see in the four commentators quoted with the poem in the anthology, *The Case for Poetry*.[2] Yvor Winters regards the presentation of "a rational critique of the paraphrasable content (roughly, the motive) of the poem" as one of the primary duties of a critic.[3] It is no part of my purpose to endorse or deny this.

Of course, *paraphrasable content* is obviously particularly apt for certain arts but possibly not for all. That is, we think a paraphrase as an aid in getting to know a particularly difficult poem or novel. But what paraphrase can we expect or demand, if any, for Brancusi's Bird, Duchamp's Nude Descending a Staircase (Chapter 15(12)), or any number of works by more recent artists such as Mark Rothko, Pierre Soulages, Hans Hofmann, or Georges Mathieu? With the Bird and the Nude the answer is comparatively easy. The author has in a sense offered a paraphrase in the title. And when we learn the titles of these we in some sense see or grasp the paraphrasable content in the work, for indeed the "bird," the sculpture itself, seems to soar or to poise for soaring, and the "nude" seems to have a head, thighs, bust, and pelvic development that easily call to mind the image of a person walking or stepping downwards. But it is not easy to say whether these paraphrased contents would have occurred to us without the prompting of the artist's title.

Supposing the artist has offered the title, should we even then take the title or paraphrased content seriously in looking at these two famous landmarks of "modern art?" With other recent painters we get what may prove to be a more honest response with titles such as No. 5 or December 16, 1959. Since the time of, let us say, Whistler, who is in a sense the author of the convention of neutral titles (cf. his "Mother," which he called Arrangement in Grey and Black), we have long since grown accustomed to titles that put us off and that appear to say to those who seek paraphrasable content, "Stop asking silly questions and look at the work."

If one goes farther back, one can find titles apparently used to entertain the listener. How indeed do the keyboard compositions called The Mysterious Barricades or Soeur Monique of François Couperin express what the names say? One might, of course, succeed in finding memoirs or other documents saying that Couperin was in fact thinking of certain real or figurative barricades or of a nun or sister named Monica. It is actually a pretty entertainment to have these titles hover in our thought while listening to these two brief but splendid compositions. But are they necessary? Has the composer added anything significant with the titles?

If an artist uses a title that seems seriously intended he invites us to let our imagination roam in a certain direction while we look or listen. The danger is, as we have said, that all this may place a barrier between us and the work. Even apparently materially non-committal titles such as Symphony IV or Arrangement in Grey and Black may not be altogether free of this.

The inevitable question that arises is: Does the artwork exist simply to illustrate the paraphrased content, or conversely, is this content merely a derivative, an *aide memoire*, a glossary or even a road map, which we may dispense with as soon as the "places" in the artwork are "located?" The artist will not be content with either formula, and yet the composer particularly may seek the benefits of both in a *program*, posing as a kind of illustrator or collaborator in a joint work of art: Liszt's "symphonic poems" or Richard Strauss's "tone poems" are ready examples. It is also entirely possible to reverse the usual order of proceeding from words (e.g., the Don Juan story) to music: that is, a poem may be composed in some sort of emulation of the music itself. In a sense ballet choreographers have done this many times over, using Chopin's piano music, Tchaikowsky's symphonies, and even those of Brahms.

It is evident that many versions of this process may be attempted and also that many fail utterly. In each case what the music expresses is rendered by the title, paraphrase or program in order to obtain for the music the benefits of the *coherence* which the tale or fable or poem already possesses. The argument appears to be: if the story hangs together, and there is a one to one correspondence with the music, the music will hang together.

All this is comparatively simple if we do not raise the rude and troublesome question *how* anything in one sense-modality *can* find a parallel or expression in another. This question, which has already been adverted to, goes to the heart of the expression problem and has never received a convincing answer other than a *solvitur ambulando*. What is evident is that transmedial or intermedial devices such as programs *are* employed to give an artwork coherence.

An artist in one art is not necessarily deficient because he deliberately borrows from another art. It affords him a stimulus to composition and he passes it along to us. But as to actual depiction, we may well ask whether any one would ever have attached the names Manfred, Tod und Verklärung, Les Préludes, or La Mer to the works that bear these names, if the composers had not done so. In every case the work we hear is affected, fatefully affected, by the knowledge of the title or program.

There are still other devices or stratagems the artist may use that fall under intentional expression. We must, of course, be careful to exclude the use of a kind of *code* to express something. As literary critics are quick to say, merely talking about an emotion usually does not express the emotion, make it real and vivid for others. So also in transmedial situations we could set up some convention, for example a triangle within a circle ⊚ (somewhat like the current symbol for peace ⊕), to symbolize, let us say, love or immortality, but it is hard to see how any such symbol could have any artistic, rather than a *conventional* semantic power to communicate this idea. The artistic use of one medium in relation to another is not that of a sign to thing signified. It must not only signify what it is about but in some manner realize it before us. *Metaphor* and *symbolism* may in this sense not only enliven a subject but lend it a high degree of meaning. The same use may be made of *myth* or *allegory*.

In each case the artist relies on our knowledge of a sequence or plot in one medium to enable us to decode another. Certain features of the one fairly readily allow themselves to be encoded in this manner, but it is apparent that if we can, as we must, distinguish between formal and material (elemental) traits, only the formal can really be encoded. How can a poem or a piece of sculpture or a painting succeed in summoning up some sort of image of a trumpet fanfare, or the strain felt in his muscles by Hercules, or the stench of the Augean stables? Questions like these must be left to be investigated on some other occasion.

This, then, is a large family of expressional devices (title, paraphrase, program, allegory, metaphor, myth, symbolism, even Eliot's objective correlative).[4] It is evident that they are employable not only for expression itself but for insuring a kind of desired coherence or order. The latter is the only aspect of the expression problem that we are here concerned with.

If, in practice, these devices lend coherence to the work, we need to ask ourselves whether the art work also can stand by itself without the prop of the program? We cannot generalize as to whether art works can or cannot. We can only say that if a work does maintain its power, it does so from the strength of the comparative, contextual and tendentive relations of its elements, from the strength of these elements themselves, and from the power of its figure or figures, for there are no other sources of strength.

(b) Another use that may be made of the term 'expression' is revealed when the expressing product is taken to be a *symptom* of a condition, either in the author or artist, or of the age, social milieu, class, or anything else which may reasonably be said to be a personal or environmental determinant of it. There seems to be no reason to suppose that anything of this sort can be thought to be responsible for an artist's coherent or incoherent expression, because a symptom by its nature does not depend on choice.

If the artist intends to express something then, to be sure, his product may even of itself *show* it. But generally in this situation he manipulates the object so as to be a correlative for what he wants to express, and this puts it into our first set of types of expression.

We do of course gain a kind of understanding of artworks when we learn what their determinants are. It is inevitable that many works will be searched in the hope of learning about what "lies back of them," particularly their authors and their social origin. They will be studied to see what they "betray" (as a symptom may be a betrayal) of such origins. If this is sometimes thought of in terms of expression, there will, of course, be a *perfect congruence* between what is expressed and the expression of it, because the symptom is by its nature produced by a given phenomenon. If such expression can be better or worse, it will be largely a quantitative matter: some products reflect or express their age or their authors only slightly, others afford a broader or deeper glimpse. In general, symptomatic expression is always successful, provided we can identify what it is a symptom of.

In general, this kind of expression is to be entirely distinguished from intended expression: some of the best expressions of, let us say, mid-Victorian England, Trollope's novels, for example, were not created to be symptoms or "betrayals" of their age. Usually, deliberate efforts of this sort are self-conscious, stilted and may prove to emphasize the wrong things. Just as we are in a poor position to characterize ourselves, so the artist who is truly *of* his age can only serve as the subject of characterization *by others*.

The understanding of the artwork through the apprehension of it as a symptom or "betrayal" may enhance our interest in it and its author and even the internal and external relationship of its parts: everything in a causal context is revelatory in this sense, and what it so reveals of artist and artwork may be altogether momentous, since the two are congruent or even identical.

(c) There are two further notions that grow out of the expression problem, and they involve such nearly fatal misinterpretations of what works of art are that the complete abandonment of the term 'expression' in criticism could only have a salubrious effect.

In one interpretation, the work of art is a kind of language or *vehicle* for the *artist* to use to express some disembodied thought or conception. In the other, some conception is thought to be an *embodiment* of the material frame of the artwork. The two are somewhat complementary to one another.

We cannot be content with the first of these since it gives a false picture of the relation of the artist to his work. An artist does not regard his work as something dispensable or expendable — to be jettisoned once his conception has reached his audience. He literally loves his paint, clay, brass, iron, wood or other form of matter; a musician loves the literal sound of instruments or voices in his ear; the poet or novelist loves words, their meaning, use, structure and so on. It is difficult to redeem the notion of expression, as it has been used, to convey these facts about artists when we think of an artwork as only a *vehicle* or a *language*. The sculptor may be accustomed to the use of the expression vocabulary, but he emphatically does not regard his material as an *indifferent vehicle* for his thought. What would be an example where the vehicle is entirely indifferent? Naval vessels communicate in a number of ways; of these some are to be preferred under certain circumstances such as weather or visibility or battle conditions. The very same message can be communicated by Morse Code, signal flags on the rigging, signalling by a seaman using an appropriate pennant in each hand, and flashing lights, all of these in addition to radio broadcasting of words. It is obvious that no artist has ever regarded his medium in any such utilitarian manner.

Neither can we accept the interpretation of expression as embodiment. This is a meaningless relic of an otherwise extinct Neo-Platonism. We can see its results in Holmes' interpretation of Emerson's poem, not so much in the paraphrase of it, which is harmless or even helpful, but in the interpretation that follows this which appears to set forth poetry as a form of *decoration* (interior or exterior). The flat, prose, paraphrased content is thought to be decked out like "Cinderella at the ball." Paraphrased content has its makeshift uses, but the equation "expression = decoration' can do no honor to poetry or to any other art, for if this *is* what is expressed, the answer must often be, "Is *that* all he meant to say? Why didn't he say it more plainly? Why did he go to these lengths?"

'Expression = decoration' is as mystifying as 'expression = incarnation' in an earlier age. To be sure 'embodiment' or 'expression' is a harmless enough *manner of speaking*, but it, along with 'form-content,' is so insidiously misleading that it deserves to be virtually expunged from our way of talking about art. Rather, we should look to the natural means for order in artworks, in all the richness of their dimensions. So long as we need a paraphrase we have not yet fully confronted the work of art itself.

Having added the immense resources of connotative relations to the dimensional, contextual, and tendentive we now have all the principal means of effecting coherence before us. We have pointed to exemplifications in particular arts in order to relieve the necessarily general character of the account, which is meant to serve as a rationale for all the arts. The more purely "abstract" arts or styles of art may appear to illustrate its formal generalizations better than those with connotative or expressive content. This we deny. "Content" furnishes only a new set of relations, as 'relations' is understood here. The apparent conflict that tempts us to interpret the classical form-content distinction in such a way as to oppose one to the other derives from the habit of regarding a form as an empty vessel that "holds" or "embodies" the content and from the almost irresistible power of connotations to usurp the center of our interest at the expense of nonconnotational relations, to which the term 'form' is sometimes confined.

These are, of course, theoretical questions which should be kept distinct from the problems of the practice of art. We must here refrain from favoring one trend over another, abstract art over representational art, or purely instrumental music over such "mixed media" as opera or song, or the reverse. Our effort must be directed toward understanding and not toward dictating what practice shall be. "Form-content" is a coinage of theory which is but an obstacle to understanding.

The relations introduced into artworks by *connotation* or expression raise singular problems. The relation to the spectator is evidently more complex for the "external world," the world beyond the gilt frame, thereby appears to enter the experience. In consequence, the force of expressive and connotational "content" tends to be centrifugal for the artwork and to shift its function in an epigraphic direction: the artwork may become a poster. While this is not necessarily an objection, it is well to be aware of the fact when it arises. The co-ordination of various families or relations resident in artworks also becomes particularly acute when connotation and expression make their appearance in them.

Connotation introduces a factor from which immense benefit can accrue to the artwork through the range of significance it opens up. It also exposes it to the hazard of a "retreat from the phenomenon," into intellectual (as against phenomenal) abstraction which cannot but be fatal to it as art. The artist is well-advised to keep this in mind when he chooses either to introduce or to avoid connotative elements in his work. There is no danger that the avoidance of connotation will entail any more diminution of meaningfulness in the artwork than that the artist has declined to avail himself of a particular pattern of inner significance.

The most momentous of all the expressive connections derives from the fact that the artist is the prime causal fact in any art, at least as we have known it until now. He has his intentions, skills, and techniques, of course, but he is revealing himself as well as expressing himself. The whole man responds as a person with a past, present, and future, and his responses spring from ultimate determinants we may know nothing about, either in general or in particular. We value the artwork because it is never wholly "detached" from the artist. It gives us not only a symbol, vehicle, or embodiment of his thought, but his thought itself. Michelangelo and Mozart thought *so*, and the "so" *is* the *Pieta* or the *Requiem*. The thought is not somewhere distant from or distinguishable from the work. This is why it can feed the soul in aesthetic experience.

SUMMARY

In addition to the devices already examined that may be thought to contribute to the unity or coherence of artworks, techniques of representation and expression are also available to the artist.

Resort to representation of nature or the environment promotes coherence because nature is itself subject to laws which make it intelligible. Resort to aleatory techniques to produce what have been called "poem-shaped objects" or other such artefacts introduces nothing essentially new so long as selection is exercised on the limitless products that chance turns up.

The artist's reliance upon lawlike associations and regularities in nature promotes order or coherence because, or to the extent that, the observer can be depended upon to make coherent inferences in accordance with them.

Expression may conveniently be considered to comprise two principal areas: what is expressed may be explained when we can regard it as the artist's intention or as the symptom of the personality of the author or artist or his social context.

Names and titles are often used to convey the artist's intention. This may also appear in the form of allegory, myth, symbolism, or an "objective correlative."

Paraphrases, like titles, are hermeneutic devices, often not the artist's, to formulate or to help reveal the artist's intention.

Neither the notion of a vehicle which bears the real work of art nor that of its embodiment in an outward form can serve as more than misleading metaphors: the artwork *is* the artist's thought, not a representative of it.

NOTES

[1] Karl Aschenbrenner: *The Concepts of Criticism,* §5.5.
[2] Frederick L. Gwynn (and others): 1954, *The Case for Poetry*, Prentice-Hall New York, p. 139.
[3] Yvor Winters: 1943, 'Preliminary Problems: Twelfth Problem', *The Anatomy of Nonsense*, New Directions, Norfolk, Conn.
[4] T. S. Eliot: 1919, 1921, 'Hamlet and His Problems', *The Sacred Wood*, Knopf, New York.

CHAPTER 10

HOW IS ART POSSIBLE? (1)

To ask the somewhat Kantian question of our title is undoubtedly to invite the expectation that a definition of art or a specification of the necessary and sufficient conditions of it, or a summative analysis of it is being proposed. But this is not our intention. Some of what may be necessary conditions have been explored here, but by no means all. We are now concerned only with what may be called the objective conditions, with that which is inherent in the objects of experience, of sense and perception, and which makes it possible to develop aesthetic objects in some sense-modalities but not readily, if at all, in others. To specify other conditions one has to proceed to a much more specific delineation of the media of the particular arts, visual, musical, literary, and other, and beyond this to direct one's thoughts to the artist himself and to the vast assortment of available techniques. Beyond what is about to be specified, all the form-giving resources already explored at length stand open to the artist.

Since we confine ourselves to the senses, the most notable mode of art that falls largely outside consideration for the present is of course literary art. Here one must look beyond the senses, narrowly construed, to uncover other necessary conditions, specifically notions such as causation and motivation: without these, human actions cannot be understood. But although motivation and causation must clearly take us beyond the senses, they are themselves but modes of what we have called *tendence* or the *tendentive*, as will become clearer in the analysis offered in Chapter 13 and in the study of narrative poetry in Chapter 14. The various dimensions of artistic data summarized in the next chapter are applicable also to the materials of literary art, but this calls for a more detailed and extended exposition than we can accord it here.

One of our principal contentions in Chapters 10 and 11 is that the basic character of the several senses helps to determine the nature of the arts: if our senses and the data of our senses were not as they are, no arts as we know them could ever have come into being.

Let us assume that art is to be located in general in the realm of perception or imagination. Classical aesthetics recognized only vision and audition, including also visual and auditory imagination, as vehicles of the arts. Without considering the reasons that were cited in the past in support of this, we can learn some important lessons about the arts by reviewing all of the sense-modalities to determine why some of them are evidently more favorable than others to the development of arts.

Assuming for the moment that we are sufficiently familiar with vision and audition, let us look first at other modalities: tactile or haptic, thermal, olfactory, and gustatory or savory. One might even have to include pain in such a review, since it is at certain levels an entirely distinct sense. We shall omit consideration of it almost altogether for the simple reason that it is obviously an abnormality to want to be afflicted with pain. We shall discuss the family of erotic sensations only briefly because they largely reduce to the others and because the subject is of so vast a scope we cannot hope to do it justice here. Kinaesthetic sense has not been extensively considered for reasons cited below.

73

Let us begin by asking about the aesthetic possibilities of *thermal* sensations. At first sight, one would say that they are by themselves of no aesthetic consequence whatever; and indeed we might not be far wrong in this judgment. Thermal data seem to have but one dimension running from hot, through warm, tepid, and cool to cold. They are also variable in their extension over the body. One can imagine a machine that would vary these data, moving from one area to another by gradual or abrupt gradations or by sudden gusts from contrasting directions, using air or water to effect these changes. Obviously, the familiar shower bath is a ready source for exploring some of these possibilities. I do not recall having heard this suggested, perhaps because the possibilities are, to say the least, not rich. Yet we may remind ourselves that the Romans, the Turks, the Finns, and the Japanese, and no doubt others, have as a matter of fact explored whatever aesthetic resources there are in baths. The mere utilitarian value of bathing to cleanse the body of the filth it is exposed to seems to have been transcended by what are undoubtedly richer values.

We have, then, at least a remote possibility of using the bath with water or air for purposes that may approach those of art. But what makes such use doubtful, if not impossible, is that it is hard to imagine what a thermal *work* of art would be, a thermal symphony, thermal choreography. Artworks are brought before the mind to render a certain satisfaction. What kind of work would a thermal work of art bring before us? We might try to sketch the possibilities of a thermal "choreography" or "score." In order to record it we must employ two dimensions, though of course the intensities of thermal experience by themselves should properly be strung back and forth along the single dimension of a straight line. We have a time dimension marking the start and finish of events events and a temperature dimension running from warm to cool;

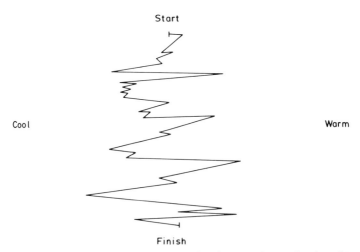

and so forth. I will not say this is not potentially pleasant, but only that if it represents a work of art, it is the thinnest that one can imagine.

I think I hear an objection at this point that even raising the remote possibility of a thermal work of art degrades all art. What has all this to do with the Sistine Chapel or the treasures of the Louvre? My answer is, not very much, and yet something undeniably. Great paintings are the result of an artist's having at his disposal a substantial variety of not only visual dimensions, such as brightness and saturation of colours, but also the more problematic, but no less real, warmth and coolness of colors. No doubt there is more involved in these works than the exploitation of dimensions, but they are the first conditions for there being any Sistine Chapels, and they are usually exploited to the very limit of our powers of perception in works we commonly characterize as great. What we can learn from our thermal "work of art" is that the resources of an art are in the first place determined by the nature, variety, and richness of the dimensions of its medium.

The possibilities of *tactile* or *haptic* works of art seem immeasurably greater than those for thermal works, and of course the tactile and the thermal are often linked with one another. We can see at once how immensely more complex the tactile medium is in the phenomenon of coordination with other modalities, for example, the visual. Without considering the many vexatious metaphysical and epistemological problems in this coordination, we need observe only that beginning somewhere in infancy we learn to read off and to predict tactile data from the visual data with astounding accuracy. (One may begin to explore the problems by studying Bishop Berkeley's *New Theory of Vision*). Hallucinations, which represent a want of coordination between the modalities, are after all extremely rare. In this process of coordination, the senses particularly of vision and touch immensely augment and enrich one another.

Taken wholly by themselves tactile sensation are, of course, far richer in scope than the thermal, for example. There are several dimensions inherent in these data. Surface *texture* (smooth, rough, oily, etc.) is fairly distinct from the total *shape* of the object when the hand or some other part of the body explores it, and its *size* is distinct from both of these. An important part of the satisfaction in tactile data derives from their coordination with kinaesthetic data. On the whole we are inclined to take tactile data very much for granted and to concern ourselves far more with the visual aspects of tangible objects than we are with tactile data themselves. We are content to "read off" the tactile from the visual; when we see a tree, we have no interest in touching every branch, twig, or leaf, and we generally forego whatever satisfactions there may be in manual contact with most things we encounter.

In recent years, the sense of touch has enjoyed a kind of revitalization not only in what one might call the New Eroticism, but also in efforts to restore literal contact between alienated urban persons through techniques of a kind of tactilism that are not necessarily erotic. It is fairly certain that early man had many fewer taboos than we have about touching one another's bodies. The erotic overtones and undertones of tactile data have, of course, been extensively explored in psychoanalytical and psychiatric literature.

There are also other synaesthetic possibilities for touch and vision. We appear to react in subliminal kinaesthetic ways to both representational and abstract pictures far more than we think, perhaps with slight and yet palpable tremors of nerves, soma, and viscera. A bad picture that appears to be lopsided for no good visual or connotative reason may contribute to a sense of disequilibrium in us that is somatic as well as visual.

Where the thermal data were dimensionally inherently monotonous, tactile data, besides being spatially three dimensional, are thus generously profuse. There are wet or watery, oily, gritty, smooth, hard, yielding, surfaces; there are light and heavy bodies involving kinaesthetic as well as tactile sensations; there are often effects of air or water in motion on the shape of a body; there are somatic and kinaesthetic sensations that do not involve external touch; and there are no doubt others as well. If there are purely tactile works of art, they are made possible, in terms of our title, by the rich possibilities in their dimensions, their size, weight, shape and surface. Unlike the thermal sense, touch *appears* to afford us a real object, which seems a very general necessary condition for there being a *work* of art.

Before we move towards other modalities, it may be well to mention *electric shock* as a distinctive sense-modality. It is most commonly a disagreeable but not always painful datum that scarcely anyone can wish to endure, although at very low intensity it is at least an interesting stimulus. Its aesthetic value? One would have to say, nil, and it has no known synaesthetic possibilities.

We may turn next to the aesthetic possibilities of *ingestion* and *savor*. Aesthetic psychologists have explored the subject extensively. The customary dimensional analysis of tastes into bitter, sweet, salt, and sour does not always appear to be an apt classification, partly because true savors (which must include the olfactory element) are highly variegated and are not really reducible to these four "dimensions," phenomenologically. Experimentally, tastes can be segregated from olfactory data, although they are normally accompanying and mingled. The pleasures and displeasures of food and drink are not likely ever to go out of fashion and are discussed ceaselessly in every civilized and every primitive community. Our question is: are we producing anything we wish to call art with good cookery, fine wine, and the rest of the menu? Let us leave aside altogether the china, glassware, silverware, tablecloths, and other accessories of an attractive table. We are not interested in the "fine art" of dining, but only in the aesthetic possibilities of gustatory data. Our question, then, reads, can there be gustatory or savory art, and how is such art possible?

I think we must answer this question by saying that it is not at art. As with "thermal art" nothing has been borne before us, *vorgetragen*, as the Germans say of an opera or drama. There is no *work* of art here. A recipe is not a score. If the menu is repeated, we eat a second meal; we do not have a second performance of the same work of gustatory art. What is necessary to art is in one word *imagination*: gustatory and savory data perish as they are had, while those of music and visual art are readily capable of lingering in imagination and of being revived in the progress of the work. If one recalls a delectable dinner, the imagination readily conjures up a *vision* of the table setting, the succession of courses, the guests, and the color or sparkle of the china or silver. But savors and flavors do not recur in this manner, nor do they organize themselves into objects.

I now wish to suggest that if the body-localized sense modalities are the source of genuine arts, they must possess the readiness to stimulate the imagination, anticipatory and retrospective, that is inherent in vision and audition. Without this they cannot rise much higher in the scale of the arts than a massage of the body. The converse of this is also interesting: the arts of sight and sound if reduced purely to their sensuous components, are scarcely more than massages themselves, rather than full arts as we know them. It is imagination which helps to call the *work* of art into being. A musical work or a poetic or dramatic composition demands of us a synoptic and imaginative grasp transcending the present, sometimes evoking a virtually instantaneous synthesis.

None of the body-localized sense modalities is well served by the imagination, and I am prepared to go even further. Speaking for myself, and I believe others will agree on careful introspection, I will say that one cannot imagine, cannot call up accurate images, nor even poor images of the tastes that were experienced at the table, whether of food or drink, with the cessation of eating and drinking. The same may be said of thermal data, and of all olfactory sensations. I believe that no one can imagine any taste or any aroma that is not now physiologically present, unless the brain is re-stimulated artificially. On only one occasion have I had an olfactory mnemonic image, an unmistakable whiff of brandy which once turned up in a dream I had. But I think dreams are very different from daytime recollections in this respect. One might explain this with the paradox that a present dream is more real than a past that is now being recalled.

We come, then, to *olfactory* works of art. I think the sense of smell is the highest of the senses "below" vision and audition. Although there is, as I have just been saying, no olfactory imagination, this sense is one where we are almost as "bodiless" as we are in vision and audition. In the previous sense modalities that we have explored, the body must be directly and in an important sense consciously involved: the datum is localized in or on the body, and we are aware of its localization. But we are not directly aware of anything "going on" in our ears when we hear something; we can only *infer* this fact by stopping up our ears. Nor are we directly aware that processes are going on in the cornea or retina of the eye when we say we see something. This, too, is an inference, although one that is remarkably certain, virtually unassailable. I submit that in this respect the olfactory sense is similar to vision and audition.

C. D. Broad has called vision a *saltatory* sense, that is, a kind of leap (*saltus*) has been made out of the body, as it were, and the datum is localized somewhere beyond it.[1] If I make an exceptionally loud noise within, say, an inch of your ear, a pain may be localized in your head. But it will be the pain or shock that will be localized, not the clang. Of the latter you will simply say, "it was *very close* to me" (let us suppose this all happened in the dark).

Unlike Broad, I would regard audition as well as vision a saltatory sense, and I believe the olfactory is also saltatory. If I enter a room that has highly aromatic flowers somewhere in it such as magnolia blooms, or stock, or nicotiana, I detect and aroma *in the room*, not *in my nose*. The nose resembles the ear in this respect. Obviously the nose is involved in inhaling this whiff, but I do not necessarily localize whatever it is that causes the smell in my nose. In this respect smell seems very clearly a saltatory sense. And it is worthy of note that some of the most delicate tastes or savors such as those of wine are really discerned in large part by the nose and not only by the palate or tongue.

There is, however, one clear consideration, already mentioned, that shows why we must draw a line between smell on the one hand and vision or audition on the other. Though all these senses are saltatory they are not equally capable of appearing or realizing themselves in *imagination*. I propose the following example from my own experience.

Let us consider the person who has smoked cigarettes for some years, long enough to experience the demand or craving for them. When such a person is denied cigarettes for a number of minutes or hours through one circumstance or another, he experiences a strong craving sensation. He is not imagining the aroma of cigarettes or cigarette smoke, although, of course, only these will quiet this demand. If such a person stops smoking altogether he experiences very strong and almost unbearable sensations of craving for some considerable length of time. Eventually, in ten days, or a month or two, he will experience such feelings only occasionally. Finally they will stop altogether. Within a year the smell of burning tobacco will very likely be nauseating to him. If, however, the imagination kept on conjuring up pleasant olfactory images of tobacco, like his earlier experiences, even after he gave up the use of cigarettes for good, he might simply go mad. The want of olfactory imagination is what saves him from this. If the exsmoker could revive *in imagination* the pleasantest moments of his smoking days he would never be able to break his habit. The habit is broken and the craving ceases simply by the cessation of smoking, though not suddenly. Imagination, or rather want of imagination, comes to our aid by obliterating the olfactory past for us. This want of imagination or imaginability is one of the principal ways in which the olfactory sense differs from those of audition and vision.

Suppose I am tormented by a desire to stand once more on a bridge over the Seine looking downstream, or to sit once more in a box at the Vienna Staatsoper or La Scala. This pleasant torment can occur because I can retain these things, visions and sounds, in my imagination. Or suppose I can scarcely wait to hear, let us say, Beethoven's Second Quartet. It is because I am now imagining strains and fragments of it as I heard it played years ago by the Budapest Quartet. I say, "it keeps running through my head." Such a "torment" every music lover is willing to endure and even to enjoy if there is a prospect of his eventually spending an evening hearing four musicians playing some particular piece, and especially to his liking.

If one is a perfectly trained and accomplished musician, on the other hand, one can almost satisfy his enjoyment of music simply by reading over the score, in an atmosphere of total silence. The 'almost' merely indicates that an actual performance would be preferable, even to such a person, to merely imagining the playing. Lay persons are usually totally incapable of believing the musician when he says he can "hear" or imagine the music merely by looking at the score. But there is not the slightest doubt that this can be done − it is not even a rare ability among thoroughly trained musicians. It is taken for granted, just as you and I can read the newspaper aloud if we have occasion to.

We see from this that the pleasures of vision and audition *do* segregate themselves decisively from those of the other senses. Olfactory sensation lies at the border between "upper" and "lower" senses: upper because it is saltatory, lower because it is not sustained by imagination. This by no means rules out the possibility of synaesthesia or *Gesamtkunstwerke*, but only that, setting literary art to one side, the core of synaesthetic *works* must lie either in vision or audition.

We should also note that vision and audition can receive data virtually without limit. The gustatory mode on the other hand is limited by appetite and satiation, excess in either direction making for physical uneasiness or even nausea that arrests aesthetic functioning at once. The aesthetic possibilities of vision and audition are in part determined by the richness of their dimensions and the sometimes unlimited but always numerous possibilities of variant elements in each dimension. They do not easily, if ever, threaten to overwhelm *the body* with surfeit as do scents, the gustatory data. Moreover, the dimensions in each of these two modalities are nicely adjusted to one another, and they are rich without being profuse in the seemingly random way of the scents and tastes.

It would be instructive at this point to consult the invaluable succinct account of the possibilities of "smell prisms" and "odor squares" devised in emulation of the double cone for colors which are given in Woodworth's *Experimental Psychology* (Chapter XX). The intermediate links joining the corners of these squares to possess do not possess a convincing scalarity such as we have with the gradation of the brightness of a given hue or with the gamut of musical pitches. A square devised by Henning, for example, proposes a series along a dimension named Spicy ⟷ Fragrant. Beginning with the first terminus we proceed through cloves, caraway, bay, hops, thyme, arnica, lavender, vanilla, and heliotrope to the second terminus. Whatever value this may have for psychology, it reflects nothing in experience which would make olfactory works of art possible as the pitch series makes musical works possible.

The olfactory series has a slight resemblance to the assortment of timbres in the several choirs of the orchestra: reed, brass, strings, drums, bells, gongs, and so on. Timbres in the classical orchestra inject a kind of random character into music which is otherwise subject to such strict organization: pitches, tonalities, keys, scales, modes; graded intensities from loud to soft; graded extensities from broad to narrow tones; various vowel qualities or vocalities; exact divisibility of durations, and so on. Until electronic devices reached their present sophistication one could only think of the existing assortment of differently timbred instruments as a "survival of the fittest" among the many musical instruments mankind has invented. At present virtually an infinity of timbres is electronically producible – the need is for composers capable of writing *music* with all these timbres to command. For the present and the foreseeable future, the expansion of dimensional possibilities presents us with an *embarras de richesses*. It is doubtful if even Bach could master the whole of the vast tonal resources that are now available.

In any answer to the question how art is possible, the richness and order of the dimensions must be a prime consideration. Another factor making the superiority of vision and audition is their "objective" character: in contrast to whiffs and tastes there is at least the illusion of a public visible or audible "object," even if epistemologists seem unable to settle this matter definitively even for vision. These modes are also virtually free of the trammels of the body and its easy lapses into fatigue. To be sure, in music and visual art, one can produce boredom through a variety of evils, such as monotonous repetition. This is corrigible in the hands of the skilled composer, painter, or sculptor. But there is no remedy for near nausea from surfeit of even good drink, food or scent except total cessation of the ingestion or inhalation of them for a certain time; even if these data were capable of the kind of variegation which the musical composer commands, the limits of palatability would remain the same. Even the best of chefs is eventually incapable of transcending them.

It is unprofitable to quarrel over the extension of the term "art," whether this is to include wine, perfumery, dining, and so on, or not. It is much more important to recognize the profound dimensional differences of the several senses, that the various arts exploit. The more varied and yet orderly a sense-modality is the more capable it is of mothering one of the arts. From this standpoint dimensionality explains why vision and audition support some of the greatest arts. Ordered dimensionality is the first consideration in answering the question how art is possible.

Our review of several of the body-localizing senses shows that they differ from vision because they do not present us with an *object*, something distinct from ourselves, ob-jected to us. This we see in their nonsaltatory nature. I am not certain why this renders a sense less rich in aesthetic possibility unless it is because objectification (in this sense) is tied up with imagination. In the sense-modalities we have reviewed here, we literally *enjoy ourselves* rather than, strictly speaking, anything other than ourselves. I do not say that they are wholly devoid of "objective" character in some respects, yet there is very little that can really be *shared* in these sense data. As a result, hedonic quality is often the beginning and the end of their aesthetic resource. Unique modes of imagination are stirred up very little or not at all. Of course, particular tastes or aromas may now remind us of some particular previous experience, but they can have no great texture of relations such as are inherent in visual and auditory data. One taste may be comparable to another (as sweet as, more bitter than) but these are but feebly "dimensional" at best, and they are never the dimensions *of an object*.

We can see even better how the organo-centricity of these data diminishes their aes-thetic potential by going on to another sense which is definitively organo-centric, namely kinaesthetic sense. There is no object here for the body to sense, project, or ob-ject, for the organ of sense is itself what is sensed. This is even more emphatically true in erotic sensation, or sense of well being. Erotic, if not kinaesthetic, functioning, is virtually definitively hedonic, the summit of "enjoying oneself." The erotic here is being taken in a deliberately narrow manner as virtually identical with the autoerotic since satisfaction in *giving* satisfaction, concern for another, may obviously involve far more of the per-sonality than merely the senses. (No doubt, it is a far more significant form of love.)

Whatever we may think of the satisfactions of erotic or kinaesthetic exertion, the point now is that neither of these, simply as a sense-modality, is aesthetic in nature, and a large part of the reason, I suggest, is that there is no object in them, and thus no *work* of art.

If, however, these exertions themselves become objects for other persons, the situation alters quite significantly, for now we are back to vision and imagination. Undeniably the performance of the athlete has aesthetic potential, although this is almost always over-looked in most of our games except diving, gymnastics, and some of the field sports. Even this, however, is no more than potential, for the purpose of games in themselves is generally to display and enact striving and strife, vitality and victory.

Erotic display or exhibition is not necessarily pornographic, that is, designed to stimulate sexual response. The great treasures of the nude in the world's art are never unerotic, though they are, I think, only rarely pornographic, if at all.

The want of an object in certain senses seems to go hand in hand with the weakness of imaginability or revivability of the data. This may appear to be less true in the instance of erotic data until we reflect that imagination in this instance is first of all visual and that this is capable of actually stirring associated erotic feelings or even response. The imagination helps create the "object."

The conditions in the several senses then that help us answer the question how art is possible come down to an array of features that are not all realizable, or at least not all realizable equally well, in all the senses. Prominent among these are richness of dimen-sionality, capacity of being revived in imagination, a certain freedom from organocen-tricity, the capacity to present an object to us, and hedonic possibility. To these we must add those which we have already extensively explored above, strength of tendence and contextual interplay in data. I think we tend to regard as arts in the strictest sense of the term only those types of realization that best illustrate all of these features.

SUMMARY

The various sense-modalities are not all equally favorable to the development of arts.

The thermal sense provides certain satisfactions to the body, but it is dimensionally poor. The effort to interpret it as a source of art, although unsuccessful, throws an interesting light on other modalities and other arts.

The tactile sense is more favorable to the development of an art, since here we have true *objects* with distinct dimensions such as texture, shape, and size, and since the coordination of touch and vision leads to important synaesthetic results for both senses. Aside from this, the aesthetic potential of this sense must be regarded as slight, because by their nature such tactile objects necessitate the contact of the body, and the imagination is but feebly stirred.

The aesthetic possibilities of savors, of ingestion, appear to be much greater than either of the foregoing senses. Savors are varied and profuse. Since they are deficient in respect to arousing the imagination, that is, facilitating the imaging and reviving of presently absent data, there is little in them of an object or work of art.

The olfactory sense has the highest aesthetic potential outside of vision and audition. Aromas are highly profuse, but like the savors, they are difficult to order, and have only a dubious scalarity. There appears to be no possibility of imaging, or imagining, in this modality, and thus little on can call an object or work of art.

Body localization or organo-centricity definitively characterize kinaesthetic and erotic data and thus remove the possibility of an *object* of aesthetic interest in them except, for example, via vision. They may, however, rank very high in capacity for hedonic satisfaction.

NOTE

[1] C. D. Broad: 1952, *Philosophy, The Journal of the Royal Institute of Philosophy* 27, 3ff.

CHAPTER 11

HOW IS ART POSSIBLE? (2)

A close comparison of the several sense-modalities in respect to their aesthetic possibilities will show why vision and audition are far in advance of all the others. Accordingly, we may construct a table to reveal such a comparison.

We have explored the senses so far in respect to their *dimensionality*, that is, the capacity of data to be ranged in certain orders (such as hue, or pitch, or intensity and extensity). We may also speak of these as the *comparative* relations of data or elements. These aspects of the data are set forth in the first three columns of the accompanying table (q.v.).

Two modes of comparison are introduced in the sixth and seventh columns that have occupied some of our attention in the previous chapter: *revivability* and *hedonic potentiality*. Revivability can also be spoken of as imaginability. It is simply the capacity of data to appear or reappear in the unique form of images in the total absence of "objects" or of the parent data themselves. Hedonic potentiality refers to the capacities of the sense to afford pleasure and displeasure.

For the sake of completeness the table also recognizes two traits which have been considered in detail above, namely *contextuality* and *tendence* or tendentiveness. The presence or absence of these traits in the several sense modalities significantly helps to determine the availability of data for aesthetic use. Their bearing on questions of form, unity, or coherence needs no elaboration beyond what has already been said. The comparative capacities of the modalities in respect to contextuality and tendence is set forth in the fourth and fifth columns of the table.

We may summarize the various modes of comparison as in Table I.

1. Elements have *comparative* relations with one another if they can be placed on one or more dimensional scales, for example, pitch, hue, size (extent, duration), intensity, and so on. The scalarity of data of the various modalities differs very significantly as we have already observed in the previous section. The sum of the comparative relations may be called the *dimensionality* of elements, comprising intensity, extensity, and quality (the last of these differentiated somewhat further below).

2. Elements have *contextual* relations if in some context of relevance (e.g., the area enclosed by a frame) their concomitance mutually generates results in them that they do not have in other contexts, or in relative isolation.

3. Elements have *tendentive* relations when, given that they differ and are in one another's spatial or temporal proximity, the tension or force in one element is satisfied or fulfilled in the other, or when the reverse motion leads to tension or instability or even frustration. (We acknowledge that tendence, although it does characterize some data of sense quite literally, often owes a good deal of its strength to learning, conditioning, or habit. This may limit the availability of these data to the artist. The question of the "objectivity" of tendence is rather unprofitable. It is sufficient to say that modes of tendence are usable resources for the artist in every community that senses or that learns to sense their feel or force.)

TABLE I

DIMENSIONALITY

	Degree of Intensity	Degree of Extensity	Range of Quality	Contextuality	Tendence	Revivability	Hedonic Possibility	Sum of the Factors
Electric Stimulus	High 5	High 5	Little or None 0	None 0	None 0	None 0	None −5	5
Algedonic	High 5	High 5	Low 0	None or Insignificant o	None 0	None 0	None −3	7
Thermal	High 5	High 5	Low 0	Significant 2	Significant at Extremes 2	None 0	Moderate 3	17
Haptic	High 5	High 5	Considerable 3	Slight 1	None 0	None 0	High 5	19
Savor	Moderate 3	Low 1	High 4	Moderate 3	Moderate 3	None 0	High 5	19
Olfactory	Moderate 3	Moderate 4	High 4	Moderate 3	Moderate 3	None 0	High 5	22
Visual	High 5	High 5	High 5	High 5	High but Limited 4	High 5	High 4	33
Auditory	High 5	High 5	High 5	High 5	High 5	High 5	High 4	34

4. The phenomenon of *revivability* in what is called the imagination appears to characterize some modalities more than others and has a decisive bearing on their availability for aesthetic use.

5. The *hedonic potentiality* of elements is never irrelevant to aesthetic considerations but it is significantly modified as it is integrated into the several modalities.

In our table the relative potential of these modalities as I think of them is briefly characterized and also supplemented by numbers. These are intended only as a rough measure of the strength of the senses in each respect, but they need not be taken too seriously. In fact, the individual reader may sense the degrees quite differently. Notice that negative numbers are assigned in some instances.

There are many further characteristics not considered here, for example, a phenomenon in the quality of musical intervals such as the octave that recurs each time that the frequency of the vibrations is doubled. Temperature shows no such phenomenon when the degree of temperature is doubled (however this might be measured) nor does color or any other modality.

One must also remember that *intensity* and *extensity* can mean only approximately the same sort of thing in each modality. It is quite possible that intensity of color is not really felt to be any kin to intensity in temperature. The same sort of thing may be said also of tendence. With sufficient habituation the succession of courses in Occidental meals may seem to us logical or somehow "necessary," proceeding from the unique quality of appetizers, through main courses, to sweets and desserts at the end. The reverse order seems to us "wrong." Much depends upon how "objective" we think tendentive traits are.

Let us now quickly compare some eight distinct modalities in terms of their dimensionality and their other powers. We have first the capacity for particular data to differ in *intensity*. Pain (algedonic data) and heat can be more or less intense and a tone of a given pitch can be more or less loud; the saltiness of a taste and quality of one and the same aroma can likewise be more or less intense. Haptic or tactile intensity, if this notion is permitted, seems applicable principally to surface qualities and to weight or pressure. The intensities in other modalities are readily understood.

Extensity refers either to sheer spatial extent or apparent spatial extent of a datum. Pains, for example, may occupy a certain area and can be sharp ("narrow"), dull, deep, diffused, and so on. Taste seems to be very poorly endowed in this respect, since, of course, it is entirely localized in the mouth. Smell can be greater or narrower in extent, almost in the same manner as warmth and cold. Extensity of tone would first of all refer to time, as duration, rather than space: in this sense, the extent of tones would be long or short. (We have long since ceased to attend to the metaphor in this.) In a quasi-spatial sense tones vary with their pitch in their "breadth" or "narrowness": high notes are narrow and low notes broad or full. Pitch and extensity may, however, be experimentally separable with modern laboratory devices. Colors of course have varying extensity in the sense of spatial extension altogether literally.

Merely for purposes of comparison, we place under *quality* all the other dimensional characteristics besides intensity and extensity: under pain and electric stimulus little can be distinguished besides degrees of intensity and extensity; heat and cold show very little more in the way of quality; touch is fairly rich in quality, for example, smooth, rough, hard, soft, oily, watery, surface, and numerous geometric distinctions, so far as the hand, especially, can grasp the whole of a body. Taste is thought to reduce to bitter, sweet, salt, and sour, but in conjunction with smell, savors develop, and much richer discriminations are possible. Smell is very rich in distinctions of qualities but not as rich as audition and vision since, as we have seen, the qualities are not really scalar; we are merely capable of distinguishing a huge and heterogeneous mass of aromas. Under auditory quality we include both pitch and timbre, and under visual quality we include both hue and saturation. The richness of vision and audition under these dimensions has already been touched upon. Only here do we seem to have true scalarity, for the dimensions of quality in the other modalities are not convincingly scalar but most often a heterogeneous assemblage.

When we turn to *contextuality* we are thinking mainly of the degree to which a quality varies with its context. Musical tones, intervals, and chords are very susceptible to this and so also hues. In a moderate degree savors and smells are determined in their quality by context. Tactile qualities are somewhat less affected than the foregoing. Thermal data are significantly determined in this respect if we recollect that even a small progression toward lower temperature from very warm can seem cool and that a contrary move can seem correspondingly warm.

In *tendence*, auditory data appear to exceed all others, as we have already noted in the instance of the cadence. All music, especially in the classical harmony, "moves" very strongly, unless a composer is utterly incompetent in managing it. Color "harmonies" and tendence are the subject of some difference of opinion. Color is highly contextual, as already noted, but it is weaker than tone in respect to tendence, at least in my opinion. Great strength of tendence and movement in visual art inheres in line and mass and in rhythm. This is not to be explained without reference to kinaesthetic factors.

Revivability, or imaginability, seems to me a strong and necessary condition of aesthetic availability, for how can one regard data as having aesthetic possibilities, if the imagination is simply incapable of bringing them before our attention in the absence of actual stimuli, if it is always in stiff lockstep with the body? One may, I concede, in rare cases have olfactory, thermal and other hallucinations and imaginings; haptic "errors" in sense are quite common (one may feel his hat as being still on his head after it has been doffed, or "feel" his watch to be still on his wrist when it has just been removed). In the usual order of things, these sensations are simply not revived or revivable without the recurrence of a stimulus.

I believe the superiority of vision and audition in respect to revivability does not, however, depend upon the actuality or reality of visual and auditory memory or other imagery. It *may* be an illusion to think we are in any sense imaging something out of the past, even in respect to vision and audition. But in the other sense-modalities I would say that we do not have even the illusion of images. Speaking only of myself, I should say that visual and auditory recollective images are sometimes of a vividness that all but rivals full illusion. The phrase "mind's eye" seems to refer to something real. I would also argue for a "mind's ear" while at the same time denying that we need the phrases, "mind's tongue" or "mind's nose," and still less an imaging faculty for the other modalities. I may remember *that* it was ever so cold last New Year's Day, and I may even say, "it makes me shiver just to think of it," but I believe this is merely one of the "far out" phrases we all resort to, to try to communicate our past sensations, knowing perfectly well that we really cannot under any circumstances do so: my sensations are not bits of information that I can store up and pass on to my future or later self in remembering them any more than I can pass them on to you like the name of Henry VIII's last wife. The want of imagination seems to me to set vision and audition far apart from the other senses: even if I only *seem* to see Mt. Vernon or hear the bells of the Berkeley Campanile, I do not in the same sense ever seem to taste and smell and shiver at vanished or distant realities.

Finally, we may consider the *hedonic possibilities* afforded by our senses. I believe that electric shock has no such possibilities, and that pain has hedonic possibilities only for malfunctioning personalities. All the other senses are very heavily endowed for pleasure and displeasure. Yet even here it is necessary to set vision and audition apart from the other senses. It is important for us to recognize the reality of pleasure in these two modalities and yet to gauge its degree of importance lower than pleasure in other modalities.

Pleasure must first be recognized to have a place in nearly all of the senses. It is well known that pleasure is not itself a sense, nor is pleasure sensed: there are no sense organs of pleasure as there are, for example, points in the skin to sense pain. The coupling pleasure *and pain* must be recognized as misleading. (Alliteration helps it along as it does the German *Lust und Leid*). Pleasure and discipleasure when they are felt are either diffused all over the human frame or if localized they are localized with sense data. When we get a pleasant whiff of a holiday dinner or of flowers or perfume, the pleasure in it is indistinguishably mingled with the sense data themselves. Pleasant tasting foods afford us pleasure, as we say, but we must not be tempted to think that pleasure is a something, an entity, a distinct datum merely because it has a substantive name. Careful introspection to "isolate" pleasure shows how elusive it is. In the end it is only the aroma itself, the taste, the touch, the warmth and coolness of the body itself that is discernible, and the same is true of displeasure, when a noxious taste or stench is discerned. Pleasure is in short not localized by itself, but is a kind of epiphenomenon upon our sense data. When, on the other hand, it is diffused throughout the frame, we resort to vague phrases for it: "feeling fine," "happiness," and so on. Pleasure and displeasure may also simply record the satisfactory or unsatisfactory, the well-functioning or ill-functioning condition of the body or of some part of it or the desire of the body-mind for the continuance of a present condition.

Turning now to vision and audition, we must first argue for the presence of pleasure there and for its somewhat lesser role in them. Perhaps one of the strongest bonds between the "higher" and the "lower senses," and one which has a decisive bearing on their aesthetic availability, is the presence, or rather the potentiality, of pleasure and displeasure in all of them. The satisfactions of the eye (and of the ear) must be particularly noted, as they are in the German word *Augenlust*, even though the most emphatic seats of pleasure are to be found in temperature, touch, taste, smell, and of course sexuality. As in the other senses, pleasure and displeasure appear in vision and audition, entirely fused with sense data themselves. Erotic pleasure fuses with erotic sensations (which are not a distinct *modality*) and may involve all the true modalities together with further internal physical sensations.

If we now experience visual and auditory data to be "permeated" by pleasure so that they are called pleasurable sights and sounds, and if we now ask ourselves what notion most readily comes to mind to characterize this response, the answer is almost bound to be phrased in terms of *beauty*. That is, at least a large part, though not the whole, of what is meant by the phrase, *pleasure in sights and sounds*, is bound to be conveyed by the term *beauty*, or some term synonymous with 'beauty'.

Thus visual and auditory data are capable of being qualified by pleasure, or displeasure. But since these data have some very unique traits, the qualification itself is markedly different from those of other modalities. These senses are, as already explained, saltatory; the data are not localized in or on the body except in cases other than normal, such as extreme intensities. The data are localized away from the body. Since we hear and see things as being there, not here, that is, in or on the body, the pleasure cannot but be localized where data are localized and thus localized away from the body. Seeing things in this way we have no need at all for mysterious processes of "objectification" such as Santayana and sometimes Kant and others speak of.[1] That which strikes us as mysterious in this so-called objectification really rests on a false view of nature of pleasure. When it is treated as *only* a kind of visceral reaction, it is indeed a mystery how *it* manages to get *out there* among visual and auditory objects. The answer is that all undiffused pleasure is localized with its data, with sight and sound no less than others.

A further observation comparing the senses is now in order. As we have seen, three senses are saltatory, the visual, auditory, and to some extent, the olfactory. The remarkable fact is we appear to speak of beauty only in connection with these three senses, and no others. Pleasurable as touch or warmth may be, we do not speak of such data as being beautiful. But it is quite possible and indeed normal to speak of the "lovely aroma" of a flower or a scent. Whiffs, aromas, scents alone among the "lower senses" can be spoken of in terms of beauty.

All of the senses can participate in some degree in aesthetic functioning, but the difference in their structure cannot but affect their aesthetic availability. Some are unidimensional, like warmth and coldness; some are tied closely to the body; some are rich and some are poor in their range; some localize their data on or in the body and others always away from the body; some are adaptable to practical and intellectual functions, while others are not.

A highly consequential difference is no doubt the last mentioned. Vision and audition present us with what, in the course of growing into adulthood, we come to treat more and more as mere cues to action. Such data are so deeply subjected to considerations of utility, so pervasively intellectualized, and so interwoven with immensely complex structures of space, time and conceptual thought that the sense of the sheer pleasure or unpleasantness of them is for most persons long since lost. The artist may make it his business to remind us of them. If the "mechanization" and the intellectualization of the visual world proceeds to the utmost limit, as it apparently has in the twentieth century, the artist may rip the fabric of an overconceptualized visual world into shreds to force us to look at it and face what he regards as the true horror of it. He has different responses at other times. He may even further the work of the intellect. We recall that Leonardo regarded art as a science! The artist is neither a permanent enemy nor ally of science; he steers his own course. Sometimes the courses of others coincide with his and sometimes not.

Pure and unalloyed pleasure-in-sight-and-sound, or what is often the core of the beauty we discern, may thus be only occasionally the center of the artist's aim. He has many other fish to fry, depending upon what at a given time there is to see and hear, upon the degree of rationalization of this world. The artist of our time most often regards mere beauty, sheer pleasure in sight and sound, as only a sickly sweet pacifier. He is saying that he has more important things to do than to contribute to a superficial aesthetic "state of coma" in his audience.

Surveying the whole of our table, we will not find it surprising that concentration has finally centered upon audition and vision. Although the primacy of these must be conceded — and they are of eminent significance for all literary art too — it may be more important for us to remind ourselves that the lower senses also deserve our concern. The neglect of them is likely to grow rather than diminish in our time in spite of the fact that the pursuit of "sensual satisfactions" may appear to have intensified. The pollution of the physical world must evidently first be made burningly vivid to us before we take the trouble to restore the atmosphere and our physical surroundings. The lower senses deserve emphatic consideration in any definition of culture.

Our survey sketches out in broad outline the basic resources from which the artist develops his media. The rest, we must say, is left to him. We can take note of the fact that the possibilities in dimensionality, contextuality, power of tendence, revivability or sustainability in imagination, and hedonic yield are thus and so, but the artist must learn to use them to good effect, not from abstractions such as we have been compelled to devise but by actually exploring and discovering what can be done with them at first hand. And this has to be done in a community of persons who command not only several senses but also a host of other powers under such abstract classes as intellect, communication, utility, sociality, morality, and many more. All of these have their effect or echo in what artists do.

SUMMARY

The data of all the senses can be compared and differentiated in respect to their dimensionality, contextuality, tendence, imaginative revivability, and hedonic possibility. The supremacy of vision and audition is apparent in such a comparison.

Pleasure establishes a link between the "upper" and the "lower senses" just as adaptability to rational ends provides an all-important difference between them. The familiar hedonic capacity inherent in all the senses yields an important ingredient of the idea of beauty, since this is in part to be identified with pleasure in vision and audition.

The senses differ in the degree to which they may be used for intellectual and practical purposes, vision and audition being particularly adaptable to this end. This adaptation also vitally affects their aesthetic availability.

NOTE

[1] George Santayana: 1896, *The Sense of Beauty*, Part One, Scribner's, New York.

CHAPTER 12

THE COMPOSITIONAL ORDER OF ART

THE INTRINSIC ORDER

We have now considered in a general manner that will permit application to particular arts the nature of the material with which the artist works. This exposition has covered the intrinsic order of art; we have said little about what the artist can do to realize this structure. Before we do so, we may review the argument so far.

We approached the problem of coherence by considering the conditions of perceptibility of objects when seen as *elements in relation to one another*. We defended the approach from the charge that it intellectualizes aesthetic experience. The most obvious relation of elements to one another is concomitance. Such elements will necessarily exhibit, and will be perceived as exhibiting, *sameness and difference*. We learned what happens, or appears to happen, when either of these relations dominates. At one extreme we encounter the void of the unielemental complex, in which the complex becomes an element, as it were. Here the element has nothing to contrast itself to. Under that condition it must eventually lose its identity. This is a condition we can only develop as a kind of thought-experiment; by its nature it is void and thus beyond perception. At the other extreme, we encounter a similar void from the interaction of an infinity of elements in a context. This is like spinning a color wheel ever faster until in the end a mere white or void is perceptible; such a white or void may symbolize for us the "infinitization" of elements.

The condition of perceptibility thus proves to be found somewhere between two voids at the extremes. But this leaves a vast area to traverse. We may begin at one end with two contrasting elements which will be either of the same or of different *size*. This effects their seeability and, as we learn later, their "gravitation" or *tendence* toward one another. As we add more elements, we compound the problems, since the elements are also at a certain *distance* from one another. Their relationship will be affected by the *extent* of the elements and the degree and type of difference prevailing among them, and by their *number*. They will exhibit one-ness, two-ness, three-ness, etc. How far may this "etc." run? To a hundred, a thousand, or only ten? This is an empirical psychological question. We may take a small whole number, about eight, as the limit of *compresent numerability*. But even this stretches seeability somewhat. In vision we find that certain stratagems of grouping will insure better seeability, and the eye will tend to resort to them, even unaided by an artist. If we have seven elements in a row, a favorite device is symmetry: three elements on either side flanking a large central member (and the flanks may exhibit secondary symmetry). There are of course other groupings besides this one.

Certainly, one of the most remarkable results that sets in whenever elements near enough to form a context is the *intervallic* phenomenon. This is most literally exemplified in spaces enclosed by lines or masses, by musical intervals, and to some extent by adjacent colors. It is entirely beyond prediction and has the startling result of both dividing and uniting the component elements. Working both above and below the level of awareness, it conditions all the other relations in aesthetic complexes.

Elements are not only contrasting and connected but they also manage to "assert" themselves, to become emphatic, to "realize" themselves. The complex now tends to organize itself along a principle line of division between an *emergent* or dominant element, the figure, and a *recedent* element or ground. This is applicable to every perceptual medium. A powerful example of emergence is exemplified by the *unicity* of the emergent, that is, when it is numerically one. This notion may also be retained when both the emergent and recedent are complexes of subordinate figures and grounds, that is, second (and higher) order emergents and recedents, provided a fairly close relationship unites the prime emergent and the prime recedent. In visual art, single prime emergents are the rule rather than the exception. Spatial complexes illustrate particularly well the results of diminishing or emphasizing emergents in the direction of either subdominance or superdominance. Artworks more often comply with rather than defy these conditions. A complete defiance can only yield chaos, whose aesthetic value is nil but which the artist may bring upon the scene as an extra-aesthetic necessity.

The *appeal* or interest which aesthetic complexes, chiefly artworks, have for us derives first from the qualities their elements have irrespective of their relation to one another. Elements, have, as a limiting case, a certain quality or character, an *elemental character*, by themselves or in isolation, provided something acts as a *surround* or limit of internal relevance. This character has a unique appeal for us which may be called *elemental appeal*. Second, elements are modified in their very nature, quality, or character by their concomitance. Their effect or apparent effect on one another, which alters their elemental character, is their *formal character*. Finally, the appeal they have when they are in the presence of other qualities, and because of it, is their *formal appeal*.

These categories and distinctions are applicable to all aesthetic complexes. So far as acceptances and rejections are implied in the foregoing, they function not as aesthetic standards, but rather as information about the rewards and penalties of proceeding in various directions. We have said that what we hope to find are such relevant questions that may be addressed to the artist or to his work.

Going on now to the sections beginning with Chapter 5, we have explored the nature of aesthetic media in much greater detail than was necessary in Chapter 2–4. What we have concerned ourselves with is what the actual resources are that are inherent in the several aesthetic media. Elements can affirm themselves in one degree or another, can emerge and recede because they are related to one another by systems of *dimensions*. Tone elements, for example, are found to resemble and differ in respect to pitch, intensity, timbre, extensity, vocality, and duration. Particularly in the instance of pitch, intensity, and duration systems of relations exhibit *scalarity*, and possibly in the other instances as well. These comparative relations of elements, constituting their *dimensionality*, being essentially "static" cannot by themselves account for the appeal of the artwork, but they deepen our grasp of it.

The formal appeal of elements, we have said, arises from their having an effect upon one another. This involves "dynamic" relations such as *contextuality* and *tendence*. Comparisons can be made even when elements are not in the same complex, but contextuality, as the term implies, involves a real interaction (though noncausal) between elements, and tendence, their attraction and repulsion. These two classes of relations are obviously more nearly responsible for the vitality or frigidity of the artwork than the others.

The first of them, *contextual* relation, shows us how elements change merely by existing in the same context or proximity. The range of effectiveness of the element defines the outer limits of the work: within this all elements may be presumed to bear on one another, but not all in the same manner or in the same degree. Such relations provide an important resource for the artist.

The other type of relation goes beyond the causal, beyond the effect of elements on one another to their *attraction* for one another, or gravitation toward one another. These are the *tendentive* powers of elements. It is in this family of relationships that the arts of vision and audition most clearly segregate themselves from others, such as taste or smell. A dinner menu in the Occident runs in a certain order, largely from custom or habit, whereas musical, visual, and literary works of art have inner connections of a much more powerful sort. These then afford the artist a potent resource, but of course he is not obliged to make use of those which have been explored up till now (for example, the classical diatonic system of harmony): he may find other or better tendences in elements, or groups of them. What he cannot do, or can do only at peril to what he is creating, is to ignore or nullify all known tendences, and to offer none in place of them. It is idle to judge such a matter a priori. As pointed out, one can only speak of the probable rewards and penalties: sometimes the artist needs or believes he ought to ignore both of these for some other end. One should then look carefully to see whether it is an end other than an aesthetic end: this too has its rewards — and penalties.

If these cover the principal relations native to or inherent in aesthetic media, we must observe that the artist may also seek to "naturalize," as it were, other devices. Here we think particularly of *connotative* devices: devices of representation and expression in several of its modes. Artists may favor or may deplore the use of them and assert or deny their aesthetic usefulness or effectiveness; what all parties agree on is the *power* which connotative or expressional devices exert, when they are present, upon virtually every level of elements in artworks. Accordingly, the power of such devices must not be underestimated.

We have finally scrutinized all of the sense-modalities to see how they compare with one another in the richness of the resources they afford to the artist. A fair appraisal both confirms our opinion as the the aesthetically most viable senses, which turn out to be vision and audition, and also shows that there are some important resources elsewhere.

THE COMPOSITIONAL ORDER

If this review of aesthetics resources is more or less adequate, we must raise the further question: *How can these resources be employed in the creation of art*? Art does not create itself nor is it secreted like the marvellous shells of sea anemones, molluscs or other organic bodies. What does *the artist* contribute? What can, what does the artist do? This is the question we must now try to answer, first in a general manner that touches all of the arts and then with more specific reference to some of them. For the purposes of exposition, we shall have to speak of artistic activity in terms of a process in time that is more suited to stages in the manufacture of commodities — we may have to speak as if first, someone conceives of a purpose, then gathers the materials, and then, works and reworks them, and so on. That such an exposition can be misleading may be seen from the work of the musical composer. Mozart, for example, was compelled to use the "materials" of music available in the closing half of the eighteenth century or devise new ones or revise some that had fallen into disuse. But what *are* the materials available at that time − just those harmonic, melodic, rhythmic, and other devices that in fact turned up in previous music or in his music, *or* an available body of them from which he drew some for his own use, letting the others lie? Our speaking of available means must obviously proceed with great caution, for if we say the means or media were just those that he used, we utter only an empty truism; but how, on the other hand, can we say that these things that he did *not* use were nevertheless part of his medium? The fact is that almost any composer even partially approaching Mozart's stature *adds to* the resources of his art − if he does not he has merely said or done what was already said or done, and then, as we have remarked before, his work is an anomaly, for it is both his own and not his own.

With these precautionary thoughts in mind, we may now proceed to ask what artists do with available means. It is obvious that they do not leave things as they found them. In fact, even with things that are now called "found" objects they inject something new into the situation simply by picking them up and saying, behold! More commonly, if the artist is working in long-established arts such as painting and musical composition, he re-orders selected materials with an eye or ear to what has a reason or justification for the place he gives it, and he omits everything else. In this sense, the artist's aim is to achieve coherence, to provide that every part of his work justifies its place in it or is justified by the presence of other parts or elements. Whether they *do* belong is, as we have seen, not to be settled by the fiat of published "intentions." What is meant by 'justification' may be illustrated by cases in which a figure of a given size justifies itself by the manner in which it is related to, or grows out of its ground, and a ground justifies itself in a corresponding manner; or where a plurality of parts or figures of apparently equal force justify themselves in the manner in which they convincingly accommodate one another or maintain relevance through conflict; or where parts are related by their tendentive roles, developing motion and rest; or where other unique "mechanisms" native to given arts establish a dependence and independence of parts. Since it is the mark of the artist never to leave things as he found them and to reorganize them for what eye or ear regards as good reasons, we now ask, not what we have already asked, what are the bonds of connection in materials, but *what can the artist do with materials with such inherent bonds*? What "moves" and "procedures" on his part are possible?

We divide procedures the artist employs to gain unity and coherence into three main categories:

> *Isolation*: centralization, concentration, closure
> *Repetition*: identity, similarity
> *Development*: continuity, climax

Thus the artist, in order to lend the artwork that degree of inner coherence that is necessary in order to insure that all its parts justify their place in it and are disposed to the best advantage for themselves and for the whole, may (1) facilitate an all-encompassing grasp of it through brevity or unicity, or focus attention on some strong centering region or core figure or element from which bonds of connection radiate; (2) facilitate inner transition among parts or elements of the complex through repetition, or promote recognition of the identity or similarity of the parts; or (3) enlist interest in all the parts by a gradation of emphasis that reveals them all as tending toward a culminating end. These devices, while distinct, are not necessarily exclusive of one another. The artist may employ them together or one of them more prominently than another. The devices should not be so loosely defined that everything exhibits all of them. Closure, for example, is absent whenever we cannot see the forest for the trees. Neither must the term 'coherence' be confined to some "formalistic" sense, although so-called formal devices may be resorted to in order to promote coherence. As there are no a priori restrictions as to the elements or materials to be exploited by these "methods," other than their inherent appeal, whatever it may be, so also there is no limit to the particular devices that may be devised to effect closure, continuity, and development so long as the "justification" of parts is served.

The techniques thus outlined for the practice of art also serve the purposes of criticism. They are the foundation of those relevant questions the artist must constantly address to himself, and after himself, the critic. Appropriately applied in each medium they can show the rewards and penalties of alternative practices.

(1) *Closure*: Isolation, Centralization, Concentration. In one form, the device of the core figure has already been explored under the name of the unicity of the emergent. We have explored at some length how aesthetic perceivability is affected by according figure and ground various sizes in relation to one another. Unicity is, of course, compatible with the other two unifying devices and in general should be. Closure is both one of the strongest and weakest devices of coherent organization, because, on the one hand, the sheer unicity, the numerical oneness of a figure or emergent, already lends a powerful presumption of unity and coherence, but on the other, just as little discrimination is needed for an artist to lend coherence with this device as there is for a respondent to apprehend it.

The relative dominance of figures by closure is most easily seen in *visual media*. Untold numbers of *paintings* obtain unity by this device. Portraits are prime examples. The most simple or simple-minded aesthetic demands for coherence seem to be satisfied with unicity, particularly when, as in portraits or other representational painting, or in photography, this is reinforced by *expression*. The real test of artistic powers and of the power of unicity itself comes when the painter denies himself this simple source of support. This is true not only of "abstract" and particularly Gestalt-free painting: it is merely well illustrated there.

It seems almost truistic to say that *architecture* and *sculpture* resort to the core figure device since we are strongly inclined to view them at just that distance where visual closure is possible. Not all buildings, however, are fortunate (or unfortunate) enough to enjoy a distinct existence. We tend to single out separate structures rather than regard, let us say, a city block as a unit, often for merely economic reasons.

Coherence by way of closure places an enormous weight on the shoulders of the individual complex. For if it stands fully alone, it has indeed gained coherence from unicity, but it may then all the more glaringly display both its inner disorganization and its irrelevance to its ground and surround. One may test this with a limitless number of examples of success and failure in public squares the world over.

By its nature, *sculpture*, far more than painting, must reckon with the space it inhabits, for it has a very real effect on it. An urban square or a garden in which sculpture is placed is its ground not its surround, and thus part of the work itself, as every ground is for its figure. This is why the marching platoon effect of pieces of sculpture in most museums (e.g. the Vatican) is so deadening. The distinction between ground and surround is of first importance in sculpture and architecture. In each case, one must decide, or better, the eye must be invited to decide, how far the limit of inner relevance (figure plus ground) extends, and where the bounds of irrelevance, the surround, begins. The physical world of course runs on and on into the surround, beyond the limit of relevance. The eye must therefore decide where the limit is, and in the ideal situation (where matters of private property can be ignored) everything within this limit, together with the sculptured figure itself, should be regarded as mutually adjustable — this is exactly the freedom a curator exercises in developing an exhibition in a museum. Of course this can only be a counsel of perfection.

Paintings fare much better in museums in the exclusion of the irrelevant because a certain restraint is nowadays observed to avoid crowding. Since the ground of a painting terminates at its frame, the surround is important only because distractions and intrusions may arise there and invade the ground and figure. (One may recall the old way of filling the walls of museums not only side to side, but top to bottom, in the nineteenth century.)

In *music* the three devices of unification are much more interlaced with one another. The core figure device is harder to employ literally here, because the limit of immediate compassability (the specious present)[1] is restricted. Very short compositions, such as songs, however, illustrate closure fairly well. Further unification of a composition over a period of time must rely on repetition of the theme (theme and variations is a simple device from this standpoint) or, what is much more difficult, on inner development towards climax that may wholly avoid repetition. Repetition in music differs fundamentally from repetition in spatial arts. It does not lay identical figures *alongside* one another: the successive appearances of the theme or figure are meant to *overlay* one another. Repetition is for the purpose of driving home *one* theme or motif as the center of attention. The composer must therefore subtly contrive not to evoke the response, "What a bore, here it comes again!" but to display one and the same musical thought in varying and interesting contexts and conditions.

The *literary* use of the core figure has been adverted to in reference to the measurable extent that leading figures may occupy in terms of the number of lines spoken. We reiterate that this is but *one* way to gain unification and centralization in the drama. At the opposite extreme a potent figure may make himself felt without appearing at all. Thus the plot of the von Hoffmansthal-Richard Strauss *Rosenkavalier* is set in motion by the absence of the Field-Marshal while his wife, the Marschallin, is dallying with her lover, young Octavian, who gaily sings

> Der Feldmarschall sitzt im krowatischen Wald
> Und jagt auf Bären und Luchsen . . .
> Ich hab' ein Glück, ich hab' ein Glück.

The nonexistence of the Field-Marshal on the stage, but his ever imminent appearance helps to sustain the tension. We see from this that there is not just one way to *realize*, to make real, a figure.

The prominence of the core figure device is especially seen and felt in European painting of human figures and scenes *prior to* the emergence of true landscape painting. A turning point may be observed in Giorgione's *The Tempest*, so-called, where the figures of a nursing mother with her child and the young man a short distance away, both in the foreground, inhabit, but do not dominate, the scene, at least not through emphatic size. These figures are not strong emergents, not "concerted." The landscape as a whole seeks to emerge as having a value in itself. But by its nature a landscape as a whole (as distinguished from the discrete figures in it) cannot be an emergent: it can only invite us into itself, as it were — a phenomenon we shall consider again below in a very different connection in recent painting. In *The Tempest* there are figures but they are not under-lined: human figures, a bridge, a stream, a fragment of an arcade in ruins, houses in the distance, clouds, lightning flashes. The mood is that of a dream.

As the core figure device makes way for landscape and other complex settings, unifi-cation must be sought in rhythmic repetition, in continuity and development with a plurality of lesser figures. Relations such as those of similarity, contextuality and ten-dence are exploited. Often however only a nameless but potent mood or emotion may permeate and unify a composition.

(2) *Development*: Continuity, Climax. Leaving the devices of repetition for the last, we turn to our third device of unification. Unification by means of unicity or core figures may be supplemented or replaced by devices that make for continuity or inner *development*.

Development is continuity that permits scalar intensification in some direction and that heightens, "escalates," or "matures" toward a culmination or climax felt to be inherent in the materials. The use of the terms 'continuity' or 'development' is, of course, a trifle metaphoric when applied to space rather than temporal process, since it is inherent in space that its points be coexistent. But this is to exalt the geometrical sense of the terms at the expense of their perceptual sense. A staggered row of bars sweeps upward we say, at least for those whose habits in vision are set by the convention of reading from left to right (possibly, those who read only Hebrew or Chinese see this as a declination).

Lines and contours are among the simplest devices to afford continuity and develop-ment in the spatial arts, and they also admit of extraordinary complexity. This resource is by no means confined to the draughtsman's line. As Professor Pepper says, "there are as many stimuli for visual lines as there are inducements to draw the attention of the eye from one point to another."[2] He distinguishes some six or seven kinds of line or rather, stimuli for line, since lines are implicitly drawn even when there are only, say, three points presented in a given space. Lines are at work as boundaries between masses, as completions of broken but implied figures, and elsewhere. Besides continuities in line we can of course also identify similar orders in masses or what count as masses since their size is a scalar quantity.

The purpose of all continuities in spatial art is to move the eye of the observer and in so doing to create the illusion that something *is* in motion. The point is that in all the data of sense enlisted in the service of art, appearance *is* reality. Seeing is not passive registry, as photographic paper accepts the image in the film, but a ceaseless exploration. Static figures, endless repetitions, and continuities that lead nowhere numb the eye. Knowing this the artist must know how to avoid it; explorations must be rewarded with discoveries. *All* areas of the work are significant, even those dark and shadowy areas, seemingly void, such as we see receding from the central figure in the later works of

Rembrandt. In them we rest momentarily before we move back to the illumined figure. The great painters are skilled guides in leading our eyes through every quarter of their pictures: they have painted every part of them, and every part is, in degree, important. Ordering lines and masses in such a way that the eye and thought are set in some kind of motion provides a fairly simple, if not literal example of continuity and development.

The most important consideration, and the one that "makes art possible," as we have already seen, is that any and all dimensions of any sense-modality, if they are convincingly scalar, provide resources for artistic exploitation. Besides line and mass we have also the coloristic dimensions for visual data, as already set forth. For tones, variable duration, and rising intensity or pitch of tones, being scalar, have, when suitably employed, almost irresistible power to move and to sweep us along with their motion: all of this of course is supplemented by the contextual and tendentive powers and the harmonic, rhythmic and other potentialities of tones. If other senses are less likely to furnish true objects and works of art, this is in part, we suggest, because of the want of scalarity in their data, though in all sense-modalities sheer elemental quality is always a rich source of satisfaction – and of course dissatisfaction. Vision and audition do not so much transcend and overstep the other senses as provide a culminating capstone for the senses in general. We must neither overrestimate the difference nor underestimate the kinship among the senses.

The devices for even more advanced forms of continuity that are true growths, developments, or maturations are of course limitless. Certainly one of the devices most heavily leaned upon both in auditory and visual art is connotation, that is, what the elements or parts of the artwork mean to one another in some broadly semantic sense, their place in a "myth" or "program" that often dictates the minutest detail to the artist. There is no ready way to spell out even the basic directions of continuity and development where this resource is employed. Their source is of course most often poetry or literature, for centuries the most dominant of the arts, especially since visual and auditory arts have allied themselves with it and drawn much of their sustenance from it.

Concerning the innumerable devices of development in literary works themselves we may here content ourselves with the observation that whatever enlists the reader's curiosity or expectancy may be put to the service of maintaining interest and tension until a certain solution or satisfaction ensues. Thus, matrimony, death, victory, and many other such outcomes may serve as the goal. We may be sufficiently interested in human destiny to see such ends achieved or avoided so that we follow a narrative of some hundreds of pages or to spend some hours in the theatre. If our interest or curiosity compels us, the author has found an audience. The popularity of the novel, drama, film, story, ballad, epic and other such forms rests on the virtually inexhaustible resources available to the interested observer of the affairs of men, women, and children and the world they make for themselves.

Since we shall consider examples of continuity and development later on, we shall observe here only that the newer music confronts the same problems in this respect as that of the great European tradition. It has refused to accept the classical solutions to the problem of providing coherence in music, but it acknowledges the same need for it. Monotony must be avoided, formal design must prevail, climaxes must be prepared and reached. So, Ernst Křenek in his *Studies in Counterpoint*, a sort of primer for atonal music, writes that a tone row must avoid the interval of the octave because it "creates the impression of a complete standstill of the musical flow, thus interfering with the *principle of continuous tension and motion essential to atonal music*."[3] (Italics mine.) Nowhere do composers and theorists like Schoenberg dispute the necessity of reaching coherence in their work, and it is doubtful if even Stockhausen, Boulez, and at an earlier stage, John Cage in our day have desired any other result.

It should be said of music and other so-called temporal arts that if, by comparison, the painter hopes to create movement in perceptual space (for physical or geometrical space, at least in a local or Newtonian sense, is essentially static), the musician's aim is, in a comparable connection, exactly the opposite. Where the painter hopes to create the *illusion of motion*, the composer hopes to create the *illusion of rest*. A musical theme by its very nature rests on the phenomenon of the "specious present" and the composer hopes always to stretch this present further and further. He hopes to arrest time: "*Verweile doch, du bist so schön!*" Since, of course, there are limits to this, he resorts to the repetition of themes in the interest of arresting time. A repetition in music is not so much a second or third something as a second or third "auditory glimpse" of the same thing. We marvel at the structure of symphonies and operas, yet what would 'structure' mean if we could not in some sense hold parts together? A flashlight illuminating a night time scene by moving through an arc of, say, 180°, is not thought to remember the scene at 30° when it reaches 60°, or 60° when it reaches 90°, for it does not remember at all. But if in fact every moment lived through (and filled with some content such as musical tones) perished utterly in the same way as the patches revealed by the flashlight, music as we know it could not even begin to exist. It is this sort of fact that makes continuity and development in music necessary.

It is obvious that development is not mere repetition. Merely saying something over and over again is precisely what we mean by not developing it. In development there must be difference, newness or even a strangeness, but not just any novelty counts as development. There must be some kind of "necessary connection," but not that which is provided by identity. The fullest paradigm of development is organic growing, which unites continuity and novelty and proceeds, as it were, from one to the other by small increments or differences. These three are jointly essential in the application of the idea of development to art: identity, novelty, and gradation of difference.

(3) *Repetition*: Identity, Similarity. Seeking for new musical forms, Debussy repudiated the familiar devices of repetition (recapitulation, reprise) exemplified in sonata form, three part song form, rondo form. When he assimilated these to the cud the cow chews, he put them in no pleasant light. Debussy may have succumbed to the temptation to universalize his own practice and there may also be a touch of Gallic chauvinism in his view of the matter, since the greatest monuments of French musical creativity lie elsewhere than in the sonata form.[4] Still Debussy's aim of a music that is unified without being repetitive is well worth taking seriously. We may suppose that it will be a music in which everything is seamlessly united to what has gone before, what comes after, and what is somehow contained in the whole, and all of it moves and develops with an inevitable continuity towards some convincing end. This is certainly not a trivial hope, as his own music often effectively demonstrates.

Such music, then, is not at all impossible. There are other processes or events in time, besides music, that are comprehensible in such terms. Take, for example, a great battle,

Waterloo, Gettysburg, Stalingrad. In a sense nothing is repeated here, and it has a beginning, middle, and end. It comes to a climax on which everything turns, and it comes
finally to a horrible or glorious end, whichever it may be for us.

Debussy was in effect saying that repetition is for the benefit of those who do not
understand something the first time it is said and so must ask to hear it again – and again.
Without judging whether he was right or not we may at least accept what he hoped for
as something that flatters our musical intelligence or at least our musical potentiality.

Repetition, however, is not likely to be extirpated from the arts, since one form of it
at least is indispensable in all the arts, but especially in music: rhythm. This is the repetition of immediately adjacent figures (not in the sense of figure as a prime emergent,
for this by definition can occur but once in one complex). Such a device creates a series
that is inherently monotonous and is generally numerous enough so that the eye or ear
does *not* fall to counting the members. A grouping of a dozen visual points, bodies or
motifs so that we perceive their twoness, threeness, up to eightness, will lead to the
perceptual creation of figures out of them. So we can see the following collection of dots,
reading them from left to right, alternatively as 1,2,3 (a triangle), 4,5,6,7 (a four-sided
figure), 8,9,10,11,12 (a pentagon); or as 1,2,3,4; 5,6,7; 8,9,10,11, and so forth.

.   .   .   .

1   2   3   4   5   6   7   8   9   10   11 12

We have already observed something of the phenomenon of *accommodation*. Accommodating figures are structures involving a very few larger, similar or identical and
mutually reinforcing forms of emergent figures. Monotonous groups, on the other hand,
are inherently quite numerous, and if they are deliberately made focal, made to emerge,
they inevitably provoke fatigue or boredom. For example, suppose I play you a new
composition of mine that reads as follows,

etc.,

continuing in this fashion for five or ten minutes, ever the same. Your response to this
(the so-called Alberti bass) will be to say, Stop! I heard you the first time: or, when
does the composition really begin? Or you are simply fatigued, bored, or even narcotized.
All of these are appropriate responses. Current music, both popular and "serious", often
comes close to such exploitation of monotony, and apparently with the deliberate intent
of narcotizing the individual (the use of pharmaceutical narcotics with such monotonies
is no coincidence). If the intent of works of art is something other than this, it is readily
apparent that monotony must either be avoided or used with appropriate restraint,
having due regard to its powers for contributing to composition constructively.

Monotony has such potency that its effects must be very carefully gauged in advance.
It has the capacity to· unify, exerting the maximum "force" that can be attained in
vision and audition. Because of this, it is its own worst enemy when it is made focal or

figural, when we are presented with nothing but a single figure. The very first presentation of the Alberti figure just shown is already unified by its unicity, encompassability, and its inner unity as a major triad (FAC), and the later repetitions only underscore this. But the inevitable result of ceaseless repetition will be a void: we have no more reason to attend to one of the component figures in it than to another, and we end by ignoring all of them, if we can.

The analogue for this in temporal arts must be carefully selected. We have *not* been observing something like a colonnade in vision in the foregoing, for in repeated musical figures, as already pointed out, we overlay the figures, one upon another. Hence each appearance and reappearance can have a force like the blows of a hammer striking in one place. The result can accurately be described as "driving it into the ground" — and the ground is indeed exactly where repeated configurations belong, if anywhere, not in dominant or emergent positions. Before we develop this aspect of monotony we may make a corresponding observation about vision.

Monotony presents a threat to vision as well as audition, but visual good sense prevents us from misusing it too often. These are some of the common forms of visual monotony: the figures of an identical print on women's clothing, the pickets of a fence, a marching company of soldiers, the perforations on postage stamps, the links of a chain, a colonnade, vertical or horizontal rows of windows, telegraph or electric power poles across a prairie, ties on a railway track, and so on. The reason these are generally not offensive is that the eye immediately turns to the *whole* the members constitute. Such a whole, being a whole, is then *one* by virtue either of its unicity or of some inner continuity or development. Our eyes turn to the figure or silhouette of the woman from the monotonously repeated figures in her clothing unless the members are either inherently offensive or in some way compete with the principal figure. (Everyone knows that the stout lady should avoid dresses with huge flowers or dots.) Or we turn to the fence as a whole, perhaps as a continuant line in the landscape, to the square or oblong or line formed by the soldiers, to the individual stamps or to the whole sheet of stamps with its regular but not obtrusive lines of perforation, to the total shape of the fenestrated building, to the dwindling line of the power poles or railway ties as they approach the horizon, to the chain as a whole forming a loop or line when it is worn as a belt, or when it runs from the ship's hawse pipe to the anchor or to the bollard on the dock, and so on. The eye is a fairly accurate instrument in deciding when the components or members obtrude and when not.

In vision, then, monotonies are benign when they are employed in such a way that attention is directed toward wholes. They may be employed either in the prime figure or in any ground. Monotony, particularly when it appears in the form of subordinated rhythm, can be and often is benign. The point is that it unites and unifies powerfully and it must be employed with this in mind. The print figures of a garment, even when slightly distorted by the contours of the body form lines of connection from head to foot, left to right, forearm to trunk, and so on. If they are so large as to become focal they no longer enhance the total figure but compete among themselves for our attention, thus dividing instead of uniting.

Turning next to audition, similar considerations obtain but with a varying emphasis. The employment of monotony in the figure, since it is so insistently, if not insidiously, intrusive, must be treated with the utmost care. Chopin Études present good examples. Thus the first Étude, in C major, with its billowing arpeggios seems for a moment to be employing a monotonous device. But we see almost immediately that each wave that breaks is subtly different from the others, in pitch, shape, chord structure, and so on. Since this is instantly perceived we turn the ear toward the marvellous sweep of the whole. Each wave is focal just long enough for us to catch what it is and to hear how it differs from the preceding and following arpeggios.

Études are a good test of what we are saying. They are often written with the dual purpose of taxing the performer's skill and perhaps training him in some one difficult manual operation (we tend to forget that an Étude is first of all a *study*) and of presenting the resources of the instrument to the highest advantage in a brilliant and possibly even profound work. A mere Hanon exercise on the other hand, is deliberately monotonous, for it is training the pianist in one small skill at a time. Every serious pianist on earth has heard or played No. 1; it is tolerable, if at all, only because of the purpose it serves in training the hand and fingers.

The use of real monotonies (monotonies which are not subtly different in detail, and thus unlike those in the C major Étude) in the musical figure or emergent is limited. A trill is one such, and there are many others. But generally they are very short, play the role of accompaniments, or are qualified in other ways. The test examples one brings to mind may turn out to be internally highly varied after all: the Chopin B♭ minor Sonata, last movement; his Prélude, Op. 28, No. 14 in E♭ minor; the first and second of Bach's 48 Preludes, and so on. In these and other cases the composer has made a gamble, and these at least I would say, have won. They suggest monotony just enough to gain its benefits in unification but vary the materials sufficiently to prevent our dozing or napping or being "drugged."

The monotonous prime emergent is the most objectionable case, and the one most fraught with danger to the order and even to what may be called the perceptual survival of the whole (cf. Chapter 3). Monotony in the ground or recedent seems to be not only tolerable but to render important benefits. Historically this was made possible only by a momentuous revolution. It will be instructive to accord it a retrospective glance at this point.

As music evolved out of the purely polyphonic style in the seventeenth century, it was moved to reorganize its inner structure completely in order to realize again the ideal of ancient Greek drama. The hope of emulating the ancients led to the invention of opera. This was principally the result of the effort of Claudio Monteverdi (1567–1643). If music-drama was to be possible it would have to elevate one voice among the *dramatis personae* at a time and also give him music to sing that bore some relation to the poet's thought. For this, polyphony, contrapuntal music, was not well suited. The solution was found in concerting a vocal line and supporting this by the combined powers of members of an orchestra, as an "accompaniment." When this procedure at length made its way into the music for the purely instrumental orchestra and then into the music for keyboard instruments alone (organ, harpsichord, clavichord, virginal), a single line or voice was made paramount, leaving the others to subordinate tasks. Although the leading voice, to be heard above the others, might shift from one register to another, the highest voice in a tonal mass tended to assert itself. This is the outcome of the *monodic revolution* of the seventeenth century: a prevailing voice, usually the soprano, or discant, and a subordinate or accompanying role for the other voices, unless they too were summoned out to perform *solo*. In the latter event the soprano might be silenced, or given a less prominent line in the ensemble, or made to sing more *piano*, or given a temporarily purely harmonic task to perform. Occasionally, of course, the old counterpoint asserted itself, but except for its final, belated triumph in Bach in the early eighteenth century, its flourishing days were at an end. The new music, also often described has *homophonic*, now had to evolve entirely different rules to govern itself.

In all of this web of history we can pause only to show how momentous the results were to be for the maintenance of unity and coherence, particularly in purely instrumental music. Briefly, it is this. The principal voice or *melody* now became, in our terms, an undisputed prime emergent. The remainder of the tonal mass was used either to form a further part of the emergent (for example, an alto voice might play or sing at a remove of a sixth or a third from the soprano), or to provide some of the necessary ingredients for the ground or *harmony* (most commonly at least three voices), or to serve other purposes (or even both of the foregoing). The harmony could be provided by a secondary bank of instruments. One further necessity was that a *rhythm* be provided. For this, one could employ a drum or other percussion instrument, or if this appeared too *ostinato* or barbaric it could be provided by the deeper subordinate instruments, such as a larger viol. Thus the role in general of all but the concerted instrument was to be henceforth that of supplying in a fairly systematic fashion the harmonic and rhythmic necessities. The "three elements" of music, *melody, harmony*, and *rhythm*, were thus provided for.

The harmonic and rhythmic functions to be performed, especially the latter, were inevitably somewhat monotonous. Rhythm is, of course, a prime example of repetition, and repetition, though it may descend to monotony, is a prime source of unification. But if care were exercised in the use of it the highest benefits would accrue for the ensemble: in addition to unification by thematic means in the concerted voice or voices, there would be a constant rhythmic source of unification provided by the comparative monotony of the lesser voices, especially the lower. Here monotony could be benign instead of harmful. To be sure the duller role for the bass voices might not appeal to high-strung or egotistic personalities, but an orderly hierarchy fairly readily evolved to solve the problem. The three functions were not always distributed to distinct "choirs" in the orchestra: all voices could at one time or another, suitably to whatever stratagem the composer was pursuing, perform a melodic function, even cellos and basses; all of them had to participate in maintaining the harmonic texture; and all, even the higher voices, might contribute to the rhythmic pattern. By the end of the eighteenth century the problems of the division of labor and of finding suitable instruments was worked out. The result was a dazzling array of performers on this great "guitar" of the modern orchestra, from Gluck, Haydn and Mozart to Berlioz, Wagner and beyond.

Our problem is to find out whether monotony may have a salubrious as well as a deleterious effect. The classical systems of harmony and composition found it not only something to be tolerated but in fact to be effectively used. Monotony in rhythm is evidenced in such obvious cases as the bass rhythms of the polka $'\cup\_\_\cup/\ '\cup\_\_\cup/$, the minuet and waltz $'\cup\cup/\ '\cup\cup/$, the mazurka $\_\_\ '\cup/\ \_\_\ '\cup$, and many others more sophisticated and subtle.

We have now, I believe, all the ingredients of the *resources of coherence* in art works, as follows. (1) The device of isolating, centralizing a poetic or artistic thought as a distinct encompassable figure on its ground, in all the artistic media. This device is always aided by the comparative brevity of the scope of the aesthetic complex either in space, time, or (the more elusive) imaginal extent. (2) The provision of continuant threads, often by devices of tendence, and of conveying the thought of a development that pervades a work through every quarter of its being. (3) The devices of repetition, simply placing like with like (and of course rhythm is like this) or of reviving and recurring repeatedly to previous details, or of assigning the task of unification to one part of a work and that of free diversification, inventiveness, and novelty to others. As we have seen, monotony is too potent a unifying device to be avoided altogether; it must be used, but with a perfect discretion.

SUMMARY

A prime necessity for the artist is an understanding of the elements and of the relations between elements in the medium in which he chooses to work. These constitute the resources for art.

What the artist can *do* with these materials is to place and organize them in complexes in such a way that they justify to the eye or ear their place with respect to one another. He places them together because he believes they belong together. This is what is in general meant by coherence and unity in art.

Three procedures may be employed by the artist to effect unity or coherence. First, he can order the figure in his composition in such a way that it may be encompassed by the eye or ear in space or time.

A second procedure of unification is to repeat the prime or other figures in the complex, thus gaining unity by their identity or similarity. (Repetition exists in varying degrees and often takes the form of a recurrence to a previous theme.) Repetition that runs unchecked is inherently harmful to an emergent. Monotony is most tolerable in a ground or recedent where in the form of a rhythm it can help to unify a complex without obtruding upon the more consequential matter of the emergent. It may, however, appear as a component even in a figure or emergent.

A third procedure to gain coherence is to maintain lines of continuity in the complex, and to pursue the process of development or growth that lead to appropriate climaxes.

Music illustrates particularly well the unification of its materials by means of an emergent melodic line, the interrelation of voices in harmony, and the maintenance of a repetitive and even monotonous rhythm in its ground.

NOTES

[1] In his *Principles of Psychology*, vol. I, p. 609, William James attributes the authorship of the phrase, "the specious present", to E. R. Clay, *The Alternative*.
[2] Stephen C. Pepper: 1938, *Principles of Art Appreciation*, Harcourt Brace, New York, p. 177.
[3] Ernst Křenek: 1940, *Studies in Counterpoint*, G. Schirmer, New York, p. 7.
[4] Debussy himself wrote also in sonata form.

CHAPTER 13

FEELINGS, FORCES, AND FORM

Our study of coherence has sought to lay bare both the potentials for form inherent in the materials the artist engages himself with and the devices and stratagems he may use to gain his purposes, making them virtually extensions of himself. But form will ever suggest "empty formalism," the "merely formal," and watchwords such as "formal" and "coherence," even when used as they are here, may too often suggest only the cerebral or intellectual if not frigidity and death.

The reason for this lies in our manner of exposition. If we have omitted saying exactly how *passion and feeling* enter into every detail of both the materials and the devices of the artist, it is only because up to now constant reminders of them would add nothing that would inherently help us to understand them or the aesthetic economies they inhabit. But we do affirm emphatically that to have any aesthetic interest at all is to be an emotional participant: *aesthetic awareness is vital awareness, is literally to be alive to and emotionally involved in what we encounter.*

Something more must now be said about the place of the affects in the arts beyond what was implied in Chapter 9. The reason is that without reference to them we cannot do justice either to literature where both familiar and unfamiliar emotions may be expressed or to arts such as instrumental music where we are unable to say what emotions in any familiar terms are expressed.

Emotions, the affects, are important in the arts in every way, but particularly as these are seen from the present standpoint. They are not themselves of course devices of coherence but rather forces in maintaining connections and in giving meaning to elements. As such they are likely to be involved in any resort to expression, even of mere matters of fact. What seems unmistakably to be emotion may be expressed also in independence of representational content in a narrow sense of the phrase, both instrumental music and abstract visual art affording copious examples of this. In order to gain some understanding of the way in which emotion functions in the arts a threefold distinction may be devised.

We may distinguish the following:

(1)   The presentation, expression, or as we may also say, the *invocation* of emotions: here they are part of the subject matter which the artist chooses to present or represent for us; for example, by the literary invention of personalities that manifest certain emotions.

(2)   The *evocation* of emotions in the observer or participant in the arts: here the artist hopes to evoke pity, sympathy, derision, or other feelings for his subjects and for his work, in whole or part.

(3)   The *provocation* of emotions, which may result from the dissemination of the artwork and may be directed toward some circumstance associated with its content in the world of reality.[1]

Thus *Romeo and Juliet* in rich array presents or *invokes* the passion of the lovers, their joy, fear, hope and despair; the aggressive wrath of the Montagues and Capulets; the compassion of the old Friar; the loyalty of friends. Further, the spectator not only witnesses and comprehends these feelings, is not only himself caught up in the tumult of love and hate, but his sympathy and perhaps "pity and terror" are *evoked* by this spectacle of both joy and inhumanity. Finally, the specator may be stimulated or *provoked* to certain actions by the moral or lesson he has drawn from what he has witnessed. In our day, the *West Side Story* version of the old theme may stimulate in the spectator a tolerance he might not otherwise feels, or it may even provoke the contrary. It is true that artists in general are not always eager to have their works serve as provocations, whether malignant or benign. But behavior or conduct can be powerfully influenced from this source. Indeed, this is virtually inevitable.

Of these three, there can be no doubt of the pre-eminence of the first, at least in literature and in certain other arts. The invocation of emotion is part of the artistic realization of any human situation, and the author must make it convincing. The emotional bonds of depicted subjects reinforce the use of the available devices to weld the elements of the fiction or myth together, always, of course, providing that the right chord of interest is evoked in the spectator or participant. The author will try to evoke a certain set of responses in us and avoid the inadvertent presence of others: sympathy for a heroine or prominent character, let us say, and not ridicule or derision; or the contrary.

Although the reality of invoked emotions is uncontested we still need to know how and whether we can identify them. If we ask what emotion or emotions Browning has invoked, that is, has chosen to make an indelible part of the subject of "The Confessional" (Chapter 14, below), the answer we shall see, is fairly apparent: the wrath of a person brutally betrayed. If we ask what emotion somehow animates the opening of Schubert's great Symphony in C Major we can neither answer, nor quite refuse to answer. It is so with virtually the whole repertoire of instrumental music. I think it would be a mistake to say "no emotion is involved," "the term is meaningless in this context," "musically intelligent persons don't ask such questions," and so forth. The fact is we are stirred by such music, but it is also the fact that we cannot say by what emotion. The safest course would be to say, the "Schubert-C-major-Symphony-emotion" which would at least not be misleading, however uninformative it might be.

This whole question deserves study at great length. For the present, we must confine ourselves to some of the fundamentals that might enter into the answer. Let us first ask ourselves what we have in mind when we speak of emotions and feelings. I think the following will cover a basic range of terms.[2]

(1)   *Appetitions and Satisfactions*: felt appetites, desires, inclinations; aversions, loathings; enjoyment, satisfaction.
(2)   *Pathic Responses*: affection, liking, loving, being pleased, feeling sympathetic toward; anger, abhorrence, disgust, dislike, hatred.
(3)   *Affects of Causal Involvement*: hope, trust; fear, dread.
(4)   *Cognitive Affects*: surprise, wonder.

It is apparent that instrumental music will rarely undertake, or succeed in, the invocation of any of these feelings *specifically*, except with the aid of associational devices (titles, programs, etc.). Hence if *this* is what we must mean by emotion then the long and short of the matter seems to be that such music "expresses no emotions." This seems scarcely any more satisfactory than saying that it "expresses nameless emotions."

Difficult as these questions are, there is yet a fundamental fact about the relatively "pure" artistic media that is easily lost sight of and that contributes something very substantial toward a closer knowledge of these nameless emotions. This fact, to which we have given considerable attention, is the tendentive power of elements. As we saw, there appear to be very definite "inclinations" and "aversions" in visual and auditory elements. Directions are pointed, motions or apparent motions are made, tendences are felt, satisfactions and frustrations are realized. If this seems still to rely somewhat on metaphor, the metaphors have by now become virtually new literal meanings as applied to these materials.

If we speak then in tendentive terms of elements in the more abstract arts we are in fact not far removed from the vocabulary of the emotions as recorded in familiar discursive language. A glance at the classification just proposed shows that at least the first three classes organize themselves around a kind of positive and negative polarity, typified in "inclination" and "aversion." This inclination, directionality or even "intentionality" is precisely what we have identified as tendence. The perfect adaptability of music to literary subject matter and the full realization of the urge and surge of erotic emotion in the "Liebesnacht" of Wagner's *Tristan und Isolde* are alone sufficient to demonstrate this.

The reality of directed motion in artworks ties together the extremes: the literary and the abstract arts. In turning from the one to the other, we are not making a leap into something foreign. The motion inherent in the human actions the narrative artist takes as his subject matter is directed and meaningful and manifests itself as invoked emotion. But this motion is no more potent than the animated and rhythmic motion of music can be in suitable hands. In a word, emotion is motion.

Tendence of elements as actually felt is thus the mark of vitality in the artwork whether this lies in the area of abstraction or of representation. In the latter, it is exhibited through the several classes of familiar or identifiable feelings (so-called emotions in a narrow sense fall largely under what we have called Pathic Responses). The fact that it is hazardous and often without significance to interpret the manifest tendence in abstract works in terms of readily identified and conveniently named emotions or feelings does not cast doubt on the basic kinship among the arts and the tendence inherent in their several differing materials: it merely reveals that we have inadequate knowledge of the prompting causes of tendence, particularly in the abstract arts. The fact is, few of us have an insight into the whole fabric and structure of the elements that are taken as the subject matter of these arts comparable to what even fairly simple persons have of the logic of human behavior. Yet such insight is what the great instrumental composers have commanded. The need is therefore to approximate ever closer to such knowledge.

Since it is easier, up to a point, to come by a grasp of human action and motivation, we may conclude by what must be a mere sketch of what is in principle relevant in that area for the participant's, the reader's, realization of the literary artwork, particularly fiction of a narrative sort.

It is obvious that we do not normally exhibit feelings of any of our four sorts unless there are precipitating circumstances. Persons who feel ceaseless fear or euphoria without being able to identify anything as the reason of it are generally deemed to be in a more or less pathological state. We may sometimes be plunged into something resembling such states without taking very much trouble to clarify our "reasons," but if the matter is important enough, and if we make a sufficiently inquisitive effort, we can generally give ourselves an adequate explanation. This is really a process of rationalization, but in both the best as well as the worst sense of the term. It can issue in discourse that *characterizes* the subject of our feelings. These are the ultimate premises of our appraisals and evaluations, and they alone give meaning to the feelings we have, *if anything can*.

Now this is exactly what the literary artist is bound to attend to. He presents us with persons in interaction with one another, not as simply atomic particles bombarding one another, but as having meaningful purposes that conflict or harmonize and that are pursued with some degree of determination. None of this occurs without the help of energizing emotions in the participants. Full awareness of the depth and quality of the motion that can animate a complex of characters and situations in fiction depends upon cognizance of certain basic factors. The author must provide us with the means of gaining a deep acquaintance with the persons and places in the tale, the quality of understanding and of self-characterization by such persons of their own nature and situation, the kinds of emotions and appetitions such persons undergo or feel in a variety of circumstances, the imperatives or commitments they tend to follow, and finally the character of the actions that actually transpire in which they participate. To know all this as the author knows it, and possibly to know it sometimes even better, is to be in a position to grasp the tendence and movement of the tale.

It is difficult for the layman to believe that the instrumental composer can have a depth and intimacy of acquaintance (really too superficial a word) with the quality, character, force, tendence, and range of relationship of the materials in the world of tones in which he spends a good part of his life, comparable to what we have just sketched as typical of the author's and the reader's knowledge of their worlds. Yet this is indeed the fact. If we try to understand the arts from the standpoint of creation and not just of consumption we can begin to grasp this, and we shall be much closer to an understanding of the unity of the arts than we can expect from an "aesthetician" whose interest in the subject has been stirred at third and fourth hand only by the speculations and analyses of philosophers.

SUMMARY

No account of art may neglect to explain the place of feelings or emotions in it, particularly one which lays a great emphasis on formal considerations. We must distinguish among the feelings art may invoke or express in its materials, or evoke in the attitudes of participants towards them, or provoke in actions toward circumstances associated with them.

The feelings for which we have a basic vocabulary are those that arise in the course of human interaction. They are a necessary part of literary arts which take their substance from this source. But feelings are no less real in any and every other art whether they are identifiable by the basic vocabulary or not.

What we have identified earlier as the tendence of elements manifests itself in narrative literary art as the emotions that accompany motivated action and in other arts in various motions among elements. In all of the arts, elements that have aesthetic potential are perceived as having tensions, inclinations, aversions that lead the participant toward frustration or satisfaction.

Since the medium of literature is human life itself, we grasp the manner in which elements in literary works (persons, their traits and acts, places, and other details) justify their place toward one another when we can make moral or motivational sense of them. All the arts, and particularly also the more abstract arts, manifest the same texture of tendence. This is the ultimate source of the emotions they evoke.

Arts are made possible when elements in a medium have an appeal in and of themselves and also in relation and in motion toward and against one another. We must be prepared to find an enormous variation among individuals in their apprehension of these media.

NOTES

[1] Karl Aschenbrenner: 1974, *The Concepts of Criticism*, D. Reidel, Dordrecht, pp. 82–84, 230–233.
[2] Karl Aschenbrenner: 1971, *The Concepts of Value*, D. Reidel, Dordrecht, § § 1.0 and 2.0.

PART TWO

THE INTERPRETATION OF FORM

PREAMBLE

We have sought to show that the form of the artwork is not a mere vessel for it but rather the sustainment of its life. Art owes its existence to the possibilities for form inherent in the materials it addresses itself to, from whatever source in sense and imagination these may be drawn. Exploration of these resources and their transformation by the processes of composition await the vision and apprehension of the artist. The concept of coherence enables us to characterize the outcome, marking one of the principal values we hope to derive from concourse with art.

The previous exposition has sought to provide an account of the intrinsic and the compositional orders in sufficiently general manner to enable us to see the essential unity and symmetry of the arts and detailed enough to make the application to each art apparent and plausible. We have shown what should count as elements in each of the arts and how in each of them we are to apply such notions as the emergence and recedence of figures and their magnitudes, basic dimensions, comparative relations, inner tendence or movement, and so on. What is now needed is to catch a glimpse of form in various works in some detail. Only so can we say more confidently what form in artworks is and whether it contributes to their value.

Always, one should seek to gain acquaintance with whatever counts as form by seeing and hearing it in the context of particular works, not as a detachable formula. Fortunately, the arts provide something for everyone, both for the definite and the indefinite listeners. Professor P. E. Vernon will speak in Chapter 16 of and for definite and indefinite viewers and readers as well. But they yield up their inner wealth only when the respondent surrenders himself to them, savoring the elements, large and small, that enter into artworks and sensing intimately their movement, direction and culmination. Analysis such as appears in the following sections is addressed solely to the perfection of viewing, listening, and reading.

CHAPTER 14

COHERENCE IN NARRATIVE ART

Attention to the structure of narrative art begins with Aristotle from whose *Poetics* we earlier took a long quotation (Chapter 4). It would be superfluous to repeat the commonplaces of extant theories about plot, and it is equally unnecessary to offer an alternative to them. What is needed is rather to see how materials of narrative or fiction and their structural use in the hands to the artist can contribute to coherence that makes the sustained life of the artwork possible.

The brevity of the examples of narrative provided is not altogether a disadvantage. We can see even better in a confined context what must count as the elements in such art, the prime and lesser *emergents*, their *ordination* and *magnitude*, their *comparative, causal, contextual* relations, and the inner powers of *tendence* in the form of the motivation and the unrolling of events. Above all, we can see how the artist deploys his developmental stratagems with them. Being in poetic form we have a characteristic resort to repetition for the purpose of effecting unity, by means of rhyme, alliteration, regular stanzaic form, and the rhythm of implicit meters. Poetry also permits the sheer repetition of key words, thoughts, or phrases which might be intolerable in prose ("Lies, lies, lies . . . lies . . . "; "Exon Wild, Dunkery Tor . . . Exon Wild, Dunkery Tor . . . "). We shall now draw attention specifically to some of the instances of the categories we have developed.

(1) ROBERT BROWNING, 'THE CONFESSIONAL'

Spain

It is a lie — their Priests, their Pope,
Their Saints, their . . . all they fear or hope
And lies, and lies — there! through my door
And ceiling, there! and walls and floor,
There, lies, they lie — shall still be hurled
Till spite of them I reach the world!

You think Priests just and holy men!
Before they put me in this den
I was a human creature too,
With flesh and blood like one of you,
A girl that laughed in beauty's pride
Like lilies in your world outside.

I had a lover — shame avaunt!
This poor wrenched body, grim and gaunt,
Was kissed all over till it burned,
By lips the truest, love e'er turned

His heart's own tint: one night they kissed
My soul out in a burning mist.

So, next day when the accustomed train
Of things grew round my sense again,
"That is a sin," I said: and slow
With downcast eyes to church I go,
And pass to the confession-chair,
And tell the old mild father there.

But when I falter Beltran's name,
"Ha!" quoth the father; "much I blame
The sin; yet wherefore idly grieve?
Despair not — strenuously retrieve!
Nay, I will turn this love of thine
To lawful love, almost divine;

"For he is young, and led astray,
This Beltran, and he schemes, men say,
To change the laws of church and state;
So, thine shall be an angel's fate,
Who, ere the thunder breaks, should roll
Its cloud away and save his soul.

"For, when he lies upon thy breast,
Thou mayest demand and be possessed
Of all his plans, and next day steal
To me, and all those plans reveal,
That I and every priest, to purge
His soul, may fast and use the scourge."

That father's beard was long and white,
With love and truth his brow seemed bright;
I went back, all on fire with joy,
And, that same evening, bade the boy
Tell me, as lovers should, heart-free,
Something to prove his love of me.

He told me what he would not tell
For hope of heaven or fear of hell;
And I lay listening in such pride!
And, soon as he had left my side,
Tripped to the church by morning-light
To save his soul in his despite.

I told the father all his schemes,
Who were his comrades, what their dreams;
"And now make haste," I said, "to pray
The one spot from his soul away;

To-night he comes, but not the same
Will look!" At night he never came.

Nor next night: on the after-morn,
I went forth with a strength new-born.
The church was empty; something drew
My steps into the street; I knew
It led me to the market-place:
Where, lo, on high, the father's face!

That horrible black scaffold dressed,
That stapled block . . . God sink the rest!
That head strapped back, that blinding vest,
Those knotted hands and naked breast,
Till near one busy hangman pressed,
And, on the neck these arms caressed . . .

No part in aught they hope or fear!
No heaven with them, no hell! — and here,
No earth, not so much space as pens
My body in their worst of dens
But shall bear God and man my cry,
Lies — lies, again — and still, they lie!

I do not pretend to offer a critique of this and the following poem. I assume that each will be thought at least a highly competent and creditable work. Nothing I say will compete with the appraisal of critics so long as they take these works seriously, nor will it tend to disprove what they would be likely to say. I confine myself to a few reflections on their structure and vitality in such terms as we have now developed at length, and as may be illustrated perhaps even more effectively when we apply them presently to music.

We have, then, in "The Confessional" an *object* that has a kind of existence in time, or that can be projected in time when it is read consecutively, thoughtfully, and responsively. It is a piece that is a characteristic production of its poet: intense, abrupt, dramatic. Lesser hands than Browning might have extended it and labored it. They might themselves have narrated the incident, pretending to objectivity and even omniscience about it and the subjects of the action. Browning chooses to hear the tale from the girl herself. It is not fully clear to me why he casts the whole of it into the form of couplets. This device might well have deadened the poem when the point of it is to be almost a shriek of rage at a morally monstrous betrayal of confidence. But it comes off, nevertheless, possibly because the exigencies of rhyme and stanza form compress and thus intensify something that is already exceedingly tense and intense, exactly as the story demands.

The girl's response to the events is so evidently the only morally proper one, the story can, in a sense, be told in but one way, her own: there is nothing further to say. Adverting to our distinction, we have here the presentation or *invocation* of an emotionally charged scene. If we ask what the nature of it is, or even ask after the name of it, the answer is best given in the *ipsissima verba* of the poem, since from first to last it issues from the person whose emotion it is.

Again, if we ask what is *evoked*, we have little difficulty in answering, although some of us might not be agreed what to think of the simplicity of the girl's trust in the father confessor. We cannot, however, but be moved by the tragic outcome of a well-intentioned deed.

Finally, it would not be difficult even for a Catholic contemporary of ours to share something of the rage, should he think of all this in something more than poetic terms, a rage and sense of shame that might be directed even at the Church itself. Thus, the poem may easily be *provocative* as well as evocative.

The story is brief enough, but even so, a structure of some complexity. "A lie," we hear in the first words, and thereafter the whole is a defense of this charge, so that when in the very last words we hear it again, the conclusion snaps tight upon the premises, like a trap. The tendence is thus to be found in the relentless progress to the conclusion of a moral syllogism which issues in convicting the Church of a dreadful wrong. It is no idle thing for a humble person to hurl such a charge, particularly at something like the Church in Spain in the sixteenth century. It involves an enormous expenditure of energy. I think it is obvious that Browning has devised a cause, the original event, that is, as philosophers say, fully adequate to the effect, the girl's response. The emotions in the narrative context in which she tells the story weld together the narrated events into a hot mass, yet they also cast an intense light into every corner of it so that we can easily trace the moral and motivational connections in it.

We are led forward from the first moment by the girl's charge that the Church, an institution devoted to rightness and goodness, is guilty of a monstrous wrong. We learn how hopes and expectations have been defeated, utterly. We readily understand her passionate involvement with Beltran, a youth of extraordinary vitality and idealism, traits that explain a generous and high-minded girl's attachment to him. These very traits, quickly limned in, explain her wanting her union with the youth to conform to the moral order of the Church. Naively, but in deepest trust, and not foolishly, she counts on contrition to rectify what she sees as her error, taking the Church at its solemn word. The frustration of all this, making her feel as if she were Judas Iscariot betraying the Savior, completes the moral justification of the sequel and her overwhelmed response.

In a narrative such as this one and the one to follow, as indeed in all art, there must be, as we have seen, a justification for everything in it that is appropriate to, or proper to, the particular medium and that satisfies the organ by which we apprehend the work. We understand how and why human events, actions, and emotive responses occur when and as they do and why their whole trend and tendence leads to what it does, only when we can make moral sense of them. Human actions can be the subject matter of art because in fact they possess these inner connections, because the movement by which we are taken from one element to another is imbued with feelings of inclination and aversion, of tension, frustration and satisfaction.

(2) THOMAS HARDY, 'THE SACRILEGE'

A Ballad-Tragedy (Circa 182–) Part I

"I have a Love I love too well
Where Dunkery frowns on Exon Moor;

I have a Love I love too well,
        To whom, ere she was mine,
'Such is my love for you,' I said,
'That you shall have to hood your head
A silken kerchief crimson-red,
        Wove finest of the fine.'

"And since this Love, for one mad moon,
On Exon Wild by Dunkery Tor,
Since this my Love for one mad moon
        Did clasp me as her king,
I snatched a silk-piece red and rare
From off a stall at Priddy Fair,
For handkerchief to hood her hair
        When we went gallanting.

"Full soon the four weeks neared their end
Where Dunkery frowns on Exon Moor;
And when the four weeks neared their end,
        And their swift sweets outwore,
I said, 'What shall I do to own
Those beauties bright as tulips blown,
And keep you here with me alone
        As mine for evermore?'

"And as she drowsed within my van
On Exon Wild by Dunkery Tor —
And as she drowsed within my van,
        And dawning turned to day,
She heavily raised her sloe-black eyes
And murmured back in softest wise,
'One more thing, and the charms you prize
        Are yours henceforth for aye.

' "And swear I will I'll never go
While Dunkery frowns on Exon Moor
To meet the Cornish Wrestler Joe
        For dance and dallyings.
If you'll to yon cathedral shrine,
And finger from the chest divine
Treasure to buy me ear-drops fine,
        And richly jewelled rings.'

"I said: 'I am one who has gathered gear
From Marlbury Downs to Dunkery Tor,
Who has gathered gear for many a year
        From mansion, mart and fair;
But at God's house I've stayed my hand,

Hearing within me some command —
Curbed by a law not of the land
   From doing damage there!'

"Whereat she pouts, this Love of mine,
As Dunkery pouts to Exon Moor,
And still she pouts, this Love of mine,
   So cityward I go.
But ere I start do the thing,
And speed my soul's imperilling
For one who is my ravishing
   And all the joy I know,

"I come to lay this charge on thee —
On Exon Wild by Dunkery Tor —
I come to lay this charge on thee
   With solemn speech and sign:
Should things go ill, and my life pay
For botchery in this rash assay,
You are to take hers likewise — yea,
   The month the law takes mine.

"For should my rival, Wrestler Joe,
Where Dunkery frowns on Exon Moor —
My reckless rival, Wrestler Joe,
   My Love's bedwinner be,
My rafted spirit would not rest,
But wander weary and distrest
Throughout the world in wild protest:
   The thought nigh maddens me!"

Part II

Thus did he speak — this brother of mine —
On Exon Wild by Dunkery Tor,
Born at my birth of mother of mine,
   And forthwith went his way
To dare the deed some coming night . . .
I kept the watch with shaking sight,
The moon at moments breaking bright,
   At others glooming gray.

For three full days I heard no sound
Where Dunkery frowns on Exon Moor,
I heard no sound at all around
   Whether his fay prevailed,
Or one more foul the master were,

Till some afoot did tidings bear
How that, for all his practised care,
    He had been caught and jailed.

They had heard a crash when twelve had chimed
By Mendip east of Dunkery Tor,
When twelve had chimed and moonlight climbed;
    They watched, and he was tracked
By arch and aisle and saint and knight
Of sculptured stonework sheeted white
In the cathedral's ghostly light,
    And captured in the act.

Yes; for this Love he loved too well
Where Dunkery sights the Severn shore,
All for this Love he loved too well
    He burst the holy bars,
Seized golden vessels from the chest
To buy her ornaments of the best,
At her ill-witchery's request
    And lure of eyes like stars . . . .

When blustering March confused the sky
In Toneborough Town by Exon Moor,
When blustering March confused the sky
    They stretched him; and he died.
Down in the crowd where I, to see
The end of him, stood silently,
With a set face he lipped to me —
    "Remember." "Ay!" I cried.

By night and day I shadowed her
From Toneborough Deane to Dunkery Tor,
I shadowed her asleep, astir,
    And yet I could not bear —
Till Wrestler Joe anon began
To figure as her chosen man,
And took her to his shining van —
    To doom a form so fair!

He made it handsome for her sake —
And Dunkery smiled to Exon Moor —
He made it handsome for her sake,
    Painting it out and in;
And on the door of apple-green
A bright brass knocker soon was seen,
And window-curtains white and clean
    For her to sit within.

And all could see she clave to him
As cleaves a cloud to Dunkery Tor,
Yea, all could see she clave to him,
    And every day I said,
"A pity it seems to part those two
That hourly grow to love more true:
Yet she's the wanton woman who
    Sent one to swing till dead!"

That blew to blazing all my hate,
While Dunkery frowned on Exon Moor,
And when the river swelled, her fate
    Came to her pitilessly . . . .
I dogged her, crying: "Across that plank
They use as bridge to reach yon bank
A coat and hat lie limp and dank;
    Your goodman's, can they be?"

She paled, and went, I close behind —
And Exon Frowned to Dunkery Tor,
She went, and I came up behind
    And tipped the plank that bore
Her, fleetly flitting across to eye
What such might bode. She slid awry;
And from the current came a cry,
    A gurgle; and no more.

How that befell no mortal knew
From Marlbury Downs to Exon Moor;
Nor mortal knew that deed undue
    But he who schemed the crime,
Which night still covers . . . . But in dream
Those ropes of hair upon the stream
He sees, and he will hear that scream
    Until his judgment-time.

Four personalities project themselves through time in this poem, their trajectories approaching or intersecting either to conflict or to harmonize. In a manner appropriate to poetic presentation much is said in few words to acquaint us with their essence: snatches of discourse, brief glimpses of actions taken or supported, reflections of actions in the experience or feeling of other persons. All of them remain vital realities to the end whether living or dead, each in a manner characteristic of himself or herself.

The story is brief and simple and need not be paraphrased. The setting is that of a somewhat footloose subculture of itinerants or vagabonds, subsisting often by theft an ever on the move from camp to camp, but less formal and less well knit than the gypsies. The host culture remains ever as a ground and comes forward only, though significantly and forcefully, in the form of the Church and the system of law when it sends one of the characters to the gallows. Without it and its laws and customs the subculture would be something utterly different from what it is. The established order is a "they" that confronts these wandering folk who are in but not of it, but who must take it into their reckoning and make appropriate adaptive moves.

The central figures are twin brothers, a girl who has been attached to one of them, and a man known as Cornish Wrestler Joe. There is a firm bond between the brothers, and this is further fortified by a pact to revenge themselves on the girl, whose vanity has contributed to a sentence of death of one of the twins. The obligation to mete out folk "justice" is accepted and never brought into question. The guilt is reckoned altogether to the girl. No action against Wrestler Joe, for whom the girl has left the brother, seems to be contemplated.

The doomed brother's figure remains potent whether present or absent. "Remember," be murmurs on the gallows to the second brother, who recounts the events and conversations, and his personality remains effective even beyond death. Keeping elements working even though they are not present is something one can do in the artistic medium of the meaningful word just as one can in the other arts, but here in a unique way. The reason is that the elements of literary works, even the places and personalities, are not sense-realities but meanings. The novelist or poet, if he has skillfully enough planted a thought, a meaning, can count on its persistence and, with proper stimulus, on its resurgence at climactic moments. This is the manner in which even a comparatively simple poem like this manages to obtain some of its effects. In long narratives, it is all important. As we have seen earlier, music seeks to defeat the time dimension and to give us the illusion that tone-filled moments do not perish but form "figures" of a certain "shape" and "extent." Literary art likewise transcends its time limitations, but with connotational means. It is unlike music in that it implies connections with an essentially mythical world that is presumed to exist before and after the events of the myth itself.

Thus in 'The Sacrilege' the scene is presented as continuous with preceding years that have bred these personalities and conditioned them to act as they have done. At the end and beyond it that world is still there. In it, the second brother is unlikely to be brought to justice for his murder of the girl, and this probability, or improbability, is a definite part of the world of the poem. In some sense, in this world of myth, he will dream and be plagued by his guilt forever.

As we think of the characters of this tale, we see how their significance, their causal and motivational potency may be independent of the extent of the figure they cut in the poem. Wrestler Joe unwittingly triggers at least the final act of revenge, and probably even more at an earlier time. He seems to bear no burden of guilt as a paramour may in more organic societies. If Joe is the trigger, the girl is the detonating powder. She herself, however, although motivationally all-important, is heard from only indirectly; we are practically teased into inventing her and giving her a character.

A disproportion of the role to the significance is shown also in the second brother's place in most of the action. Although he narrates the tale and even makes the logic of revenge his own, he is rather a willing instrument for what others determine. His primary significance emerges only at the very end. Here it is not clear whether the brother truly feels anguish and penitence for a crime or the recollection of the drowning girl, and her screams of death merely plunge him into a ghastly mental state. Although his conscience may bother him, his unexpiated guilt is likely to be buried with him.

If, as in all art, the literary artist wishes to invent and develop figures in relation and interaction with one another he must discover in them those traits and powers that sustain interest. Our study of the relation of elements has shown that whatever success or failure the artist has, however this is reckoned, will depend upon any or all of these considerations: the number of *effective* elements that come upon the scene and whether they stand toward one another in relations of coordination or subordination, of accommodation, complement, or conflict; the *magnitude* of the elements in relations of extent to one another, where extent need not be restricted to dimensions of time or space but can manifest itself in significance; the degree of *similarity* or difference of elements in their intrinsic dimensions; the effects of *contextual* compresence upon identical or resembling elements; the inner *tendentive* power of elements to move, to attract and to be attracted to one another, to gravitate toward and to be repulsed by one another. It is evident even from the necessarily brief examples considered here that literary characters stand in all such relations to one another and that the relations are the very ones the artist is most concerned about in his compositional efforts, and after him, the critic. Both the elements and the relations have an essentially moral quality, since this is intrinsic to all *human* relation — if they were but physical bodies to one another, they would not be subjects of literary art.

In "The Sacrilege," only a moral grasp of the personalities and their situation enables us to see how and why the story develops as it does. The same would be true, and indeed fairly emphatically so, in comic situations. We understand this if, at the risk of oversimplifying, we sum up the moral and emotional energies that move the principal figures. What moves the first brother? If we may answer in the briefest terms, we must say love, perhaps lust (as common sense distinguishes these); then agonies of jealousy, hatred and revenge; twinges of conscience, as shown in the hesitation to rob "God's house." The girl? Lust, or at least a somewhat thoughtless surrender to inclination; vanity, a touch of cupidity; in general, a person living the shallowest sort of existence, never or never as yet stirred to any great depths. The second brother? Loyalty to his twin brother and identification with the latter's vengeful response, but also a reflectiveness that leads in the end to an awakening of conscience, at least "in dream." Wrestler Joe? So far as we can catch a faint glimpse of him, he is, like the girl, a mere smudge of lust.

These and other appraisals of the figures in the piece are the ways in which we sum up their characters and offer moral explanations of what they do. The elements are relevant to one another and not merely laid alongside one another as we found them to be in the subaesthetic modalities.

Turning to the interaction of these figures, we see an all-important focal moment of the action in the fifth stanza of Part Two. We are almost certain by this time what the second brother is charged to *remember*, and we know what events have prompted it, what in the first brother's mind has seemed to fully justify his demand that he be avenged. This is like the winding up of a spring. We know what exertions have gone into the winding and how much energy is now stored in it. Our curiosity about how it will be sprung makes us remain to hear the rest of the tale.

As we expect, the girl soon goes off with Wrestler Joe. Although the second brother has until then had some hesitation to avenge the brother he now shakes himself free of it. He waits until the river swells and dispatches her.

The tale is simple, even sparse, and well-knit, every turn of phrase limning in an essential detail. The lines of development that are illustrated in the concatenations of causation and motivation are unbroken and lead inexorably to the outcome. The poet is wise and skilful enough to know that he must make his reader expect or divine, as he reads or hears, how the events of the poem are to unfold but not to know them so precisely that his interest in them is extinguished when they occur. If a poet manages all this well he will hold his reader to the very end.

There is also another strand of development in what we may call the moral logic of he poem. Revenge is one of the expected ways in which human beings administer the moral economy. But it is not a moral solution since it only raises up another wrong. Human beings may see that moment of revenge as the finish of an action, but the moral economy demands an expiation.

This is provided for in Hardy's poem. The murder of the girl is unexpiated formally and the second brother escapes a fate such as his brother's.

> But in dream
> Those ropes of hair upon the stream
> He sees, and he will hear that scream
> Until his judgment-time.

The agony of the fate he has chosen for himself thus proves to be as bad as death itself. The characterization "tragedy" which Hardy attaches to the poem is accurate to the extent that the second twin, being not merely left to be stamped out of existence by the law as another criminal, "owns" his crime, his "deed undue", for this is the first condition of moral redemption. But if he falls short of this, the term 'tragedy' is mis-applied since as noted he may be stricken less by guilt of conscience than by agony of recollection.

We can learn a great deal about the fictional or narrative art from this and our previous brief example. This medium inhabits the imagination almost wholly. In poetic form, sight and particularly sound can help determine the artistic reality, but it is the mind's power to project and to remember that enables a work to come into being endowed with spatial and temporal properties of a nature altogether *sui generis*, but possessed also of formal properties analogous to those of other arts and media.

In "The Sacrilege" figures are projected over and emerge from the ground of a social order and relate themselves to one another. The very place in which the actions occur, under craggy Dunkery Tor on Exon Moor, seems to participate in the moods and re-sponses of the characters. As individual elements the characters possess an elemental quality and appeal, drawing our attention to themselves to attract or repel. They have a formal appeal in their interaction with one another and even in their mere presence to one another, working both causal and contextual interpersonal effects. The compositional devices the artist employs are the familiar ones of repetition or recurrence and lines of development toward minor and major climaxes. Finally, the whole possesses a shape and order toward which the participant's attention may reciprocally move from scanning the individual moments, movements, persons, and places.

Looking back we see that these are the literary variants of the moves and motions that are open also to artists in every art. Even our modest but genuine examples from the vast sea of literature enable us to see how each of these moves is made by the literary artist at work with his own glimpse of the human event. He must keep before himself every slightest element in the whole and know the directions in which they move; in literature this is to say the direction in which human life in all its variety moves, the fulfillment and frustration of enterprise. Study of this example may help us to answer the question how literary art is possible, and if it does, it will also help us to learn how art itself is possible.

(3) JAMES DICKEY, 'THE SHARK'S PARLOR'

Memory: I can take my head and strike it on a wall   on Cumberland
    Island
Where the night tide came crawling under the stairs   came up the first
Two or three steps   and the cottage stood on poles all night
With the sea sprawled under it   as we dreamed of the great fin circling
Under the bedroom floor. In daylight there was my first brassy taste of
    beer
And Payton Ford and I came back from the Glynn County
    slaughterhouse
With a bucket of entrails and blood. We tied one end of a hawser
To a spindling porch pillar and rowed straight out of the house
Three hundred yards into the vast front yard of windless blue water
The rope outslithering its coil   the two-gallon jug stoppered and
    sealed
With wax   and a ten-foot chain leader   a drop-forged shark hook
    nestling.
We cast our blood on the waters   the land blood easily passing
For sea blood   and we sat in it for a moment with the stain spreading
Out from the boat   sat in a new radiance   in the pond of blood in
    the sea
Waiting for fins   waiting to spill our guts also in the glowing water.
We dumped the bucket, and baited the hook with a run-over collie pup.
    The jug
Bobbed, trying to shake off the sun as a dog would shake off the sea.
We rowed to the house   feeling the same water lift the boat a new way,
All the time seeing where we lived rise and dip with the oars.
We tied up and sat down in rocking chairs, one eye or the other
    responding
To the blue-eye wink of the jug. Payton got us a beer and we sat

All morning sat there with blood on our minds   the red mark out
In the harbor slowly failing us   then   the house groaned   the rope
Sprang out of the water   splinters flew   we leapt from our chairs
And grabbed the rope   hauled   did nothing   the house coming
    subtly
Apart   all around us   underfoot   boards beginning to sparkle
    like sand
With the glinting of the bright hidden parts of ten-year-old nails

Pulling out   the tarred poles we slept propped-up on   leaning to sea
As in land wind   crabs scuttling from under the floor   as we took
    turns about
Two more porch pillars   and looked out and saw   something
    a fish-flash
An almighty fin in trouble   a moiling of secret forces   a false start
Of water   a round wave growing: in the whole of Cumberland
    Sound the one ripple.
Payton took off without a word   I could not hold him either

But clung to the rope anyway: it was the whole house bending
Its nails that held whatever it was   coming in a little and like a fool
I took up the slack on my wrist. The rope drew gently   jerked   I lifted
Clean off the porch and hit the water   the same water it was in
I felt in blue blazing terror at the bottom of the stairs and scrambled
Back up looking desperately into the human house as deeply as I could
Stopping my gaze before it went out the wire screen of the back door
Stopped it on the thistled rattan   the rugs I lay on and read
On my mother's sewing basket with next winter's socks spilling from it
The flimsy vacation furniture   a bucktoothed picture of myself.
Payton came back with three men from a filling station   and glanced
    at me
Dripping water   inexplicable   then we all grabbed hold like a
    tug-of-war.

We were gaining a little   from us a cry went up   from everywhere
People came running. Behind us the house filled with men and boys.
On the third step from the sea I took my place   looking down the rope
Going into the ocean, humming and shaking off drops. A houseful
Of people put their backs into it   going up the steps from me
Into the living room   through the kitchen   down the back stairs
Up and over a hill of sand   across a dust road   and onto a raised field
Of dunes   we were gaining   the rope in my hands began to be wet
With deeper water   all other haulers retreated through the house
But Payton and I on the stairs   drawing hand over hand on our blood
Drawing into existence by the nose   a huge body   becoming
A hammerhead   rolling in beery shallows   and I began to let up
But the rope still strained behind me   the town had gone
Pulling-mad in our house: far away in a field of sand they struggled
They had turned their backs on the sea   bent double   some on their
    knees
The rope over their shoulders like a bag of gold   they strove for the
    ideal
Esso station across the scorched meadow   with the distant fish
    coming up
The front stairs   the sagging boards   still coming in   up   taking

Another step   toward the empty house   where the rope stood
     straining
By itself through the rooms   in the middle of the air. "Pass the word,"
Payton said, and I screamed it: "Let up, good God, let up!"   to no one
     there.
The shark flopped on the porch, grating with salt-sand   driving
     back in
The nails he had pulled out   coughing chunks of his formless blood.
The screen door banged and tore off   he scrambled on his tail   slid
Curved   did a thing from another world   and was out of his
     element and in
Our vacation paradise   cutting all four legs from under the dinner
     table
With one deep-water move   he unwove the rugs in a moment
     throwing pints
Of blood over everything we owned   knocked the buck teeth out of
     my picture
His odd head full of crushed jelly-glass splinters and radio tubes
     thrashing
Among the pages of fan magazines   all the movie stars drenched in
     sea-blood.
Each time we thought he was dead   he struggled back and smashed
One more thing   in all coming back to die   three or four more
     times after death.
At last we got him out   log-rolling him   greasing his sandpaper skin
With lard to slide him   pulling on his chained lips as the tide came
Tumbled him down the steps as the first night wave went under the
     floor.
He drifted off   head back   belly white as the moon. What could I
     do but buy
That house   for the one black mark still there   against death   a
     forehead-
toucher in the room he circles beneath   and has been invited to
     wreck?
Blood hard as iron on the wall   black with time   still bloodlike
Can be touched whenever the brow is drunk enough: all changes:
     Memory:
Something like three-dimensional dancing in the limbs   with age
Feeling more in two worlds than one   in all worlds the growing
     encounters.

"Memory is the first word of this poem and also virtually the last. What is the significance
of it? The poet leaves no moment for us to reflect on this striking fact; instead he plunges
on with the narrative, losing not an instant of time.

We learn of the events in preparing for the fishing adventure; maybe they will land
a shark. They tie a hawser "to a spindling porch pillar", row out with the pitiful remains

of a run over collie pup as bait over the "windless blue water" of Cumberland Sound, and drop a wax stoppered jug as a mark of the whereabouts of the intended catch. There is more than a hint of the purpose of the adventure with the mention of a "drop-forged shark hook." But the outcome is a surprise to everyone: not just a shark but one of monstrous size and strength.

Having landed the shark they are obliged to cling to it with determination. Since the whole house is built on spindly pilings in the water, it threatens to be reduced to splinters — to say nothing of danger to the life of the participants. And near disaster comes suddenly when the narrator, left alone, is lifted "clean off the porch" and splashes into "the same water it was in", referring to the fish. He scrambles back up the steps "dripping water" to relative safety. His companion meanwhile has gone to seek help leaving him alone to fight for his life. He returns with the townspeople in sufficient numbers to lend muscle to the ensuing tug of war. They man the hawser and gradually bring in the shark, a mammoth hammerhead. Since the people are out of the house and out of earshot, they tug at the line in a nearby field and succeed in pulling the beast into the house, into the parlor! There its thrashing about reduced the room and contents to sheer trash, "cutting all four legs from under the dinner table."

"Let up, good God, Let up!" he cries. After this monstrous, relentless destruction is complete, the shark is near death. At last they get him out by greasing his sandpaper skin and tumble him down the steps. He floats belly up as the tide comes in — "belly white as the moon."

These are the bare bones of the narrative, with dozens more said or implied in the poem. The movement is brisk and told at progressively breakneck speed. A first climax comes when

> The rope drew gently   jerked   I lifted
> Clean off the porch and hit the water   the same water it was in
> I felt a blue blazing terror at the bottom of the stairs and scrambled
> Back up . . .

He possibly doesn't know at that particular time what the "it" is that precipitates the terror he feels. But all too soon he learns that the beast is

> A hammerhead   rolling in beery shallows

Another climax ensues when they realize the imminent danger that they face, with the hammerhead coming up the stairs, drawn relentlessly by a "pulling mad", unseeable throng of townspeople, "some on their knees"

> The rope over their shoulders like a bag of gold.

He screams, in a state that borders on panic, and well he might, since the destruction he and his companion are forced to witness is truly awesome. "He unwove the rugs"

> knocked the buck teeth out of
>   my picture
> His odd head full of crushed jelly-glass splinters and radio tubes
>   thrashing

> Among the pages of fan magazines   all the movie stars drenched in
>   sea-blood.

It is a scene that ends in the death of the shark, but what lasts forever for both witnesses is summed up in one word:

> Memory!

This word gains a new dimension for it signifies the perpetuation of the present into the
future.

> What could I
>   do but buy
> That house   for the one black mark still there   against death . . .
> Blood hard as iron on the wall   black with time

Compulsion, yes, but who is not a victim of compulsion — all of us, some more, some
less. Remember, in that moment of "blue blazing terror" brought on by himself, the
shark "has been invited to wreck" the premises. But the beast is innocent! Saying that
the shark has been "invited" in is vastly ironic. It signifies remorse. Therein lies the
tragedy of the whole event.

The outcome is close kin to Thomas Hardy's 'The Sacrilege', sub-titled 'A Ballad-
Tragedy', though the shark episode is less poignant. The murderer will be haunted by
guilt-feelings forever after.

> In dream
> Those ropes of hair upon the stream
> He sees, and he will hear that scream
> Until his judgment time.

It is true that the crime is murder for revenge, which is much more reprehensible than
killing an animal, but it means the death of an innocent being nevertheless.

Where is the tragedy? In Hardy's poem it lies in the fact that "he will hear that scream
until his judgment time", that is to say, he will feel his guilt for the rest of his days, and
even beyond. In Dickey's poem, the narrator's remorse manifests itself in the death of
an innocent victim caused by the lack of foresight, and by a certain thoughtlessness.

CHAPTER 15

COHERENCE IN VISUAL ART

The small selection of works included here exemplify artistic procedures that may not at first seem to be those developed in the foregoing theory. In few or none of the illustrated works does the artist resort exclusively to closure, to repetition, or to development. Yet the distinct modes of organization, isolation, simply symmetry, symmetrical and asymmetrical accommodation, flanking symmetry, centralization of figure, radial symmety, and pervasive development to climax represent different ways in which our three general procedures of compositional ordering are carried out (or defied), separately or in concert.

1. *Isolation*. The Gattamelata statue (2) and its setting, or virtually any piece of sculpture in the round, illustrate the use of closure as the solution of the problem of finding a suitable ground for the figure and of the termination of the ground at some limit of relevance that defines the surround. Control of not only the figure but of the ground and surround rarely lies in the hands of the artist alone. Considered only as figure, sculpture such as the Gattamelata in side profile or the Horse of Selene from the Elgin Marbles (1) presents figures whose coherence we can trace first to what is instantly coherent as expression, a familiar animal form. Beyond this, the figure of animal and rider owes its force to inner development. This is true likewise of the head of the horse of Selene even when taken in independence of the lost members of the whole figure. Virtually all of the architectural examples cited here exhibit the same phenomenon of closure and of solutions, with one or another degree of success, to the problem of providing or finding appropriate grounds and surrounds.

The closure found in the map of Paris (3) is, of course, altogether owing to the cartographer's art and his decision where to draw limits, but it is art nonetheless. The map illustrates also how the limit between dominance and superdominance in a figure over its ground may be set.

2. *Classic symmetry*. The urge towards symmetry was virtually irresistible in antiquity and it is unlikely we shall ever see the last of it. Both the front and side elevations of ancient temples such as the Parthenon are symmetrical. Classic architectural symmetry involves inverse repetition, the center of the pediment subtly dominating with the gentle inclination of the roof. When this is steepened the subtlety is lost (cf. the Madeleine in Paris). Considering the figure as a whole, closure is also obviously present. The peak of the pediment represents a culminating development, particularly if sculpture fills the triangular space of the tympanum. Perhaps the most important aspect of all is the manner in which the monotony in the columns is made much more than merely tolerable: the rectangles of the totality of the columns in each elevation and stand forth as figural. The inner repetition and rhythm participate in concert with the enclosing shape to produce an effect of serene power. As often observed, the total form is at peace with the earth and not, like Gothic, in a state of nervous agitation to flee from it. Although the form is obviously symmetrical, it should not be confused with our next two classes,

since in the present case the form is entirely one and whole and not a central symmetry arising out of discrete side members.

Classic symmetry is by no means confined to architecture but is exploited also in painting. The familiar Renaissance pyramidal form for portraits and even-grouped figures (e.g., Raphael's Madonna del Prato, Vienna, or his La Belle Jardinière, Louvre) is employed with striking effect by Velazquez in several paintings of the Infanta Margareta Theresa (7). Symmetrical group paintings, however, tend toward our class 4. The essential difference is that in the latter the central figure serves as a climax (hence the mode of procedure is developmental) for the flanking members, whereas in 2, the complex is not to be thought of as having discrete "side" members.

The continuing use of symmetry can be seen in literally thousands of instances, Oriental as well as Occidental: not only the Eiffel Tower but most skyscrapers and private dwellings.

Radial symmetry. The ordering of visual space need not always reflect motion in a horizontal direction. Visual art has sometimes adopted coordinates other than the rectangular or Cartesian. Radial coordination provides an alternative, as we see in After the Hunt of William Harnett. Centralization and culmination are even more potently present but in a new guise, for which reasons Harnett's restraint in the adoption of this scheme renders his success even more impressive. Rigorous or rigid centralization would have deadened the enterprise.

3. *Symmetrical accommodation*. We have discussed this at length in Chapter 3. The most effective examples are more or less monolithic pairs of members. Although it is present in the repetition and reinforcement of more than two identical members, the more numerous the members, the more an effect of monotony tends to prevail which must then be made up for in other ways.

Obvious examples of 3 are the front elevations, that is, the towers of Romanesque and Gothic churches: for example, Durham Cathedral, Notre Dame de Paris, York Minster, and many others. The members repeat, echo, and reinforce their essence by their near proximity. The intervening area is interesting but generally quite recedent except that when there are three doorways, the size of the center may be emphasized and with the other two make a flanking symmetry.

Our expectations of paintings are such that comparatively few examples of successful symmetrical accommodation can be found. Slight asymmetry at least seems to be demanded and this brings us to a variant of 3.

Asymmetrical accommodation. In this mode, which is often thought or felt to be an error or blemish, the two accommodating members differ markedly but boldly assert themselves against one another. Obviously, a certain conflict is inherent in this mode which is, of course, something altogether different from the classic. The prime example is no doubt the west face of Chartres Cathedral and after it Amiens. Whereas symmetrical accommodation connotes an almost classic composure, asymmetry always involves disequilibrium, potential rotation, and thus motion, if not conflict: the eye is not permitted to absorb a single figure of two nodes, but is ceaselessly thrown from one member to the other.

In painting we have limitless examples of this, painting being essentially not a *classical* art form. What must prevail in all asymmetrical accommodation to preserve it from mere error or defiance of expectations of symmetry is that there be a kind of ceaseless reciprocity of development (that is, as one of our three basic compositional procedures) and a kind of tendence of the members toward one another in the very moment of their conflict or otherness. This is amply demonstrated in painting. A familiar body of examples is provided by the many Annunciations where the Angel and the Virgin are united in the utter difference but mutual necessity of their roles. One should recall Fra Angelico's Annunciation frescos in Florence and Cortona, as well as the Annunciations of other painters.

Going farther afield one may ponder the illustrations from de Kooning (13) and the child's drawing of a stilt race below (11), and finally, the example which nature herself has obligingly provided in the twin monoliths in the breakers on the Oregon coast (5).

4. *Flanking symmetry*. This mode has numerous examples, and contrast with the preceding is easily seen. The distinctive mark is generally the three-fold division, in which right and left flanking members are clearly distinct but also as clearly dependent upon the central members. Besides the Perugino Crucifixion (9) illustrated below, one may mention any number of other examples: the Master of the St. Lucy Legend, Madonna and Child Enthroned with Angels, San Francisco Palace of the Legion of Honor; Jan van Eyck, The Virgin with St. Donatien, St. George, and Canon van der Paele, Bruges. Architectural examples range from the west face of Siena Cathedral to Sacré Coeur in Paris. In painting, if symmetry is too strong, the eye's quest for form is too easily satisfied.

To the extent that a triptych may be regarded as one work it may frequently be appropriate to regard it as an instance of flanking symmetry: it depends upon how high a degree of mutual necessity prevails among the members.

5. *Centralized figure*. The character of this mode may often resemble the preceding in that a more or less central area or figure is intended as of central interest, but here rigorous, evenly balanced symmetry is abandoned. The parts are generally numerous and ordered in subordinate hierarchies and also point as a whole in a central direction. A brilliant example is provided by Poussin's Triumph of Neptune, Pennsylvania Museum of Art, or Raphael's The School of Athens (6), the Vatican. In these two instances expression or connotation is a powerful contributory formal device, but no purely visual aspect of the form is subordinated to it in any way.

6. *Pervasive development to climax*. What has in general been almost unanimously deemed essential to the spatial artwork is *first*, that it be limited in extent, however large — so long as the size is compatible with visual apprehension as a whole; *second*, that it culminate in one figure or region — preferably one, but at least in a very few; and *third*, that all areas establish relevance to one another and to the principal figure. Modern use of development, a matter of some centuries, has moved progressively away from insistence on these features. Progressively encompassing apprehension, unitary or limited emphasis, and thoroughgoing relevance have been challenged or abandoned, though in no sense universally. The point is that we have been progressively invited to expect something different of vision and the visual. But the three "essentials" are not abandoned all at once.

What we have called development is not altogether a new mode since in literal terms it is involved in all of the foregoing. The procedure has been given a different emphasis in Duchamp's Nude Descending a Staircase, No. 2 (12). There is a strong seeking after movement (inherent in the Futurist procedure) and a strong tendency towards a region of culmination at the right. There is also a tightly knit scheme of relevance in the figure, or rather what we are invited to think of as several stages of the motion of the figure. Culminating asymmetry, though its futuristic exemplification in this instance is uncommon, has been the rule rather than the exception in thousands of paintings as we approach the modern age. The Nude is compatible with this trend, particularly in the sense in which asymmetry and motion become acceptable and highly sought after.

In culminating asymmetry all three essentials are still present but the challenge to them in the "envelopment" procedure becomes ever more insistent. In fact, a challenge to any of the three essentials mentioned above challenges all of them. As Yeats says in 'The Second Coming',

> Things fall apart,
> The center cannot hold.

Motion and conflict become perpetual, and resolutions based upon inner relevance are looked upon as illusory. Life, vitality, and eventually, power or force alone become the supreme values.

7. *Connotation.* A further word may be added to what was said in Chapter 9 regarding the use of the connotation of large or small elements as an organizing device. For reasons already cited, this is not to be regarded as simply "content," to which the ancient mechanical metaphor of the container and the contained relegates it. The bonds established between parts of artworks are frequently apprehended as a " . . . ," where this is a part or the whole of some myth, or a history of persons or events, or a shape familiar in reality, a woman, a street, a river, and such bonds are commonly of enormous strength, sufficient to contribute almost effortlessly to holding the complex together. Thus, the fact that in a familiar sense a certain depiction is offered in some of the artworks that follow contributes powerfully to their internal order, because the respondent's expectations being aroused in one part of the work are satisfied in another – this is always a reliable clue to form. We have the head of a horse depicted, a knight on his horse, a child in elegant dress, several male figures, three children on stilts, the Crucifixion, numerous male figures in a grand edifice, and an infant as the center of interest among several human figures. Visually, the resort to connotation as a resource for form has always been subordinated by the artist to more "abstract" procedures, such as those already described. In our illustrations connotation is in fact so subordinated, but it is not difficult to find examples, even in art galleries, in which the reverse condition prevails. The ultimate degradation of this mode is, of course, the poorly composed photograph which may have a purely sentimental or nostalgic interest for someone. This is by no means to be despised, except when it, or anything like it, is put forward as art.

8. *Envelopment of spectator.* The final challenge to the classic spectator's eye begins even with the emergence of landscape painting. The classic mode promoted the spectator's synoptic and encompassing view. In landscape painting, on the other hand, a larger world

is implicated than the artist presents. The spectator now becomes a participant; he is invited *into* the artwork as it were; he is encompassed by the whole rather than encompassing it himself. We are asked to step into an enchanted world in Claude le Lorrain and Watteau, a world of elegant make-believe in Fragonard, a world of rural charm in Constable, a world of visual magic in Corot. We do not look about for strict balance of mass against mass. We are induced by the painter to accept nature in the casual form in which he finds it or pretends to find it.

The development from landscape painting to the artwork into which one is invited to immerse himself visually and thence even to step into literally (e.g. Edward Kienholz's works) is a well-known phenomenon of the last century. Here too, and even in purely aleatory proceedings, one can detect the insistent re-emergence not only of the need for development or closure, but even of the more particular stratagems of gaining coherence just recounted. Our selection of visual artworks for somewhat closer inspection is of course very broad and confines itself to the most salient and typifying artistic procedures.

(1) HORSE OF SELENE (ELGIN MARBLES, BRITISH MUSEUM)

The horse of Selene is nothing short of magnificent! Profile view of animals and persons are prime examples of nature's resort to closure. It complements the axial symmetery (or as we might also say, converse repetition) of a direct front view. In a comparatively great expanse such as the head of this horse, when we turn from the total closured form, we can appreciate the manner in which the eye, ear, nostril, mane, and mouth of the animal must each play a partly figural or emergent role without, however, reducing the brow and cheek to mere grounds of recedents. Since there is in lateral profile essentially no repetition (except for the textural repetition in the mane, which however, is an eminently "tolerable monotony"), closure is of the first importance. It proves in the end to be the most "ultimate" of the compositional orders, both in art and nature. It rarely, however, stands alone, perhaps never in the organic world.

(2) TEMPLE OF NEPTUNE (SO-CALLED) AT PAESTUM

The temples of Paestum (south of Naples) antedate the Parthenon by a century or so and are marvelously intact in outer form. Scarcely any Greek temple conveys so well an impression of the device we have mentioned several times in the text, the use of repetition even of monotony but in a benign manner in the colonnade. The front with six Archaic Doric columns, suggesting Egyptian antecedents, is of extraordinary mutually reinforcing strength, the result of what we have called Accommodation. The side colonnade is more inevitably monotonous, but perfectly benignly, because attention is immediately drawn toward the rectangle the whole side forms, and because at the angle at which we here view the side there is culmination in the corner nearest the eye and another at the far right corner. Here as with all free-standing buildings, we are likely to regard a view at a sufficient distance to permit closure to be "definitive" of the building itself. But the definition is highly qualified, because a view of a colonnade, even from virtually under the eaves, has its own merits. The monotony of the frieze divisions differed from that of the colonnade in ancient Doric temples by the varying narrative content of the metopes. In this as in other examples, we draw attention to the use of compositional orders simply as devices of unification, but we do not forget that none of these orders guarantees the aesthetic excellence, or beauty, of the subjects. Other considerations must enter into this besides the formal orders we have studied.

(3) DONATELLO, GATTAMELATA

Donatello's Gattamelata, one of the glories of Padua, is unified not only by closure but by the powerful continuants of the X-lines that run from the baton through the sword to the right rear leg of the horse, and from the left front leg through the figure of the general's body (viewing from the left side of the horse). Connotative connections (that these are a horse, a military commander, a sword, spurs, bridle, and so on) are always at work and Donatello never forgets them. The connotations of horse and field commander are a serviceable armature on which the work is hung and the unifying thought which the observer cannot fail to carry away; but what has individualized the work is not this but the execution in its great lines and its details. It has not only the presumption or promise of unity which closure confers but has also made good the realization of it.

(4) MAP OF PARIS

Although what, in our terminology, amounts to a superdominant form for the central city of Paris, as presented in this fine old travel map, has issued from a mere painter's necessity, we may take our forms wherever we find them, even when they are not the result of artistic intention. (Who would not wish to see around every city a continuous "greenbelt" such as this cartographer has devised?) The map not only presents an example of superdominance (not clearly visible in black and white copy, which is unfortunately necessary because of the cost of reproducing it in full color) but anticipates a vista that could have been realized before the age of air and space transportation only in distant views from hills or mountains. In fact, however, visions from aloft of cities were projected even in medieval times. Such a visual realization contributed to the apprehension of the city as itself a work of art. While unity by means of closure is often trivially easy in some arts, it has been a kind of ideal vouchsafed only to the imagination when the subject is a city.

(5) TWIN ROCKS, OREGON

These great monoliths on the Oregon shore are a joy to contemplate, either separately or as enjoying each other's company. They embody the essence of the inorganic together with the functioning of laws of both cause and chance. Here we have in the right twin an order of closure and almost nothing else. Nothing repeats itself, top or bottom, side to side, endwise or sidewise. Chance and causation have helped in both cases to taper the monoliths towards the top, thus rounding them off with a mere suggestion of development. Nature seems to be most partial to the frustum as the dominant monolithic form. (The view of Mt. Hood, also in Oregon, from directly east or west at a distance of fifty miles, is a splendid exception to this.) The left twin adds the almost comical touch of an arch, with the result of a rough and ready inverse repetition of the outer in the inner profile. One may think for a moment of Henry Moore and also reflect on what may be learned about form from nature left to its own devices. Nature's forms are, of course, governed also by a factor of time. The photograph of the twins dates from about 1915.

This is as good an occasion as any to point out that, seen from appropriate points of vantage, the sea and sanded areas of beach or desert offer the best examples of subjects in which there is in effect no closure at all. Here one sees one undulant pattern interestingly varied, yet repeating itself endlessly. The individual elevations, the ripples of sand or water are scarcely individual enough to count as figures. One looks *into* such a complex, not *at* it, as one does at many landscape paintings and recent giant canvases. Dunes exhibit also another aesthetic potential, since they show large undulations as well as very small ones, and thus may sustain an interest in themselves from development in line of mass.

(6) RAPHAEL, THE SCHOOL OF ATHENS (ROME, VATICAN MUSEUM)

Of the many aspects of Raphael's School of Athens one might single out the use of line. The alignment, if not line, of the heads of the philosophers standing on the top step of the portico may at first be little noticed. On reflection one sees what immense difficulties such a line presents: it might totally deaden the whole composition by its fixity. But Raphael has spared no pains in rising above the problem, varying the line, spacing the figure, varying the color, countering the force of the horizontal with virtual diagonals of standing and seated figures. Then again the vertical axes of the bodies are continued upward in the pilasters of the receding nave. Finally, the figures are, as it were, tied by the loops of the concentric Roman arches of ceiling, which enclose an immense and truly sublime space. Coherence is effected by the arch series, a development towards or away from the observer, by the force of a horizontal line so potent that it must be qualified in innumerable ways, by the sheer repetition of variegated figures which includes also those in sculpture or relief. All of this, and much more, the painter has in mind, first of all, quite apart from the "myth," the erudite connotation connections that abound everywhere: Socrates, Plato and Aristotle stand out from the throng. The device of a crowd in such a space had been attempted before, and has been since, but more often botched than made even passable. The magnificent painting has been reproduced from a "cartoon" drawing by Joannes Volpato. Raphael himself is visible next to the bottom right.

(7) VELAZQUEZ, INFANTA MARGARETA THERESA (VIENNA, KUNSTHISTORISCHES MUSEUM)

We draw attention only to a few of the enchantments of this masterpiece of Velazquez. The painting possesses a subtle psychological appreciation of the subject — a child, yet one that cannot be thought of for herself alone but must be associated with a dynasty, a nation, an empire — and at the same time pursues a tremendous "architectural" plan that might have been bungled in other hands. Development of a great pyramidal figure culminates upward first in the rosette at the breast and then in the head, seemingly already too wise for its years. Conversely, we descend in ring after ring through collar, bodice, and waist to seven great rings in the hem. Closure and repetition work into one another at every stage. There is nothing mechanical or forced at any point despite the severe architectonic of it. Subtle touches of slight asymmetry appear everywhere. The painting succeeds not only formally but in its elemental appeal as well. Cool rich blues are offset by the warmer tones of the furry muff and the interior, and the gold of the sash and the hair.

(8) GIORGIONE, ADORATION OF THE SHEPHERDS
(WASHINGTON, NATIONAL GALLERY OF ART)

Visual art, as painting, in its long alliance with poetry and myth, broken only in our century, has relied on them as the prime resource to insure unity, often at catastrophic expense, since this has too often entailed neglect of the resources of unity that are inherent in the media themselves. If connotative resources are employed, we must demand that the inner movement and direction of myth (or reality or history, as the case may be) coincide with those inherent in the physical of perceptual medium. The grandest triumphs of Renaissance painting certainly meet this demand.

In this Adoration of Giorgione one will grant the painter immense license to present the story as his imagination desires it. We will not resist his flight into the novelty of landscape painting even though its detail may seem unrelated to the adoration scene itself. Others may have knit the tale together visually in stricter fashion.

In a crucifixion, deposition from the cross, and adoration or annunciation scene, in fact almost any episode drawn from the Gospels, the painter will generally arrange to have all lines, connotative or painterly, culminate in the face, figure, or body of the Savior; and in fact, this area of interest, because of the power that the narrative exerts, will be culminative often in spite of the fact that the work may be formally a botch in which the purely plastic lines, masses, and continuities run in one direction and the connotative in another. That is, the narrative draws us toward the figure of the Savior even when the painter's medium may itself have failed to do so. Twentieth-century painters have resorted to drastic measures of prevent connotation from taking control of the observer's exploration. For, as we have noted, expressive and connotational devices furnish "instant coherence" but at a price that the artist may not wish to pay.

(9) PERUGINO, THE CRUCIFIXION
(WASHINGTON, NATIONAL GALLERY OF ART)

Perugino's Crucifixion illustrates many of the concepts and artistic procedures we have under consideration. In fact it may seem to illustrate them rather too well or in so obvious a fashion that it may soon exhaust our interest. The division as a triptych is manifestly necessary because without it the rigidity of the symmetry would be even more apparent to us. As it is, we can pause for a moment with St. Jerome at the left or the Magdalene at the right before we are drawn both by the lines and by the connotations of the larger elements to the center panel: all eyes, except the Virgin's, are on the Savior and the inclination of his head reciprocates. The emotional tone throughout is, as Berenson says, quiet soothing: "the air is soundless . . . a sight inaudible, a look of yearning, and that is all." Perugino gains his effect principally by means of his space composition. We should take the figures chiefly, he says, "as architectonic member . . . not as if they were persons in a drama, but as so many columns or arches." When we do, we cannot fail to take satisfaction in the power of the adjustment of figures to one another. The exaltation of the central emergent is perfectly (perhaps all too perfectly) supported by its correspondent receding ground in the immediate center area but also in the contributory stances of the side figures. These in turn become secondary emergents with their own recedent regions.

(10) ALBRECHT DÜRER, THE APOSTLES (MUNICH, PINAKOTHEK)

The two panels presenting the Apostles combine both C–C and S–S orders (v. Chapter 3) and are in effect a diptych. Their union derives from the fact that while each picture is by itself in S–S order the dominant figures in them are of almost equal (C–C) power and size. In the left panel the lead figure is that of St. John, the recedent is St. Peter. In the other we see St. Paul with St. Mark in a recedent or dependent position. (St. Mark, of course, is not an Apostle, although he is one of the Evangelists.) The paintings seem to have grown out of the bitter Reformation struggles over heresy. The four biblical authors represent the enunciation of the true faith. They are also thought to present the four humors: sanguine, phlegmatic, choleric, melancholic. These imposing and powerful superdominat figures (cf. Chapter 4) particularly, St. John and St. Paul, which are some six or seven feet high, tax to the limit our powers of comprehening them in one view. The two panels complete one another without either of them being dependent upon the other. Rather, one should say, great as they are by themselves, they are even greater in coordinate relationship and they should show us what ability is requisite to success in an attempt at C–C order.

(11) MARC HAEGER, STILT RACE

The spatial or geometric intervallic phenomenon is an example of the mutual exclusion of figure and ground. Although both of them are, of course, necessary for the figure to appear, the ground cannot appear to us in the same moment as the figure without the roles of the two being reversed. This is seen in this seven year-old child's charming picture of stilt race, especially its lower two-thirds. It is apparent that the figure and ground of stilts and intervening space are not blended but held in suspension with one another like two or more tones. In a blend both elements merge altogether in a third thing. In a musical interval we hear both of the elements by themselves and their sum, or product, as well. Color intervals are visual phenomena that bear resemblance to musical intervals. The principal interest of the picture centers on the stiltwalkers themselves, their apparent height above the spectator or viewer, their sure grip on the stilts and above all the sense of lively competition conveyed. Every line is alive and vital. The unity of the whole is assured through the repetition of the stilts and their human figures. Their plainly varied detail softens the stark C–C phenomenon and makes it almost unnoticeable.

(12) MARCEL DUCHAMP, NUDE DESCENDING A STAIRCASE, NO. 2
(NEW YORK, MUSEUM OF MODERN ART)

Duchamp's Nude has long since acquired the status of an Old Master. It is interesting for us for several reasons. Since it employs the Futurist technique of realizing motion by a quasi-cinematographic rendering of positions of a moving body, it dispenses altogether with the device of closure. The artist invites the eye to help create the artwork. The nude sweeps swiftly before us and we are intrigued to try to make out a single form in several positions, and not only in several, for in fact a limitless number of positions are suggested. For reasons suggested, the motion has direction, from left to right. This reveals also that the device of development is employed in this same process, for the "nude" gains distinctness as proceeding from upper left to lower right. Illumination augments to a maximum in the lowest figure. In the course of the "movement" repetition is also, of course, evident. Finally, the dimension of connotation is integrated with the painting in the attachment of the title, which is as famous as the picture itself. As we have pointed out, the sculptor and painter should always reckon with the possible loss of the title, as in countless instances of relics of the ancient world. One may say that the Nude would be likely to survive even such a loss.

(13) WILLEM DE KOONING, LITHOGRAPH

Almost any scribble will show continuities if there are explicit or implicit lines intersecting or turning upon themselves. But if a scribble in a discommending sense can be at all defined, we must surely say that it seems to present nothing to hold our attention either through closure or through a series of continuities making for some culmination. This is an essential part of the difference between what the unlettered eye sees as the chaos in works of "modern art" and what artists themselves believe they see in them. The artists in effect are saying, a scribble may be identified from the fact that it isn't "going anywhere," but this is emphatically untrue of our work.

The de Kooning lithograph illustrates the foregoing and also goes beyond it in its mingling of chance with design. It is a dramatic result of *action*, deliberately taken — indeed, the strokes seem almost to be enacted before our eyes, the very point of "action painting." What appears to be chance in the result comes forward as spontaneity: nature as well as the artist is allowed to assert itself.

In the end, even when a high degree of vitality, of vital movement and action, is achieved, as in the present work, it still yields only what an object in two dimensions can yield. Like bonds or other securities, it must be judged by what it yields, not by what was invested in it in the way of action, of design or want of design, in its creation.

(14) JACKSON POLLOCK

Among our most prominent examples, we should have at least one which is apparently a complete counter-instance to our generalizations about emergence, recedence, coherence, monotony, and so on.

The works on which Jackson Pollock's fame rests are classical cases of what Sir Herbert Read spoke of as Gestalt-free order. Words of this kind seek to revolutionize our way of looking — literally. As we have seen in our opening account in Chapter 2, and as we shall see further in the application of Gestalt ideas to music in Chapter 14, perceptibility means being able to apprehend emergents synoptically in a relatively undifferentiated field. This assumes, of course, that there is some totality to begin with: a figure, a ground, a surround.

Suppose, however, that we are invited by the artist to "enter into" the picture, to roam at will in it, to turn up what we can. Such an experience is not prestructured, or not apparently so at least. From the standpoint of what normally counts as "percepti-bility" artworks calling for this kind of inspection will seem singularly random if not scrawly. But the experiment has been worth the trial, when we think of Jackson Pollock and others. Such artworks are, and are meant to be, baffling, but they defeat only the demands we have in the past been in the habit of making of perception: they hope to reward a new mode of attention. What one may, as a result, find in them may turn out to be subtly worked out figures, but more commonly, they try to do something very different. Of course, as in any other genre, these works can be rank failures. They are, an are meant to be, sight-bending.

It is apparent that when our customary mode of viewing senses a want of an emergent in this painting of Pollock, and in many others of his, this is owing not so much to a deficiency as an over-supply of emergents. Pollock does not so much defy the traditional caution that limitless multiplication of emergents leads to monotony as propose a new mode of vision. It is something new under the sun, and we are free to judge with what success.

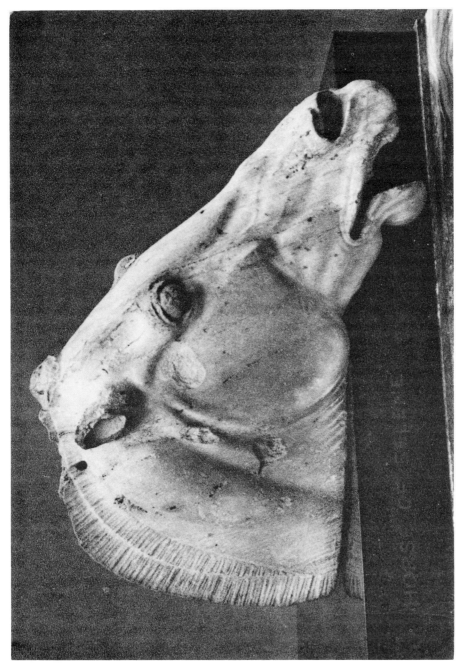

(1) Horse of Selene (Elgin Marbles, British Museum)

Paestum – Tempio a Nettuno

(2) Temple of Neptune (so-called) at Paestum

(3) Donatello, Gattamelata

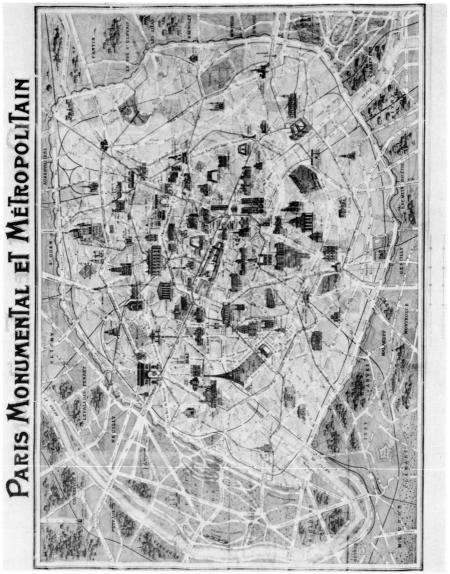

(4) Map of Paris

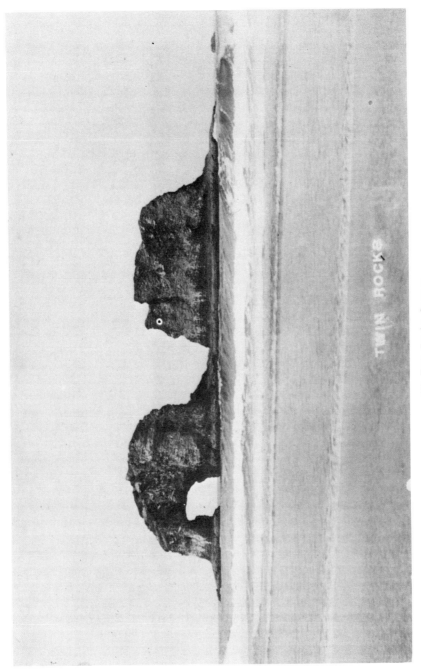

(5) Twin Rocks, Oregon

(6) Raphael, The School of Athens (Rome, Vatican Museum)

(7) Velazquez, Infanta Margareta Theresa (Vienna, Kunsthistorisches Museum)

(8) Giorgione, Adoration of the Shepherds (Washington National Gallery of Art)

(9) Perugino, The Crucifixion (Washington, National Gallery of Art)

(10) Albrecht Dürer, The Apostles (Munich, Pinakothek)

(11) Marc Haeger, Stilt Race

(12) Marcel Duchamp, Nude Descending a Staircase, No. 2 (New York, Museum of Modern Art)

(13) Willem de Kooning, Lithograph

(14) Jackson Pollock

CHAPTER 16

COHERENCE IN MUSIC

At the very outset of our study we expressed the belief that the ultimate satisfaction that is to be gained from art depends upon the perfectibility of our modes of apprehension, and that the artist's use of the compositional order is for the attainment of this end. Our exposition has now perhaps made sufficiently clear how vision is served by the artist's use of methods of unification such as closure, recurrence, and development. Our brief examples of narrative art hope to illustrate how analogous purposes are realized in literature. The ground here has, of course, been thoroughly traversed by critics and literary theorists. Music, on the other hand, presents certain special problems and demands an approach that is unfamiliar. Although musical form has long been the subject of intensive study, what has been wanting is a comprehension of the way in which the compositional order is employed in this art of tone and time and of its parallelism with the other arts. This necessitates first a study of coherence in music and then a sampling from the musical literature that will be more extensive than our references to the other arts. The emphasis in that direction is only for the purpose of redressing a balance.

Returning now to the very beginning of our exposition in which we introduced the notion of emergence and recedence generally for all the arts, we shall first show how an application of this may be made to music. This may be shown by studying certain important pieces of research in the earlier twentieth century in which the Gestaltist conception of figure and ground first received an interpretation in musical terms. We can then see how in general the musical composer employs the three compositional orders. With this we shall be in a position to proceed to the actual analysis and interpretation of musical compositions.

Sceptics often scoff at the idea that there is any common order that underlies musical composition, pictorial and sculptural design, dramatic and narrative form, the several arts, in short. Clearly, they have not looked very hard, or hard enough. The application of the figure-ground principle, not only to music but to other arts as well, is so completely fitting and natural that what is surprising is only that so little appeal to it has been made.

When we speak of a figure-ground principle we mean, in the words of a psychologist, that "one of the chief psychological characteristics of visual perception . . . is that a figure or some striking feature in the total field, tends to stand out from a more indefinite background." "These characteristics," he goes on to say, "may be duplicated in auditory perception." These observations are taken from P. E. Vernon, 'Auditory Perception,' which appeared in 1934–35.[1] He distinguishes what he calls *definite* and *indefinite listening*, which are, of course, akin to modes of the psychological notion of attention. He then extends the application of figure and ground respectively to definite listening and indefinite listening (explained below).

Although the connection of perception with figure-ground may be even older, the first important psychological investigation of this sort seems to have been that of the Danish psychologist, Edgar Rubin, who published *Synsoplevede Figurer* in 1913. (There is a German translation: *Visuelle Wahrgenommene Figuren*, 1921.)

Not only does Rubin explore the connection between figure-ground and perception, but he also makes several interesting applications of it to aesthetics. He is perhaps less emphatic than is Vernon about the degree to which the power of aesthetic works is determined by their seeability and hearability as defined by figure and ground. (In supporting this idea it may again be said that we do not formulate it as an "aesthetic principle," but rather that the observance of it yields a possible reward and its defiance a penalty.) Rubin does, however, point out, as we have done in effect, that content (expression, connotation) may stand in inverse relation to the painterly (*malerisch*) virtues of a work; he quotes William James' remark that one may only be able to appreciate such values if we turn a picture upside down and temporarily destroy or nullify its connotation. Surprisingly, Kandinsky's abstract paintings are cited in this early work to reinforce the same point. Rubin also cites the danger a painter incurs if he neglects to make his grounds recede, or perhaps better said, if he permits them to become emergent. The pale grounds that surround the heads of St. Barbara and St. Sixtus on either side of the Virgin in Raphaels' Sistine Madonna resembles crab claws if the eye permits them to become emergent, or may seem to do so if one turns the picture upside down.

It is, however, Vernon's work rather than Rubin's that I wish to cite in the present chapter, since he is apparently the first to make an explicit and fruitful application of the figure-ground principle to auditory perception, particularly to music. He devoted two articles to the subject. (They were a revelation to me when I first read them about ten years after they appeared.) The reader interested in aesthetic questions should read particularly the first article of the two; Vernon is also interested, as the title indicates, in a more extended field than musical aesthetics.

Psychologists have concentrated, Vernon says, on responses to single tones instead of what is actually heard in music by anyone with even the minimum skill to carry a tune or a melody. This is as if we were to restrict what we hear in language to single noises or words and to neglect whole meaningful sentences. Here as in the subject of vision, the work of Gestalt psychologists marked a turning point. Vernon rejects the conclusions of both Helmholtz and Seashore; neither the older elementaristic psychology nor purely physical research in sound succeeded in explaining what it is we hear in music.

Music, Vernon finds, affords opportunity for many levels of listening from mere "reflex, physical, soothing or stimulating effects on muscular activities and metabolism of the organism . . . general euphoria," and the like, on the level of indefinite listening, to "visualization of notes on the pianoforte keyboard, and . . . intellectual processes such as technical analysis of formal and theoretical aspects of the music," on the level of definite listening. Finally, in the highly trained musician, definite listening approximates to our ordinary perception of languages; owing to his familiarity with the "grammar" and "syntax" of music, "he can follow or anticipate the structural relations of the interwoven themes and harmonic progressions much as we follow verbal arguments."

We may now look at Vernon's very instructive example of musical analysis that illustrates the application of Gestalt principles to music and enables a musically prepared listener to proceed to further interpretations of his own. A certain extension of Vernon's analysis compatible with his intentions is necessary and suits the facts.

The musical example he uses is the Allegretto Scherzando from Beethoven's Eighth Symphony. A mere glance at the score (even a piano score) of the symphony is sufficient to confirm the points Vernon is drawing attention to. To be brief, I will cite only

Ludwig van Beethoven, Symphony No. VIII, Opus 93

the nine points he makes about the music and then expand them with some further discussion:

(1) The figure is higher in pitch than the ground.

(2) The figure has greater intensity than the ground.

(3) The figure possesses a different timbre from the ground.

(4) The figure moves relatively to the ground.

(5) The figure begins before, or after, the ground.

(6) The figure has different dynamics from the ground.

(7) The figure contains many notes which are dissonant with ground.

(8) The previous occurrence of the figure as a "good Gestalt" helps to emphasize it when it recurs later with a more prominent ground.

(9) The figure possesses an unanalysable unity in its 'melodic line' which differentiates it from the relatively structureless ground.

I shall comment mainly on the general purport of these generalizations and then move toward a more general account which I think will make Vernon's account more serviceable and also reinforce and confirm our own discussion of just these matters earlier in this study.

All of Vernon's "principles" particularly the first four and the sixth point out that music *such as this* has a prime emergent. A number of devices of both the intrinsic and the compositional order are involved in making this emergent emerge. The structure is homophonic, and what is said would, in general, be true of virtually all homophonic music.

We must immediately ask whether one can also extend them to other compositions besides this one and to other types of music such as polyphonic. In fact, they would have to be revised before such extension were made. For example, the third principle is formulated only for ensembles of instruments and would not apply to an instrument such as the piano.

Yet revisions could easily be made. For example, the first six might be combined and rephrased somewhat as follows: what counts as figure must emerge over its ground by virtue of a certain distinctiveness which it may gain through its pitch, intensity, or timbre, and through motion independent of the ground.

Application to polyphonic music can readily be made. A motif in a fugue is generally permitted to speak out with some emphasis: it begins by itself alone, and then the voice in which it appears falls into a weaker, more groundal stance as another voice sounds the motif, and so on until all the three, four, or more voices have in turn spoken. This we can see in the simple fugue quoted on page 28. This does not preclude the occasional competing or even conflicting appearances of the same motif in two voices at once. The figural power of the contrapuntal motive is generally affirmed by its independent appearance in a given voice which at least for the time becomes emergent. Frequently, of course, even in homophonic music voices other than the highest are made emergent, generally with the application of (2), or in ensemble music with (3), or both.

The fifth principle obviously needs qualification in order to be made more general. An accompanimental device such as is used by Beethoven in the first bar has been remarked on earlier as an example of a *tolerable monotony* that is allowed for a few moments to be emergent and figural, perhaps in order that we shall hear it in just its proper subliminal place when the main thematic figure supplants it in the second bar and becomes emergent. The same device serves as a characteristic four bar prologue to many a Strauss waltz. The point of it is to display the monotony of the ground prominently for a few moments in order to enhance the figure and make it by comparison or contrast even more emergent when it enters. Hence we should regard (5) not as an invariable but rather a useful device that may on occasion be employed to make the figure more emergent — which is the desideratum. In fact, the very opposite device may also serve to gain the same end. Thus, in Chopin's Étude in A minor, op. 25, no. 11, a solo voice is heard before every thing else with a kind of insistent "message." Many other examples could be cited. Neither of these, however, is as common as the simultaneous entry of ground and figure where the soprano has its customary prominence. The point is that the figure must emerge either through the intrinsic order such as pitch, intensity, timbre, or duration, that is, (1), (2), (3), or (6), or through some use of compositional order, such as (8) or (9).

Principles (4), (5), (7) and perhaps others are general observations on structural features which may enable the emergent to gain prominence. Number (8) is perhaps more important since it introduces the notion of repetition from the compositional order. But a fundamental extension of (8) in Vernon's analysis must be made to provide for the emergence of the figure in relation not only to its substructure as in the homophonic and harmonic order generally but also as a theme, melody or motif of a finite length (which Vernon recognizes to some extent in the ninth principle) in relation to preceding and following material (e.g., bridge passages). This produces an emergence of the figure in the horizontal dimension; that is, emergence in relation to earlier and later material, as against emergence in the vertical dimension. In Gregorian chant, being single-voiced, if a figure emerges at all, it must do so in the horizontal dimension. That is, it must either be figural throughout its length or somewhat more emergently figural in one place than another, since the single voice precludes a ground in a vertical relation. We also have an opportunity to see how this can be dealt with in the example of the Bach Courante for Solo Cello in 16.2 (1). The figure being ceaselessly audible, there is scarcely a ground even in the horizontal sense, except for a few moments that are slightly more monotonous than the rest, such a, possibly, bars 31 and 32. We should also notice that virtually ceaseless prominence of the figure can be a strong instance of unity by means of *closure*, if the composition is comparatively brief.

Principle (7) also deserves further mention. The device of dissonance to set off the figure is present in many kinds of ornamentation, for example in the mordent:

Here the shake that sounds Db momentarily with C, a dissonant minor second, only serves to set off C as the intended (figural) tone. Professor Vernon mentions an interesting example in a footnote, the so-called 'false horn entry' in Beethoven's Eroica Symphony. "The first horn plays the main theme of the movement against a completely dissonant chord played by all the violins. The result is not an ugly dissonance, but an electrifying figure-ground musical experience." That virtually any thematic material will form dissonances with some part of the accompanying material can easily be shown. Unless harmony changes with every note, even so innocuous a figure as this

will show dissonance on the second, fifth, and seventh soprano notes. Of course, as explained elsewhere, dissonant intervals are tension-producing and thus absolutely necessary to the vitality and continuity of music. Composers are, of course, not indifferent to what will appear as dissonant with their melodic lines. Although to the average ear Schoenberg will appear to have offended in this respect, in reality the atonalists or serialists by no means abandoned the concept of dissonance *or consonance.*

We thus have a key to the application of the figure-ground idea to music. Since music of most sorts is complex and stratified it is readily seen that some such principle must be followed to enable the listener, not to "understand" the music, but to gain a clear perception of what he is listening to. Emergence and recedence as a governing idea is almost certain to continue making itself felt in any foreseeable music. We may expect the ear to accustom itself to many new things, but these will progress rather by assimilation to and progressive departure from the kinds of aesthetic tonal masses we already know how to listen to.

The value of Professor Vernon's discussion of music, as already said, lies in the possible extension of the figure-ground idea to more and more parts of music and to arts other than the visual. We have already gone beyond him in extending the idea of the emergent to thematic display in the horizontal structure of tonal masses, and other extensions are also necessary. It could be shown that the more orchestral complexity there is, the more composers are generally at pains to come to terms with the idea of a hierarchy of emergents, although, of course, there are pages of the later Romantic repertoire that are relatively opaque from overstructuring and that harbor what may be gems of purest ray serene lost in an orchestral thicket. In general, however, no tone is ever really lost: if it can sound alone it makes a difference that is at least electronically detectable and may be effective in some measure on the listener. The more attention the artist pays to questions of emergence and recedence the more effective he will be. Making certain that the observer or participant of the arts *perceives* something is infinitely more important than all the words the artist can declaim or murmur to explain it.

Our discussion of figure and ground at the very beginning was undertaken mainly to introduce a useful vocabulary in which we could eventually make our notion of coherence precise. This we sought to do with the several devices of *compositional order.* The significance for music of the three procedures of isolation (or closure), repetition, and development should now be apparent.

(1) *Closure.* Every musical composition in some degree relies upon closure to try to convince the ear that every part of what it hears *belongs* where it is, and in some manner coheres with every other part. One finds good examples of this in the fact that every composer can, in some fairly high degree, count on most listeners trying to hear a connection or coherence in whatever is assertedly one composition. Closure is a presumption

of unity, though nowhere as strong or as convincing as the comparable phenomenon in painting or sculpture.

The most potent aid to closure, that is, synoptic apprehension, is brevity. Further, habituation almost invariably comes to the aid of closure even if nothing else does. One can in some manner "hold together" almost any string of nonsense words or random tones if they are heard in the same order often enough. This principle will appear to have less significance for music in the received sense, ancient or modern. Yet it is never ineffective. It is just that other devices (tonality, rhythm, recurrent figures) will be more potent agents of unification and the power of closure may not be very explicitly felt. If one is unaccustomed to the dodecaphonic system he may make trial of something like the Schoenberg Klavierstück, op. 33a, quoted in 16.2 (4), to see if it becomes somehow more "convincing" after repeated hearings. Even here, I believe the recurrence of the six basic chords through large parts of the composition takes precedence over mere memorization. Any string of elements can be memorized, but grasping identities and relations is something else. In general, the serialists are much too keen on structural unity and coherence to offer many examples, except to the altogether untrained ear, of coherence by mere isolation or closure, the mere togetherness of tones, or by mere unicity of figure.

Closure is inherently a more convincing device in spatial than in temporal arts since space is inherently the order of coexistence. Anything which is fully in the presence of something else spatially either forms a figure *with* it or *against* it so to speak, that is, it is either in some manner absorbed by it or absorbs it; in rare cases it stands in full competitive equipollence towards it. Nothing altogether like this occurs in temporal arts, although this may depend on the range or reach of one's musical intelligence.

(2) *Repetition.* The power of repetition in temporal or musical art can be interestingly discussed only with actual examples. We may point out once more that the effect of repetition is basically different in space and in time. Thus, if one relies too closely on a spatial model one may interpret the familiar ABA form of composition as being like bilateral symmetry. Usually in spatial complexes the middle member of what we may again call ABA form is the most emphatic: the dome of the Capitol as against the wings, the peak of the steeple, a classical pediment, the central member of a palatial building like Versailles, and so on. But although the central figure is important in music, certainly in the sonata form, in general that which is most significant is oftenest repeated. The B figure in song form or the B or C members of a rondo form that runs, let us say, ABACABA do not appear as often as the A figure, because in some sense they will bear repetition less often than the A *in such a context*, or perhaps the composer has himself committed himself to A somewhat more sympathetically or enthusiastically. A is unquestionably the "central" figure.

It is for this reason that we have throughout emphasized that repetition of prime figures in music is not like the ranging of a series of figures in space. A colonnade is a tolerable figural monotony because the columns together form a supporting facade proportioned in a certain way. But five identical and massive obelisks, pyramids, domes, and so on, all identical in size and shape and near one another would be intolerable. The reason that repetition on this scale is tolerable in music is that each recurrence is a recurrence only in the sense of a more or less identical "auditory glimpse" of the "same thing." We do not see the figures as a series or multiplicity of identicals, for there is *only one* such figure. But a repeated spatial figure is literally two or more figures.

The theme and variations device, so often used in music, affords a good example of this, particularly the older and simpler sort, but not excluding, let us say, the fourth movement of the Brahms' Fourth Symphony, which is an overwhelming passacaglia, thirty variations on a ground bass. In the older sets of variations, the theme is revealed in ever new garments. The harmonic frame is ever the same. At its most superficial we see the same person but only clothed differently. Eventually, a profounder kind of variation writing appears with Beethoven. Rather than more and more glimpses of one person the composer proceeds to a real development or even a kind of complex "deduction" from the original premises, the theme, to show what its possibilities are, what "truths" are contained in it awaiting only a great "logician" to infer them.

The most astonishing feat of this sort is the Beethoven Diabelli Variations. Here we go beyond our second device of unification, and we are already in the midst of the third, development. They compel us to ask whether the variations added to the theme are evolvements from the potential latent in a humble original or new additions to an old frame. This is admittedly not a clear alternative but perhaps worth reflecting on. Either method of answer is difficult. Diabelli was a popular composer of Beethoven's day, and his sonatinas are still played. The music is well constructed though in itself utterly unlikely to produce revolution. Yet this music afforded Beethoven what turned out to be a matchless opportunity not only to dazzle his contemporaries but succeeding generations as well.

What may be learned here is that a borderland between repetition and development has been reached. Even the device of Schoenberg in the Klavierstück is only in a certain structural sense repetitious: after the six chords are announced on the first two pages they reappear only in the sense that successively a figure of a bar or two is created from the chord components of each of the six types. This, too, is already a kind of development. It is perhaps characteristic of the newer music to avoid verbatim repetition: there is a horror of appearing to be unoriginal.

(3) *Development*. With the foregoing, we have already introduced our third type of unification. I shall not attempt to trace the evolution or devolution of the devices of development through several hundred years of European music. Here again the *variation form* might provide an interesting nucleus to expound such an evolution. Professor Nelson, in his *Technique of Variation*,[2] distinguishes a number of types of which the more prominent are these:

The baroque basso ostinato variation. It is characterized thus: variations continuous without cadential breaks into isolated units; the theme is a short melodic phrase of four or eight bars; the melodic phrase is utilized as a bass. A prominent example is Bach's Passacaglia in C minor.

The ornamental variation of the 18th and 19th centuries. There is figural decoration of the theme, the distinctions are mainly stylistic, and there is greater simplicity than in the previous period. An example is the variation movement in Schubert's Death and the Maiden Quartet.

The nineteenth century character variations. Profound alteration of the theme is common. There is development of motives from the theme. It is more dramatic than the predecessors. Examples, Beethoven, Diabelli Variations for Piano and even the earlier Goldberg Variations by Bach.

Free variation of the late 19th and early 20th centuries. The bond between variations and theme is more frequently a theme motive than a whole theme; the theme is altered materially. Examples: Franck, Variations Symphonique for Piano and Orchestra; Strauss, Don Quixote.

Professor Nelson's study should be consulted in detail for the general exposition of the variation form and for specific analyses the results of which are far too varied to be summarized or reproduced here. It is evident that one of the greatly expanded powers of the last type of variation is its challenge to its audience. It intrigues its audience, and enlists their interest in the complex fortunes, transformations, and transfigurations of the theme. The composer has long since abandoned the mere ornamentation of a theme. However, the tone-row technique revives older devices (as in general it, somewhat para-doxically, represents a sort of Neo-Classicism) by the fragmentation, inversion, reversion, retrograde inversion, and all kinds of canonic transformation of themes, for a manner as complex as, and in fact learned from Bach's magnificent Kunst der Fuge.

In all of these evolvements it is difficult either to distinguish perfectly between our three types of unification and equally difficult to abandon them. It seems intuitively evident that one must draw a line between mere continuity in our third type and true development. A dynasty or in fact any family tree may be used to illustrate both this movement and also the previous two. A dynasty shows an exemplary form of *closure*, since it is by definition closed and clannish; maintains *continuity* through blood relation-ship of the members; exhibits *repetition* through the physical similarity of individuals and may retain its *identity* through its possession of goods or lands; frequently *develops*, for good or ill, certain traits from one generation to another or expands in definite stages its power or influence through time or space, and so on. At the same time, the question is whether we can either *use* or *afford to dispense with* such an analogy in speaking of what we mean by continuity and development and the rest in music or the other arts. The fact is, I think, that we can neither take nor leave the analogy: in other words the analogy of life and growth is the richest and best that we have ever devised for the art work, yet it must always be treated with caution. Every artwork is a challenge to us to unlock its secrets which it will really never give up but our very concourse with it is nevertheless a ceaseless probing after them.

16.1. SONG

Our musical examples fall into two familiar classes, song and instrumental music. The division being made depends upon whether the voice is employed not only as a musical instrument but as a vehicle for thought and feeling.

The acutest questions about expression probably arise in the intermedial relations between music on one side and thought, image, fact, myth, or whatever may be conveyed by words on the other — we must be extremely careful as to what we take "convey" to mean here. Kinaesthetic clues alone may help the painter to arrive at a reliable visual interpretation in a narrowly formal sense of a myth or fact he chooses to portray, and there are numerous other ways in which visual "form" and "content" in the pedestrian sense can be accurately adjusted to one another. In music, however, explanation of how the music can express thought or feeling is more difficult. We cannot attribute this either to resemblance, except in comparatively crude cases (the drum roll and thunder), or to mere association or convention. The one explanation is too strong, the other too weak to account for the power and success of even comparatively simple musical examples.

Song may perhaps lend itself somewhat more reality than instrumental music to a solution of this problem, since it can plausibly be traced ultimately to aboriginal and even animal, yet human, vocal response — the cry, shriek, murmur, moan, coo, and so on. The expressiveness of instrumental music, in my opinion, can be explained ultimately only via the expressiveness of song. But I must emphasize "ultimately", since explanation even in the case of song involves great difficulties if not only feeling (which may be traced to animal response) but thoughts, facts, events, and situations, real or fictional, are to be expressed. We have of course addressed ourselves to expression questions only where these bear upon the form and coherence problem. This applies also to these final sections on music.

The examples of song are drawn from two extremes, devotional or liturgical song of the middle ages and the "art song" of the nineteenth century. The differences between such musics will not be fully set forth until our concluding chapter [17] summarizes the subject. The extraordinary formalism of the first type will be set forth in detail, with numerous references to questions of expression and expressiveness as they arise.

(1) *The Ordinary of the Mass*

Kyrie II

Kyrie III

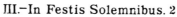

Gloria VIII

pax homí-ni-bus bónae vo-luntá-tis. Laudá- mus

te. Be-ne-dí-cimus te. Ado-rá- mus te.

Glo-ri- fi-cámus te. Grá-ti- as á-gimus ti-bi propter

mágnam gló-ri- am tú- am. Dómi-ne Dé- us, Rex cae-

lé-stis, Dé- us Pá-ter omní- po- tens. Dómi-ne Fí-

li u-ni-gé-ni-te Jé- su Chrí-ste. Dómi-ne Dé- us,

Agnus Dó- i, Fí-li-us Pá- tris. Qui tól-lis pec-

cá-ta mún- di, mi-se-ré- re nó-bis. Qui tól-

lis peccá-ta múndi, súsci-pe depre-ca-ti- ó- nem nó-

stram. Qui só-des ad déxte-ram Pátris, mi- se-ré-re

nó- bis. Quó-ni- am tu só-lus sánctus. Tu só-lus

Dó-mi- nus. Tu só-lus Al-tís-simus, Jé- su

Chrí- ste. Cum Sáncto Spi- ri- tu, in gló-ri- a

Dé- i Pá- tris. A- men.

GLORIA VIII. Musical phrase pattern

a	b	c	d	
a_1				Gloria in excelsis Deo.
a_2	b_1	c_1		Et in terra pax hominibus bonae voluntatis. Laudamus te.
		c_2		Benedicimus te.
a_3	b_2		d_1	Adoramus te. Glorificamus te. Gratias agimus tibi
a_1				propter magnam gloriam tuam.
a_1	b_3		d_2	Domine Deus, Rex caelestis, Deus Pater omnipotens.
a_4	b_2		d_3	Domine Fili unigenite Jesu Christe.
		c_3	d_4	Domine Deus, Agnus Dei,
a_2	b_2		d_3	Filius Patris. Qui tollis peccata mundi,
a_1		c_2		miserere nobis. Qui tollis peccata mundi,
a_4	b_2		d_3	suscipe deprecationem nostram.
a_1	b_1	c_2		Qui sedes ad dexteram Patris, miserere nobis. Quoniam tu solus sanctus.
		c_4		Tu solus Dominus.
a_4	b_1		d_3	Tu solus Altissimus, Jesu Christe.
a_2	b_2		d_3	Cum Sancto Spiritu, in gloria Dei Patris.
a_5				Amen.

(Subscripts indicate slight variants.)

Sanctus XII

(M. M. ♩ = 126)   XIII. s.

2.

Sán- ctus, * Sán- ctus, Sán- ctus
Dómi-nus Dó- us Sá-ba- oth. Plé-ni sunt caé-li et
tér- ra gló-ri- a tú- a. Ho-sán-na in ex-cél-
sis. Be-ne-díctus qui vé- nit in nó-mi-
ne Dó-mi- ni. Ho-sán-na in ex-cél- sis.

Sanctus XIV

Agnus Dei XVII

Agnus Dei XVIII

mi- se-ré-re nó- bis.   Agnus Dé-   i, *qui tól-lis peccá-

ta múndi: mi- se-ré-re nó- bis.   Agnus De-   i,*

qui   tól- lis peccá-ta múndi: dó- na nó-bis pá-   cem.

The origins of plainsong or Gregorian chant go far back into the middle and dark ages. They may even in part derive from the chant of the ancient Hebrew synagogue liturgy, although this traditional view has been challenged.[3] Knowledge of these masses and of the manner in which they were rendered vocally in the middle ages has been greatly extended by such commanding plainchant scholars as Dom Joseph Pothier, Peter Wagner, Dom Gregorio Sũnol, Dom René J. Hesbert, the Monks of Solesmes, and Bruno Stäblein. Our purpose in considering these traditional melodies is simply to see what devices are resorted to in them to gain unity and coherence. Much that it would be necessary to say about the masses in a full account will be left to others to say.

The Ordinary of the Mass consists of five movements, each distinct in its thought and emotional content: *Kyrie, Gloria, Credo, Sanctus*, and *Agnus Dei*. Hereafter, I use such terms as "*Kyrie VIII*" and "*Agnus Dei IV*." In modern plainchant research terms they refer to chants of the Ordinary of the Mass which appear in the *Kyriale* portion of the Gradual (Lat: Graduale), the book of chants of the Mass used by the celebrant and the choir. This anthology is a set of Ordinary chants approved by the Vatican's Congregation of Sacred Rites designed to meet the specific pastoral liturgy of the twentieth century. The *Kyriale* now in use reflects the liturgical and musical reforms approved by Pope Pius X in his famous decree of November 22, 1903, the Moto Proprio "Tra le sollecitudini." This *Kyriale* was first published as a separate liturgical book in 1905, then incorporated into the *Graduale Romanum* of 1908. This first edition of the *Graduale Romanum* is commonly referred to as the Editio Vaticana, or the GR.[4]

The GR *Kyriale* is an anthology of *Kyrie, Gloria, Credo, Sanctus, Agnus Dei*, and *Ite missa est* melodies. These melodies were composed over many centuries, from the earliest MSS with neumes (musical notation) of the early 10th century down to the 16th century.

Originally, the oldest Ordinary chants often had various poetic or prose texts added to the ancient texts. These are called tropes. By the end of the 11th century these accretions were beginning to fall into disuse. By the late 16th century, the Council of Trent (1542– 63) banned them from the Roman liturgy altogether, with a few notable exceptions.

The first movement of the Mass is a nine-fold acclamation consisting of two phrases. The words are the only ones in Greek in the Mass: *Kyrie Eleison, Christe Eleison, Kyrie Eleison*, (Lord have mercy, Christ have mercy, Lord have mercy). The brevity of the phrases readily contributes to coherence as does the repetition of the *Kyrie*; however, this is an altogether abbreviated form of the words which were in use in the early Middle Ages.

Musically, the structure may not be like this at all. *Kyrie III*, for example, using the numbering of the GR and the modern *Kyriale* published by Fischer, 1927 (this melody is numbered 142 in Landwehr-Melnicki) is approximately of the form aba/cdc/efeg. There are also interior unifying connections and slight variants of phrasing that are not shown by this analysis. *Kyrie XIII* is musically of the form aaa/bbb/bbc (number 194, ibid.). *Kyrie XIV* has the unusual order ababab/cbcbcb/dededf (number 68, ibid.). In *Kyrie XVIII* the first motif recurs as something of a reprise, aaa/bbb/aad (number 151, ibid.). *Kyrie II* (number 48, ibid.) is varied in the structure, relying not only on inner repetition but also like *Kyrie III* upon a strophic end-phrase. The form is approximately abc/dd'bc/ ebc/e'ebc. The recurrent phrase, which always comes on the word *eleison*, lends insistence and pathos to the plea to the Intercessor. The unity of the *Kyries* derives in part from sheer unicity, since they are brief, easily encompassable thoughts, party from repetition. (This is still more evident in the *Agnus* movements.) There may also be a slight development of intensity as the pitch rises to a slight peak, which is scarcely a climax, however.

The last movement (*Agnus Dei*) may likewise be short. The verbal structure is simple:

> Agnus Dei, qui tollis peccata mundi:
> Miserere nobis. (Repeated)
> Agnus Dei, qui tollis peccata mundi:
> Dona nobis pacem.

The verbal form is thus abc/abc/abd. The musical form differs. *Agnus Dei XVIII* consists of a single phrase sung three times (GR, *XVIII*). The whole movement has a range of but four tones. *Agnus XVII* again repeats in the same way except that the notes for the word *agnus* are altered in the middle line. But for this, it would read abc/abc/abc and thus AAA. This kind of repetition is virtually the same as the resort to unicity, especially in short compositions, since as we said, repetition in time arts results not in *laying one thing alongside another*, as we find in visual art in the architectural colonnade, or accommodation, but rather *overlaying one and the same thing* several times.

Leaving aside the *Credo*, which does not appear in this series of masses, we have two rather more elaborate movements, the *Gloria* and the *Sanctus*. The words of the *Sanctus* are as follows:

> Sanctus, Sanctus, Sanctus
> Dominus Deus Sabaoth.
> Pleni sunt caeli et terra, gloria tua,
> Hosanna in excelsis.
> Benedicuts qui venit in nomine Domini.
> Hosanna in excelsis

Musically, *Sanctus* II runs aba c/def/def (number 203, Thannabaum). Combining the last groupings of lines, the general form in ABB. The three opening words are frequently set in the form aba, and the remainder of the line is given a musical thought of its own. (The opening lines of the *Sanctus* of *IV, V, XIV, XVII*, numbering them according to the GR and the Fischer edition, also illustrate this characteristic order for the solemn opening phrase. Often, the occurrence of the same words, *Hosanna in excelsis*, in the last line and two lines earlier leads to an identical setting for them. Besides *II*, one may observe such a form also in *Sanctus XII*; for example, abc d/efg/efg. One should not overlook climax in pitch as it appears, for example, in *Sanctus II* on the word *in* (*in nomine domini*)).

The *Gloria* has some of the most joyful words of the mass, and except for the *Creed* it is the longest movement. The composition dates from the sixteenth century, that is to say, very late; it sounds "modern" to our ears. The penitent gains a sense of exaltation from the words, which themselves exalt all three members of the Trinity. The words are as follows. I shall break them into phrases, which are distinctly ordered in the musical setting.

> Gloria in excelsis Deo.
> Et in terra pax hominibus bonae voluntatis.
> Laudamus te.
> Benedicimus te.
> Adoramus te.
> Glorificamus te.
> Gratias agimus tibi propter magnam gloriam tuam.
> Domine Deus, Rex coelestis, Deus Pater omnipotens.
> Dominie Fili unigenite Jesu Christe.
> Domine Deus, Agnus Dei Filius Patris.
> Qui tollis peccata mundi, miserere nobis.
> Qui tollis peccata mundi, suscipe deprecationem nostram.
> Qui sedes ad dexteram Patris, miserere nobis.
> Quoniam tu solus sanctus. Tu solus Dominus,
> Tu solus Altissimus, Jesu Christe.
> Cum Sancto Spiritu, in gloria Dei Patris.
> Amen.

Perhaps none of the *Glorias* exceeds *VIII* in a certain sense of exaltation, and we may profitably concentrate our analysis upon it (number III, ed. Vat., and in Schalz, p. 526). Following the line divisions just given, *Gloria VIII* is spaced out to show and compare the basic components in notation and then in a more schematic musical phrase pattern.

The *Gloria* no doubt lends itself to further analysis by the musicologist, but this diagram will show such details as are important for our purposes.[5]

We notice the basically simple order. There are just four phrases, but each one appears with greater or lesser modifications in several forms. The opening phrase, a, appears twelve times, with the Amen thirteen, and establishes itself as the focal figure. By its firm contour and its affirmation of the tonic at the end (which is reached by the tonic trend of the falling fifth, from the first note, C, to the last, F), it serves as the principal point of departure and return. The modifications of all four phrases are subtle and apparently determined by their changing contexts. The range tones is an octave. The higher F is reached only in phrases c and d and always with an uplift of feeling. The organization, once it is grasped, is found to be both controlled and free: a limited range of materials is employed but then deployed *as if* without constraint.

The thought of the poem breathes a deep inner joy and, to return to the term still another time, exaltation. This is not without foundation in the music for several reason. Phrase b is always rising and expectant; c and d circulate on or over the upper dominant C, as if hovering in the air, occasionally reaching the upper tonic F but never remaining there. Phrase a gives stability to the whole: there is a lift to the heavens, but from an earthly condition.

One may pursue further comparisons of the sort we have undertaken. Most persons with a nodding acquaintance with music will have heard of this sort of "alphabetic" analysis. It is meant to be addressed to the ear, not, as it would appear, to the eye or to reason. A keen understanding of the form cannot but increase satisfaction in the work itself.

What we learn from the masses is that unity is rarely left to be attained by simple closure, by simple unicity and brevity. One would expect that the simpler the aesthetic complex the less structure in the form of repetition, development, or theme and variations would be resorted to. Yet we find that even in very short complexes, such as the movements of the mass, there is evidence of *Gestaltung*. This is confirmed thousands of times over both in folk and more formal music for singing. Even in very archaic music the musical lines are organized in ternary form, ABA, whence it is only one step to accommodating the quatrain of European poetry by means of a repetition of the first A, yielding AABA. The grace of plainsong is its more freely flowing line, inventing forms as it goes, adapting itself to the words and yet also transforming the words and thought by means of the music.

We have remarked earlier that one may readily gain unification by making the expressive or connotative thought pre-eminent, in painting for example: if such thought is sufficiently emphasized, little or no attention will be paid to the perceptual medium. Here we can speak of "art" only with apologies, because the perceptual medium has been put wholly at the service of connotation: it contributes nothing of its own, it "makes no difference." But when the purely musical or painterly medium is vital it asserts itself. If the artist resorts to an accompanying medium, there should be a good reason for doing so; and also a good reason in other cases for not doing so.

In no single instances we have examined has the music been somehow allowed to run alongside as a mere "accompaniment" where it might merely heighten a thought or decorate a feeling. It has not abandoned the task of unification to the expressed thought or connotation but has contributed its share, or even more, to this end. This order is therefore both hidden and not so hidden, and it makes its power felt even to the most unlettered ear. In contrast to the Mass, we have in the *Dies Irae* a strict rhyme scheme. Yet the composer has not allowed this to dominate the sequence. The *Durchkomponierung* for which Schubert is so justly praised is already a reality in this finished sequence. In the Mass, both verse and music enjoy a freedom that is the more remarkable in that the two are fully compatible with one another.

(2) *Dies Irae*

(M.M. ♪ = 160)
Seq. 1.

Dí- es í-rae, dí- es íl- la, Sólvet saé-clum in

fa-víl-la: Téste Dá-vid cum Si-býlla.   Quántus tré-

mor est fu-tú-rus, Quando jú-dex est ventú-rus, Cún-

cta stricte dis-cussú-rus! Tú-ba mí-rum spár-gens só-

num Per se-púlcra re-gi-ónum, Có-get ó-mnes an-

te thró-num. Mors stupé-bit et na-tú-ra, Cum re-súr-

get cre-a-tú-ra, Ju-di-cán-ti responsú-ra. Lí-

108 Missa pro Defunctis

ber scríptus pro-fe-ré-tur, In quo tó-tum continé-tur,

Unde múndus ju-di-cé-tur. Jú-dex ergo cum se-

dé-bit, Quídquid lá-tet apparé-bit: Nil in-últum re-

mané-bit. Quid sum mí-ser tunc di-ctú-rus? Quem

pa-tró-num ro-ga-tú-rus? Cum vix jústus sit se-cú-rus.

Rex treméndae ma-jestá-tis, Qui sal-ván-dos sálvas gra-

tis, Sál-va me, fons pi-e-tá-tis. Re-cordá-re Jé-

su pí-e, Quod sum cáusa tú-ae ví-ae: Ne me pér-

das íl-la dí-e. Quaérens me, se-dí-sti las-sus:

Missa pro Defunctis

Red-emísti crú-cem pássus: Tántus lá- bor non sit cás-

sus. Júste júdex ul- ti- ó- nis, Dó- num fac remis-

si- ó- nis, Ante dí- em ra-ti- ó- nis. Inge- mí-

sco, tamquam ré- us: Cúl-pa rú-bet vúltus mé- us:

Suppli-cánti párce Dé- us. Qui Ma-rí- am absolví-

sti, Et la- tró- nem exaudí-sti, Mí- hi quoque spem

de-dí-sti. Pré-ces mé-ae non sunt dígnae: Sed tu bó-

nus fac be-nígne, Ne per- énni crémer ígne. In-

ter ó- ves ló- cum praésta, Et ab haédis me sequé-

Missa pro Defunctis

stra, Stá-tu- ens in párte déxtra. Confu-tá-tis

ma- le-díctis, Flámmis ácri- bus addíctis: Vó- ca

me cum be-ne-díctis. O- ro súpplex et accli-

nis, Cor contrí-tum qua-si cí- nis: Gé-re cú-ram mé-

i fí- nis.   Lacrimó- sa dí- es íl-la, Qua re-súrget

ex   fa-víl-la   Ju-di-cándus hó- mo ré- us: Hú-

ic ergo pár-   ce Dé-us.   Pí- e Jé-su Dómi-ne, dó-

na é- is réqui- em.   A-   men.

Dies Irae (in English translation)

Day of wrath and doom impending!
Heav'n and earth in ashes ending:
David's rede with Sibyl's blending.

O what fear man's bosom rendeth,
When from heav'n the Judge descendeth,
On whose sentence all dependeth!

Wondrous sound the trumpet flingeth,
Through earth's sepulchres it ringeth,
All before the throne it bringeth!

Death is struck, and nature quaking
All creation is awaking,
To its Judge an answer making!

Lo! the Book, exactly worded,
Wherein all hath been recorded;
Thence shall judgement be awarded.

When the Judge his seat attaineth,
And each hidden deed arraigneth,
Nothing unaveng'd remaineth.

What shall I, frail man, be pleading?
Who for me be interceding,
When the just are mercy needing?

King of majesty tremendous!
Who dost free salvation send us,
Fount of pity! then befriend us.

Think, kind Jesu, my salvation
Caus'd thy wondrous Incarnation;
Leave me not to reprobation!

Faint and weary, thou hast sought me,
On the Cross of suffering bought me;
Shall such grace be vainly brought me?

Righteous Judge of retribution,
Grant thy gift of absolution,
Ere that reckoning-day's conclusion!

Guilty, now I pour my moaning,
All my shame with anguish owning;
Space, O God, thy suppliant groaning!

Thou who Mary hast forgiven,
Who the dying thief hast shriven,
E'en to me a hope hast given.

Worthless are my prayers & sighing,
Yet, good Lord, in grace complying,
Rescue me from fire undying!

With thy favour'd sheep O place me!
Nor among the goats abse me:
But to thy right hand upraise me.

While the wicked are confounded,
Doom'd to flames of woe unbounded,
Call me, with thy Saints surrounded.

Low I kneel, with heart-submission;
See, like ashes, my contrition:
Help me in my last condition!

Ah! that Day of tears & mourning!
From the dust of earth returning,

Man for judgement must prepare him!
Spare, O God, in mercy spare him!

Lord, all pitying Jesu blest,
Grant them thine eternal rest!

Amen.

Dies Irae (*In Latin*)

Dies irae, dies illa,
Solvet saeclum in favilla: α   a
Teste David cum Sibylla.   b₁ A
                                     c

Quantus tremor est futurus,   a
Quando judex est venturus,   b₁ A
Cuncta stricte discussurus!   β   c

                                     d
Tuba mirum spargens sonum
Per sepulcra regionum,   a B
Coget omnes ante thronum.   b₂
                               γ

Mors stupebit et natura,   d
Cum resorget creatura,   δ   a B
Judicanti responsura.   b

Liber Scriptus proferetur,   e
In quo totum continetur,   ε   f C
Unde mundus judicetur.   g

Judex ergo cum sedebit,   e
Quidquid latet apparebit: ε   f C
Nil in ultum remanebit   g

Quid sum miser tunc dicturus?   a
Quem patronum rogaturus?   α   b₁ A
Cum vix justus sit securus.   c

Rex tremendae majestatis,   a
Qui salvandos salvas gratis,   b₁ A
Salva me, fons pietatis.   β   c

Recordare Jesu pie,   d
Quod sum causa tuae viae: a B
Ne me perdas illa die.   b₂
                               γ

Quaerens me, sedisti lassus.   d
Redemisti crucem passus: δ   a B
Tantus labor non sit cassus.   b₂

Juste judex ultionis,   e
Donum fac remissionis,   ε   f C
Ante diem rationis.   g

Ingemisco, tamquam reus: e
Culpa rubet vultus meus: ε   f C
Supplicanti parce Deus.   g

M

N

(A)

M

N

(A)

Qui Mariam absolvisti,
Et latronum exaudisti, α a
Mihi quoque spem dedisti. b_1 A
                                         c

Preces meae non sunt dignae:
Sed tu bonus fac benigne, β a
Ne perenni cremer igne. b_1 A
                                         c
                                                    M
Inter oves locum praesta,   d
Et ab haedis me sequestra,   a B   (A)
Statuens in parte dextra. b_2
                                γ
Confutatis maledictis,   d
Flammis acribus a̤ddictis: δ a .B
Voca me cum benedictis. b_2

Oro supplex et acclinis,   e
Cor contritum quasi cinis: ϵ f C   N
Gere curam mei finis.   g

Lacrimosa dies illa,   h
Qua resurget ex favilla j_1 D

Judicandus homo reus: k
Huic ergo parce Deus. j_1 E

Pie Jesu Domine,   l
Dona eis requiem. j_2 F

Amen.   m

Giuseppe Verdi, Requiem

№ 2. Dies iræ

The medieval sequence 'Dies Irae,' which forms one movement of the Mass for the Dead (*Missa pro Defunctis*), is attributed to Thomas of Celano, who lived in the early thirteenth century. The origin of the music is obscure. The poem is a realization of the Last Judgment of immense emotional power, and its imagery suits the transcendent nature of the subject. The music has reappeared many times, especially among nineteenth century composers. Prominent among these are Hector Berlioz, who uses it in the last movement of his Symphonie Fantastique, Liszt, who uses it in his Totentanz, and various composers of requiems. The force of the tune is not particularly enlarged or enhanced in the settings of it (generally, a small part of it) by Berlioz and Liszt. On the contrary, the gain is all on their side: they and not it are the beneficiaries. The mere volume or the variety of timbres afforded by the modern orchestra is not much to the point here. The sequence is most effective when sung a capella in an earnest and subdued manner by male voices in unison. (The deity to whom it is addressed must not be supposed to be hard of hearing.) Even in this form, the potent, but sparse references to the Last Judgment in the Scriptures are here exceeded by far. This is true of the spirit of it, both in the words and the music.

Verdi uses the words but makes his own setting. This is often thought too theatrical and operatic, if not melodramatic. It may, however, catch the spirit of the original better than the new renderings of the old tune such as those mentioned above. It begins with a colossal crash of tympani and full orchestra and the tension is scarcely diminished throughout its length. It is an essentially Italian or Latinate and Catholic sense of the "last" event, the "youngest day" (*der jüngste Tag*) as the German has it (since it stands at the end of time and cannot grow old?). One should also remind oneself of Michelangelo's vision of it in the Sistine Chapel and Rubens' Great Last Judgment and Smaller Last Judgment, and his Descent of the Damned into Hell in the Pinakothek in Munich. All this has its counter-part in the equally profound though less dramatic version of the event in Protestantism from Luther to Bach and beyond.

Close inspection of the original sequence and its music reveals a work of remarkable construction. It is in fact so elaborately done as to make one marvel that its effect is so robust and not somehow manufactured and academic. Every nuance of form contributes to the result. But this "hidden order" of its art must first be brought to light. It is in fact easily revealed if we take the trouble to seek it. I will confine myself almost wholly to the musical aspects of the sequence.

The beginnings of the hidden order are revealed as soon as we are aware of the re-appearance of the motif of the first line

which strikes like the thrusts of a dagger or shoots of pain. There is no mistaking the motif and we may readily count its occurrence twelve times over. If this then is the "theme" of the melodic aspect of the sequence may hastily conclude that the form is strophic and that the repetition at such inordinate length is in keeping with the almost brutal message of the poem, the inevitable consequences of human guilt.

But although there are such recurrences of the motif, there are also some seventeen rhymed tercets. Hence the recurrences of the musical motif twelve times are not identical with the first lines of the stanzas. With this we must now discriminate the structure in more detail.

Putting appropriate letters for each melodic phrase we obtain first the series a, b, c, d, e, f, g. Here a is the opening *dies irae* motif. It is apparent that the stanzas run:

$$abc \quad abc \quad dab \quad dab \quad efg \quad efg.$$

These, however, obviously reveal a more encompassing identity:

$$
\begin{array}{cccccc}
A & A & B & B & C & C \\
abc & abc & dab & dab & efg & efg.
\end{array}
$$

Proceeding now into the seventh stanza we see that this entire series (we may call it (A)) is formally repeated in stanzas seven through twelve, and almost wholly repeated again in thirteen through seventeen. In the latter, C appears only once instead of twice as in the first two series. Ignoring the absence of the second C in the last series, we have therefore a still larger order (A) three times.

A prime figure, as we have seen tends to emerge particularly if it is centralized and repeated. With virtually three full occurrences of (A), the whole figure appears vigorously emergent. There can be no doubt of the cohesion or centralization of each of the (A)'s provided, of course, that the pattern is not only something on paper, but is also heard. There can be no doubt that it is.

When we look at the structure of (A) we observe that it actually falls into two parts: AABB, which is united by the fact that ab appears in each A and B; and CC, which introduces altogether new melodic material. Hence CC appears after each occurrence of AABB. This yields a kind of song form, which is easily grasped by the ear, thus:

$$
\begin{array}{cccccc}
M & N & M & N & M & N \\
AABB & CC & AABB & CC & AABB & C.
\end{array}
$$

Nothing pleases the ear more than a well-prepared and thoroughly desired recurrence. It is a kind of flattery to the ear: "Ah, yes," we say, "it's a pleasure to meet you again," and we show that we recognize a familiar, or even a not-so-familiar face.

The return to M from N seems to me the real key to the unity of the sequence. Each appearance of M is marked by four occurrences of a (the *dies irae* motif), and the repetition of N (that is the new material, *efg*) serves to further mark the reappearance of M. One may suppose that each a, being what it is, is to be sung slightly more *forte* than the other phrases.

There is still a further feature of unification in the groupings $\alpha, \beta, \gamma, \delta$. This is not the least astonishing aspect of the succession of these episodes. It is distinguished clearly by the fact that it begins with the main motif, already quoted, but these beginnings do not coincide with the first lines of the tercets: they are of unequal length, being three, four, three, and two lines in length. It is as if one had banded a series of rods first by a cross-tie at every third rod,

$$x\,x\,x \quad x\,x\,x \quad x\,x\,x \quad x\,x\,x,$$

then with further bonds holding the first three, the next four, the next three, and the next two lines:

$$x\,x\,x \;|\; x\,x\,x \;|\; x\,x\,x \;|\; x\,x\,x.$$

In this way, except for the gap between the third and fourth lines, and the 12th and 13th the stanzas (and thus the rhyme) endings are bridged by musical arcs. The process then continues:

A	A	B	B	C	C
a b c	a b c	d a b	d a b	e f g	e f g
α	β	γ	δ	ϵ	ϵ
M				N	
(A)					

And, as noted earlier, (A) reappears nearly twice again. The bonds are so numerous that nearly every juncture is jointed at least once, and the whole is therefore not permitted to break at any point. There are larger junctures at the end of the sixth, twelfth, and the seventeenth stanzas.

A further unification has been taken for granted, the rhyme in each tercet. But there seems to be no further pattern among the rhymes. There is but one recurrence, the second and seventh stanzas ending in -urus.

Finally, we come to the three closing couplets. I do not think this is a mere coda. By its nature, the sequence being addressed or declaimed to the Almighty, can only end in one final plea after which the penitent must resign himself, and consign the dead including himself inevitably, to his fate. The close of the sequence hymn conveys this feeling musically and verbally. God is not addressed directly, but by the way of the Intercessor – "Pie Jesu Domine,/Dona eis requiem."

Some small variants, e.g. b_1 and b_2, and j_1 and j_2 are noted in the analysis. One may also detect in the music of the second, fourth and sixth lines of the *envoy*, as we may call it, a kind of conflation or condensation of the ab lines above. Placing one above the other, we observe the kinship of:

(The bracketed notes in the second staff do not coincide.) The final line before the Amen is reasonably similar to this, differing principally in that it does not quite rise to the dominant (A) as do the previous j's. The massive force of the sequence is now spent; the Amen sinks even a degree below the tonic in the closing cadence.

The sequence is in the Dorian mode, that is, the Gregorian mode bearing that name, with an unmistakable tonic on D and Dominant on A. It falls once to the lower dominant and rises once momentarily to the upper tonic. B natural appears only in phrase d and in k, a variant of d. B flat appears but once, in the first couplet. Except for the first couplet every phrase ends on the tonic. Final cadences either rise by a whole tone (C–D), or fall a fifth (A–D) or a whole tone. Tercets and couplets end on cadences.

We now have the sequence before us in articulate form. There is no doubt whatever of a masterful artist's hand behind it. The wonder is that so elaborate and formal a composition should serve the purposes of one of the most emotionally gripping trains of poetic thought to be found in the liturgy.

The principal devices of unity are our second mode and in a lesser degree the first. The principal figure is M, and in this the recurrence of ab four times in each M (that is, in beginning α, β, γ, and δ) cannot fail to impress itself on our thought. Here c and d are variant ways of closing off the phrase: once C, then ce, then d. These cadential phrases therefore represent a kind of primary recedent to the primary figure, ab. The primary ground is thus N, or *efg*. After two appearances of N in the form *efg, efg*, it is shortened during the third appearance to one *efg*.

The sequence like any musical structure employing repetition shows us why we must not regard the principal figure as multiple. Rather, in the manner we have been trying to make clear, we have been afforded several glimpses of one and the same figure. A figure, as we know, entails a ground, and this too we find here even in the absence of polyphony, in the careful subordination of c and d to ab, and in a larger manner, of N to M.

Beyond the suggestions we have made, we may leave to liturgists the difficult question of the mutual use that thought and music make of one another in the sequence. In a manner that is not easily explained, the principal figures make a lasting impression upon us and the envoy closes out the hymn in a manner to assuage our grief and reconcile us to the judgment that is said to await us, knowing that, whatever it is, it will be just. Once we have made the substance of the sequence part of our thought, with or without the imagery of the Last Judgment, the musical effect must remain.

In a work of such beauty we see how musical effort and imagination have helped to bring the "hidden order" of its totality before us, exploiting both the comparative, contextual, and tendentive relations that inhabit the materials themselves and the compositional orders the artist himself can command. He is moved by a relentless Gestaltungstrieb, disposing of these resources in accordance with a sublime vision.

(3) *Schubert: Die Winterreise, Op. 89.*

Der Leiermann

Der Leiermann

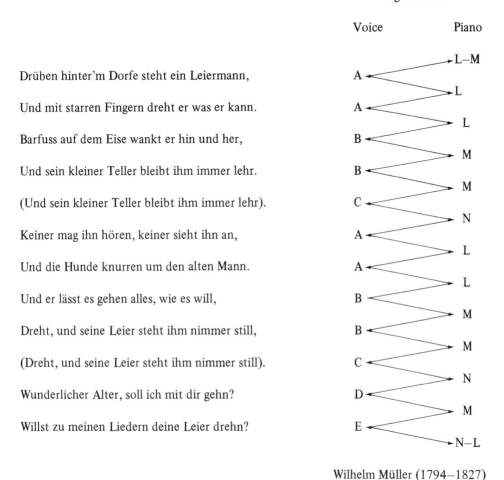

Musical
organization:

	Voice	Piano
Drüben hinter'm Dorfe steht ein Leiermann,	A	L–M
Und mit starren Fingern dreht er was er kann.	A	L
Barfuss auf dem Eise wankt er hin und her,	B	L
Und sein kleiner Teller bleibt ihm immer lehr.	B	M
(Und sein kleiner Teller bleibt ihm immer lehr).	C	M
Keiner mag ihn hören, keiner sieht ihn an,	A	N
Und die Hunde knurren um den alten Mann.	A	L
Und er lässt es gehen alles, wie es will,	B	L
Dreht, und seine Leier steht ihm nimmer still,	B	M
(Dreht, und seine Leier steht ihm nimmer still).	C	M
Wunderlicher Alter, soll ich mit dir gehn?	D	N
Willst zu meinen Liedern deine Leier drehn?	E	M
		N–L

Wilhelm Müller (1794–1827)

The poetic value of the poem is of less concern to us than the setting, but the poem cannot be ignored if for no other reason than that it served Schubert to create one of his finest *Lieder*. The poem creates a picture, and since there is no action portrayed, there is no narration as there would be in a ballad. The picture is presented from the standpoint of a speaker or poet who observes, describes, and comments on it, and sees in it a meaning or application to himself. Let us first think of the poem independently of the music.

The subject, of course, is an organ grinder who is said to be standing barefoot in midwinter somewhere near a village cranking an organ and expecting alms from passersby. In the icy weather few will be passing. His fingers stiffen in the cold.

Images of an icy desolate scene, a ridiculous jingle on the crisp air, and the hopelessness of the lone figure in it are readily evoked. If we adopt the notion of an objective correlative, the poem as read, as sounded out by the reader, should itself bring to the ear some turns of rhythm, or sonorous effects appropriate to the thought that is being uttered. In this respect the poet has made little effort to make the sounded vehicle reflect very much of the thought. What may first come to mind is the unending repetition of one tune, but the *poet* makes no effort to evoke this image. (The composer does.) He concentrates on the visual.

Although the picture is that of a pathetic, lonely old man, the poem is fairly free of sentimentality, and in fact the figure is treated with scarcely any sympathy. We are only made to *see* bare feet on icy ground and the always empty tray. Only for a moment do we hear the village dogs that murmur threats as they pass by.

If there is a thought here distinct from the imagery that vivifies it, it is perhaps in a word, the desolation. No one is afoot in this gray atmosphere, or if they are, they act as if the old man were not even visible. He is bereft of friends, his fingers and feet are unprotected from the cold, the dogs regard him vaguely as a menace. The old man is resigned to his fate, come what may; what will be, will be.

The poet is thinking of him at a cool distance. *Drüben hinter'm Dorfe*: over there somewhere, not here, where he is sitting by a warm fire. He is stirred less to compassion than to philosophical reflection about an odd or strange sort of person: *Wunderlicher Alter*. He thinks, in fact, only about the plight of his own soul, as poets are wont to do, which he fancies is as desolate as the old man. The song and song cycle end on this desperate note. Perhaps, says the introverted poet, I should go along with the old man. The monotony and despair that I pour out in my poems will be perfectly attuned to the mechanical whine of the barrel organ with its empty, soulless jingle. But this again is only another "image" to be contemplated. The despair and dereliction which are fully conveyed by the desolate landscape are not overdrawn in the poem. Its brevity is meant to insure that the reader will not forget a single detail. But it is in the end heartless. A picture — and that is all.

Whatever we think of the quality or value of the poem, and of the rest of the cycle, it is virtually inevitable that the song writers of the time would contemplate setting it to music. It had the good fortune to fall into the hands of Schubert. Who would think of trying to improve upon his setting with one of his own?

In the composer's setting, another equivalent of the thought is being devised. The mere "imagism" of the poem, its want of sentiment, comes through also in the music. The composer grasps the sense of the poem, and of the poet in the poem, perfectly. The musical expression is not just an "equivalent" for the poem, as if someone had to find a garment whose size corresponded to the dimensions of a body. The composer rather reads the poem, digests it, and then gestures musically in the manner of the song. We can say, this is the way Schubert felt, these are the musical thoughts of a man gifted in just his manner thinking about such a subject. Other people might respond by declaiming it to their friends with such and such rhythms, facial expressions, intonations and emphases of voice, or gestures. Schubert may not have been much better at that than most persons. His responses took a different form: his setting of the poem is a record, a gesture of *his* kind of thought, for he seems to have had almost no time for any other than musical thought.

If we now look at the Schubert setting and find in it a dozen subtle and highly expressive details, we may be asked whether Schubert was aware of all these details, of their consequences and interactions in their context. The answer is, I think, that he was aware of it in the way we are aware of what we say when we write letters to our friends: many details of expression are, as it were, hidden from our eyes, even if *we* write the letters, for the reason that all letters not only *convey* what we want them to convey (if we are skillful) but also *betray* many a symptom of ourselves and "the way our minds work" that we do not catch because they can only be caught by persons other than ourselves. Music is action, gesture, and a gesture is something different for performer and observer.

The Leiermann begins with a motif that is repeated, at least rhythmically, throughout the song. The monotony of the organ, and the blank and void of the northern winter are not only portrayed, but virtually conveyed or quoted. An open fifth (a singularly "vacuous" interval, unlike virtually any other, unless it be a fourth) provides a drone bass, that is persistently if quietly sounded in every bar of the whole setting, fifty-six measures. The interval is effectively used; after a dozen measures we begin to divine that it will never change before the end. An added dissonant grace note in the first two measures adds just a tremor of uneasiness. The song of the organ is as it were condensed into a pathetic sing-song figure:

Rhythmically, the figure reappears every four measures except at the beginning, between stanzas, and at the end. Two variants of this same rhythm are interspersed, lending a slight softening of the monotony but after we recognize them we know that nothing further will be done to relieve the monotony. We sink back, with the poet-speaker, into our own gloom.

Regularly, after the organ figure is heard, the voice speaks in an almost identical rhythm throughout. A few dotted eighths with succeeding sixteenths afford but a tiny alteration in the figure, and virtually none in the rhythm. The words are virtually spoken as if *recitativo*; the only accompaniment is little more than the cold and relentless open fifth in the bass:

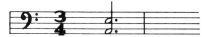

As we see from the sectional analysis, the musical organization is intended to be as transparent as possible. Simple figures occur and recur. There is virtually no development. The situation seems lifeless and desolate, as if the pulse of the heart were the sole sign of life.

Yet while the composer has taken the trouble to make the monotony to be felt as monotony, he has relieved it just sufficiently by small variances, so that he and his composition will not appear to have been monotonous themselves. Thus when we listen closely we find that the two stanzas are identical in their pattern. The pattern of the lines in the two stanzas themselves runs AABBC. The closing couplet is slightly variant.

What is remarkable is that the composer has managed to make the idea of monotony

palatable. He lets some aspects of the setting unmistakably suggest it by *being* monotonous, but he has relieved it just enough so that we take an interest in it: had he not done
so that whole world would have been monotonous in the deadly sense. It is easy enough
to depict monotony, but how does one enlist a listener's interest in it? This Schubert has
succeeded in doing. Both the poet and the composer have given us just enough desolation;
any more would be too much, any less would be too little. The song ends about as it
began. The void stretches beyond both the beginning and the end, into a hopeless past
and future.

The couplet deserves an extra remark. With the words, *wunderlicher Alter*, the poet-
speaker begins to see that there is something poetic in the scene. He sees the old man
and the whining organ as a perfect expression of his own bitter disappointments: to
grasp something that expresses our feelings is already to relieve us, if only slightly, of a
burden. That is, we bear our sorrows better when we see them, "embodied" in "correla-
tives" to our feelings. This is precisely the kind of response that one may expect to poet
to have. The poem conveys a small but instructive lesson in poetics. The cycle seems to
end on a note of an apparently endless void, a kind of desperate, suicidal note that all
Romantic poets sounded. But in fact the poet is really enjoying his pain, for he finds
redemption in anything that affords him the means for poetic interpretation.

This response is scarcely calculated to improve the old man's lot. His modern day
equivalent in Vienna or Munich can go to a publicly maintained *Wärmestube* on any
wintry day, furnished for just such persons by a benevolent socialism.

We have in effect given answers to our questions about unity and variety, development
and climax, figure and ground, but they may be pointed a little more.

The unity of the poem is achieved with simple means: a picture appears to be flashed
before us; even without a musical setting we may hear the mechanical clang of the organ.
The sketch is finished readily but unhurriedly in the two quatrains. In the couplet, the
picture is contemplated by a poet who sees the scene as reflecting his own fate and state
of mind.

Of far greater interest than the poem is the composer's setting of it especially in reference to unity. The almost silent bond of connection is found in the ground: the drone
bass is never varied. It works its effect, even if we do not focally hear it. The rhythmic
pattern likewise unifies by means of repetition, as already shown. The pattern of the
vocal line is set by the continuous alternate appearance of voice, two bars, and the jingle
of the organ, two bars, with two minor extensions of the organ interlude. At the end
(ninth and eighth bar from the end) a deft variance is effected, with a quarter note rest
dividing the verse into two parts spread over three measures, instead of the two continuous
bars in the verses of the quatrain. Even here the rhythm is virtually unaltered.

Melodically, as already noted, the pattern runs AABBC in the two quatrains, with the
very same A's and B's in each. The alternating appearance of the voice and the "organ,"
each time rhythmically the same and melodically similar, serves to enforce the shape of
the melodic figure. As is common, the reappearance of A or of B serves to make them
more highly audible or perceptible: in each appearance A (or B) is laid congruently over
the preceding A's (or B's), and the flanking of B by A serves to show the more contrasting
and groundal function of B towards A and the more dominant character of A. The couplet
is united to the rest largely by rhythmic means but its function is largely one of a climax

from one standpoint, or a coda from another. In any event, the balance of variety and unity is critical in the song since its theme *is* monotony in a real sense. This is clearly represented without a trace of the boredom entailed by actual monotony.

In terms of development to climax, the *Lied* has to maintain interest through subtle means. Everything is perspicuously or even nakedly revealed in this simple vocal and piano setting: nothing can be concealed. After the two strophic quatrains appear, identical in form, the couplet is varied just sufficiently to maintain our interest. This is fortified by the fact that in the couplet the melodic line is altered by a fairly emphatic rise to the upper dominant and even a half step higher. This upper dominant has been reached only in passing previously: here it is clearly relied upon for emphasis and climax (although "climax" is of course rather too strong a term for this kind of emphasis). The voice also ends on the upper dominant: although the dominant is resolved by the piano, the feeling of a void, open and desolate, remains, conforming to the thought.

One shudders to think what banalities a "popular" composer might have fallen into in setting the song. But Schubert seems to have solved all the problems, and to have steered safely between several abysses, and all without a sign of effort, although I would think the *Lied* even more remarkable had it not resolved the final dominant. But clearly Schubert could not see his way to ending not only the song but the whole cycle on an unresolved dominant. It is just possible that Schumann might have done so.

(4) *Hugo Wolf, 'Zur Ruh', zur Ruh'!' Lieder nach verschiedenen Dichtern, Number 18*

If one is inclined to think that a selection of European music such as the present illustrates various formal devices that make for coherence only because the numbers have been selected with this in mind, let him make the effort to turn up music that manages to do without them. It goes without saying that he will be well-advised to avoid anything and everything that falls into familiar classifications such as suites, sonatas, fugues, passacaglias, theme-variations, and so on. But neither is there any more reward in searching among things that bear titles such as *fantasia, impromptu*, or even *improvisation*. Three such pieces readily come to mind from different eras: C. P. E. Bach's Freie Fantasie für Klavier, Mozart's C Minor Fantasia for piano, and Chopin's F Minor Fantaisie, Op. 49. Each of these is not only highly structured. It is so remarkably organized that one marvels at how it can appear to be a freely improvised flight of imagination. One cannot resist the maxim, *ars celare artem*. Until one reaches far into the twentieth century, with its "discovery" of chance and the performer's caprice one is hard put to find "unstructured" music. (I am by no means relying on any metaphysical notion of structure, such that any and every thing music have structure if it has parts in some relation to one another, however cluttered the effect. Structure is here taken to mean strictly what falls somewhere among the several techniques we have expounded.)

When we reflect on what we usually have in mind with *improvisation*, this result is not surprising. Improvising, recently so astonishingly perfected in the jam session of popular music, means skill at something, not a mere potluck serving that agreeably occupies time. The impressive thing is to be able to intuit connections and relations and making everything appear to *fit* together as if it had been planned with forethought. With modern replicating devices we can readily verify our first impressions about such performances. Would that we had such a record of the famous encounter between Mozart and Clementi in 1781 or any of Bach's or Beethoven's keyboard feats of this sort.

Zur Ruh', zur Ruh'!
To Rest, to Rest!
(Kerner.)

With all this well in mind, one may yet set up two polar limits between which music and probably all of the arts move, even though neither of them is mercifully ever fully reached. At one extreme we have art in which the entire appeal is elemental: satisfaction is taken only in the qualities of elements themselves, without reference to one another. According to our taste, we find details to be rich and fruity, or dry and piquant in endless succession, until we feel a surfeit of them. At the other extreme, we are enchanted by the marvelous formal appeal of the elements, their ceaseless tension and release, their perfect fittingness in each other's company. We lose sight altogether of the fact that the elements taken by themselves (if this were possible) have no individual appeal at all. Surely there is no art at either of these poles: but we can take our bearings from them nevertheless.

One is tempted to say that art of the first sort is romantic and that of the other, classic. This is a harmless dichotomy so far as mere directions are concerned. In fact, of course, the nineteenth century Romantic school of composers was never given over to mere elementalism: no one was. ever more formally circumspect than Chopin or Mendelssohn, though they were Romantics of the deepest dye. Our categories must therefore be bent to fit the facts so far as history is concerned. It remains even now to be seen whether fully elementalist art is possible. Our century seems to be determined to find out.

What we see in the latter part of the nineteenth century is not a weakening of formalist inclinations so much as a vast intensification of the emotional dimensions of art. An ever-richer diet was being served, and it is not surprising that this should have reached a limit. This is only to say that the last Romantics, Wagner, Liszt, Brahms, Bruckner, Mahler, Strauss, Saint-Saens, Fauré, the Russian, Czech, Scandinavian, and British schools, and so on, reached this limit, not that they overstepped it. They are, in fact, a satisfying climax to a great development.

It is rash, if not foolish, to select one page of music as being typical of this development. At best one may choose an example that is genuine and that serves to remind us of its glory. For this purpose the songs of Hugo Wolf can scarcely be improved upon. We select a brief, intense, and wholly remarkable example of his work.

Hugo Wolf's mastery of the art of the *Lied* is universally acknowledged. His power to wed and weld song and thought is fabulous. Every syllable is weighed in the finest balance. His choice of poets is faultless. The Mörike poems might be the envy of every language, and even so they are transcended in the Wolf settings.

Kerner was a doctor of medicine and thereto something of a mystic, his wife being a clairvoyante. The mystic's resort to paradox is evident in the poem: *Nacht muss es sein,/Dass Licht mir werde*; and *Glanz der tiefsten Nächte*. The unseen is more-real than this world. The poem breathes the metaphysical atmosphere of the age of Hegel, and no such poem is conceivable in any other western European language.

I have ventured a translation that seeks to do justice to Kerner alone: here one cannot serve two masters, both poet and composer. But since few would think of singing any but the German words, certain inequities may be ignored. Thus, for example, the word *Nacht* in bar 13 would have to appear on that very note as 'night' in any singable English translation (as it does not do in mind) because Wolf is evidently conveying something very unique with this B♮ when the song is sung in the original key. It is the lowest note in the *Lied* and appears only once. Similarly, *Licht* in the following bar, or

Traum in bar 30, and so on. I have perhaps caught the paradox but only by transposing Kerner's sly reference to Genesis, *mir werde Licht*, to (in effect) *es werde Nacht*. Such are the surds of translation. (See appendix for the translation.)

The poem is an interesting mingling of inner and outer aspects. It speaks about the inner from an external standpoint but also realizes it, for example, in the paradoxes already alluded to. The retreat to the mother's heart is for us fraught with Freudian symbolism and doubly interesting coming from the hand of an early-day poet-psychiatrist. The familiar Romantic stance is evident: *Ich bin allein,/Fort ist die Erde/Raum der Erdenschmerzen.*

The *durchkomponiert* aspect of the song is immediately apparent. Although there are interesting recurrences, as we shall see, the poem is, in the first place, made to cohere through closure rather than repetition and recurrence. It thus has a form that is invented solely to satisfy the particular purposes of this occasion and no other. (Wolf elsewhere uses the strophic form effectively when it is suitable.) The form of the song, in this general sense, is a great sweep of line that descends through the first stanza and ascends through the second, with a shimmering climax as we reach bar 30. The descent is evident in the retreat into the night, as the ultimate source of life, and of light! The ascent is the flight into the dream. At the end the sleep motif of the beginning reappears in instrumental form, the only sectional recurrent. In the musical profile, we reach the nadir of *Nacht* (B♮) near the end of the first stanza and a climax nearly two octaves higher (!) near the end of the second. It is not song for an ordinary voice.

The pace is slow from the beginning, the rich harmony envelops the sleeper like eiderdown. In bar 9 the chord cannot but suggest the *Liebesnacht*, and the association may be deliberate, since Wolf supported Wagner with ardor. The falling line from the outset realizes weary members and closing eyelids. In bar 13 "night" is reached in a dark minor ninth chord; this quickly resolves into "light," and this is graphically represented in the open fourths and fifths of the tonic in bar 15. There follow fifteen remarkable bars of more or less chromatic character. The melodic line is a rather undulant stepwise ascent. The tension mounts as the dream approaches. It is the dark but brightening, night of the soul. Although the tonality is firm, it seems eclipsed by the chromaticism, and the outcome of the harmonic development is veiled until the very and when at *Traum* the vision opens out in full brightness.

Few passages in such a brief compass could illustrate so well what we have had in mind under *development* as a way of insuring coherence. Every sinew of the fabric is tautened, and every irrelevancy set aside. The pitch gradually rises as does the intensity. The harmonic development moves as if by a secret code that is only divulged as we reach the peak. If so short a passage can so fully satisfy, we may come to understand what effort and ingenuity are necessary to work out successfully a development that may run a quarter of an hour or even much longer in a symphony or opera.

Only at the very end of the song is the device of recurrence resorted to. With *Mutterherzen* we hear again the open fifths that presented *Licht* at the end of the first stanza. The passion of the dream resolves itself in a recurrence of the *Ruh'* of the opening bars.

This *Lied* thus epitomizes every device of unification we have been speaking of. It displays the fullest depth of Romantic thought and feeling and the last richness and ripeness of the tonal medium of the closing century.

Finally, we must recur to our discussion of the use of connotative content to gain "instant coherence." The song and the operatic medium rarely fall prey to the hazards that beset visual representational art. We may lose sight altogether of what is on the picture plane itself, treating it as a mere symbol of some distant represented reality, but we can never in the same degree lose "sight" of the musical medium when we are absorbed with Carmen and Don José, Faust and Marguerite, and so on. Wolf was as deeply absorbed with his poets as Wagner was with poet Wagner himself. Hence, his songs are never "accompaniments" nor are the poems mere "librettos."

Yet this intimate welding of two inherently distinct media must not suggest that the music lacks of compelling logic of its own. It is rather as if a kind of pre-established harmony had joined two disparate but perfectly compatible monads. Although poetry of the stripe of Kerner's may be long since out of fashion it is nonetheless genuine and competent. *Zur Ruh'* stands easily on its own feet. By contrast, one feels that *Der Leiermann* is borne along only by Schubert. He has transformed and transfigured it. Wolf is much more fortunate or was, perhaps, a better educated reader. But if we lost Müller's poem altogether and kept Schubert's music the loss would be greater than the loss of Kerner's, despite the easy superiority of the latter. The reason is that Schubert's setting is wholly dependent on a weaker poem. One could not make much of it if it were rediscovered as a *Lied ohne Worte*, but Wolf would satisfy us even in this guise, and Kerner, in the corresponding case nearly as well.

If this is correct, it teaches us something important about *Gesamtkunstwerke*, namely, that like other partnerships they are only as strong as the partners themselves. This is a moral that opera has all too often defied.

16.2 INSTRUMENTAL MUSIC

Our examples of instrumental music are drawn from the standard literature. They illustrate various modes of musical organization which are without difficulty seen to fall under the general procedures that we have studied in detail and that have been illustrated in visual and poetic art. The analyses are partly borrowed deliberately from or lean heavily upon the studies of musicologists and partly devised by the present author.

It goes without saying that the organization of purely instrumental music must be accomplished in purely musical terms. Our two classes, of song and instrumental music, do not of course exhaust all the genres that ideally ought to be examined in respect to coherence or form. So-called program music, for example, provides a kind of hybrid example of the two. The composer's program (one should think of, let us say, Liszt, Tchaikovsky, or Richard Strauss), whether explicitly promulgated or only held *in petto* by the composer, serves as a kind of explicit-implicit libretto. All the difficult problems of expression arise here anew, but there is perhaps a tilt of the scale toward reliance on pure or non-representational devices of organization, because the composer of program music is or ought always to be aware that most of his listeners may have only a vague knowledge or interest in his plot or program and that he must accordingly make certain that his musical logic is even by itself convincing from the beginning to the end of his composition. It is the "logic" of music as an art unfolding in time that is decisive. For the purest examples of this, we must turn to instrumental music. Lest it be thought that our examples are merely hand-picked to illustrate coherence, let the sceptical reader undertake to find, if he can, music from the grand tradition down into the heart of this century that dispenses with all of the procedures of the compositional order.

I do not undertake to speak of what may succeed as music here and hereafter.

(1) *Johann Sebastian Bach: Suite 1 in G Major for Violoncello Solo, Courante*

The purpose of our studies of musical works is not offered to provide exhaustive pains-taking analysis of compositions; but rather to gain a sound view of their internal order and to interpret this in the light of the general considerations we have developed. Analysis attends to such questions as why the work is as it is, what holds it together, and what if anything justifies the choice and placement of each element, but fully convincing answers can be given only if appeal can be made to some general theory of coherence such as we have attempted to provide in Part One. The study of individual works will bring to light some of the devices or procedures which composers have employed to order their works. Our discussion in Part One has identified them only from a general and theoretical standpoint.

In general, I would prefer to consider analyses already made by musicians, critics, or musicologists. A valuable source is Diether de la Motte's recent *Musikalische Analyse* which contains analyses of some twelves works ranging from the Agnus of Joaquin de Pres' Missa Pange Lingue and Contrapunctus I from Bach's Kunst der Fuge, to a move-ment from Mahler's Symphony VII and Alban Berg's Stücke für Klarinette und Klavier, Op. 5, No. 1.[6] In this instance we shall be able to rely on another person's analysis. The interpretation will, however, look for the same things we have sought in our analyses.

One of de la Motte's studies is devoted to the Courante from the Sonata in G major for Violoncello solo by J. S. Bach. The Courante occupies a single page and consists of forty-two bars. It is a work of extraordinary compression of thought, conveying from the outset the sense of an absolute mastery of the medium for this instrument. It is serene and has a warmth that derives from the nature of the instrument itself.

In an unaccompanied string composition both the melodic or thematic and the struc-tural and harmonic aspects must be conveyed at once in a single melodic line. Since these two may not always be at ease with one another, a successful solution to the problem is needed from the very outset. If the thematic figure concedes too much to the harmony, it may confine itself to arpeggios that make the harmony explicit: but in that event the theme is either slowed considerably, or it may be lacking in the ease and grace that can come from the use of intervals more closely related to scales than to chords.[7] If, on the other hand, the melodic line must itself alone define the harmony without constant resort to arpeggios, the result may be architectonically weak or adhere too steadfastly to tones that particularly define the key, such as the third and the sixth. One solution is, therefore, to mingle the two extremes, gaining strength from the larger intervals that definite the key, and grace from a freely ranging line. Bach has succeeded in just this way in the Courante, and, of course, he handles this problem successfully also in his other unaccompanied string works. The cello offers a particularly excellent opportunity to attack the problem, since the tones, especially in the lower two octaves of its range, are situated exactly where the harmonically strong tones are expected, while nearly its whole range is full of rich melodic potentiality. All of this is instantly recognized as being at Bach's command.

Courante.

It is not surprising that the key structure is itself a formidable unifying device. Of the forty-two measures, over half are in the tonic G, others are in the relative minor e, in the subdominant C, and, of course, in the dominant D. This kind of key structure is emphatically favorable to the tonic since the subdominant, dominant, and relative minor are as close to a tonic as a neighboring key can be.

The work would ordinarily be thought to be in binary form. The first part (to the double bar and repeat) leads to the dominant on which it closes with a firm cadence (that is, beginning in the key of G and closing on D, a fifth above G). The second part begins on the dominant (bar 19) and moves through several keys to return to the tonic G major. Thus a strong dominant position is established at the end of the first part and there is room for a kind of development in the first portion of the second part.

The principal theme or motif appears at the outset and reappears at least once in all the component keys. But there are further and subtler differences in its reappearance in the rhythm of the motif. Some six forms of it can be established:

The form in which the motif first appears turns up only two more times, while the form ♫ ♫♫♫ | ♫ ♪ appears no less than seven times. Bach has thus managed to free himself from the almost cramped condition of a limit of forty-two bars and shown a great variety in the shortest period of time. This he does by conveying the thought that "the theme" is not to be defined simply as the motif in its first appearance as the four notes, GGDG, but is even more to be defined by a range of rhythms. Of the fourteen appearances of the motif in one form or another only one revives the actual pitches of the opening bar and only one other repeats verbatim the time values of the first four notes. The remarkable thing here is the range of variety, but very carefully controlled, in a very short stretch of time.

de la Motte further draws our attention to the ratio between the number of eighth and of sixteenth notes. The sixteenths are used both for structural and for melodic purposes. The former is illustrated in the implicit chords in bars 31, 32, 33. The smaller more melodic intervals and the broader are nicely mingled even in the same bar, e.g., 15, 39–41, and elsewhere. The movement is basically not in rapid time, but the shift to sixteenths facilitates the gain in what we may call apparent speed. de la Motte in fact seeks to show that there is an increasing tendency toward this apparent acceleration, so that in the last dozen bars there is only rapid motion, whereas when the motif is presented at the opening the time is often but half (in eighths) of what it tends toward as we proceed. Reckoning the bars in which the motif appears as against those on which, as he puts it, there is a "power balance in favor of the sixteenths" (*Machtgewinn der Sechzehntel*), we have fourteen bars of the former compared to twenty-eight of the latter. This he characterizes with what appears to me to be considerable exaggeration as the downgrading of the motif and the rise of the motion in sixteenths to prominence, *Degradierung des Motivs und Krönung der Sechzehntelbewegung.*

This point is important and deserves a different interpretation from our standpoint. As we have seen, the notion of figure and ground, or emergent and recedent, can be and indeed must be given an interpretation suitable to the time arts as well as the space arts. The first consequence of any such notion is of course the necessary complementarity of the two notions. A emerges in view of the recedence of B, and conversely. What we have then in the Bach Courante is this. The motif appears and reappears in some fourteen of the forty-two bars. Since nothing counts as a true secondary motif, the twenty-eight non-thematic bars should be observed carefully to see whether in fact they are not meant to be recedent and groundal. (Since we have only one melodic line or voice here, it must bear both the figure and the ground since there is no homophonic "accompaniment.") When we do so the recedence of the twenty-eight bars becomes apparent. They are not without interest in themselves but they verge toward "tolerable monotony" — tolerable since we hear such measures as recedent and not as figural. Even casual inspection shows that the twenty-eight bars harbor monotonies that more commonly appear in grounds and may superficially remind us of the Alberti bass. (The Alberti bass is a true tolerable monotony but it is more characteristic of work later in the century rather than that of Bach's time.) We suggest that a truer interpretation of them would be as *toccata* figurations, which Bach is very fond of. This is how these otherwise groundal figures can here appear in an otherwise emergent voice. They have also a strong air of decorating cadences and approaches to cadences.

The first such device that appears is saved from monotony because it is short, but more importantly because there is tendence in it that moves quickly on to the next bar or to something that can serve as a terminus. In bars 5 to 8 we move quickly from V to I to V to I. In short, a cadence.

After the cadence in 7–8, the principal motif returns again and then the toccata figure reappears, this time for at least five full bars. de la Motte characterizes the cadential fall, with an interesting delay at 14, as a development that "tumbles over itself breathlessly." Strong lines of continuity and development set in at 14. Here the motion is relentlessly forward as the last notes of the figure in sixteenths drive toward the cadence; comparably in the second part, from 36 on, there is an exact parallel of this toward the final cadential development.

Whether we now regard the development after the cadence in 8 as altogether groundal, or as a kind of secondary motif in toccata style, there can be no doubt that the importance of the main theme has been enhanced, not diminished, by this. As we saw very early in Part One, a figure most effectively dominates when it is neither overdominant nor underdominant, either in quantity and extent or in its qualities. I must, therefore, disagree with de la Motte's notion that the briefer space accorded in the motif here entails the "downgrading of the motif and the rise of the motion in sixteenths to prominence."

After the double bar, a similar pattern appears but it is longer, and more animated, or as de la Motte puts it, more dramatic. This is true both of the motif and the toccata sequence. The motif now reappears eight times in five different transformations and in different keys. It thus appears ever in a new light. Similarly, the passages in sixteenths are virtually twice as long as in the first part. The height of agitation is reached just before the last four cadential bars are reached. With these stability and rest are restored.

de la Motte draws attention to the unique role played by three bars in the Courante. Bar 14 would ordinarily serve to conclude a four-bar phrase such as has begun in 11. With 14, however, a new phrase begins, this time of five bars. Hence the preceding phrase has one fewer and the second phrase one bar more than what normally accrues here. Thus 14 is a kind of pivot, or we might say an ambiguous measure. The effect is one of further animating the movement at this point.

But if the action only pivoted here, the result would be a cadence in 16. de la Motte suggests this might conceivably read as follows:

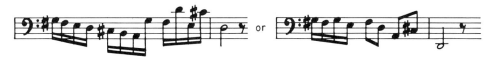

Instead, however, the close is reached only in 18. Thus, one phrase has been robbed of a bar and the second has gained one, with the vitality of the movement enhanced thereby.

Similarly, at the comparable point in the second part (bar 36 as compared with 14), we may expect the preceding phrase to come to a cadence in 36. Instead a new four-bar phrase *begins* in 36 and with the trill in 38 we expect a close in 39. Again, instead of a close, another phrase begins, ending at 42. Thus, there are two more pivots or ambiguous turns in the second part, namely, in 36 and in 29. All this, says de la Motte and perhaps rightly, increases the energy of movement at these points.

We have in this work the record of a kind of effort to transcend the very medium in which it is written. Many demands must be met and are met. Bach elects to define his tonality by a chordal framework, but without resort to explicit chords (there is only one double stop), supplemented by a scalar and smaller interval development compatible with this. Where the main motif is large and muscular, the secondary development lean in the direction of suppleness and motion.

The sections are not merely laid alongside one another in contrasting fashion. Similarities in all the figuration comes readily into view. There is already a hint of sonata form emerging out of binary in that the principal figure undergoes important transformations immediately after the double bar. There is, however, no formal reprise of any sort.

As we look back over the types of relation we have developed in Part One, we see virtually all of them illustrated here. Figures emerging from, or being set off from, their grounds and yet remaining related to them are illustrated in principal and secondary motifs. The same figures are partly altered by subtle changes in composition but also simply from finding themselves in a variety of contexts constituted by several keys in which they may appear. There is virtually no slavish imitation anywhere in the Courante: each bar has a kinship or resemblance to some other but it remains itself in its own place. The power of tendence is supplied most often by motions or cadences, but also by direct scalar lines, for example, in 14–15 and 36–37. And still other applications may readily be made.

(2) *Beethoven: Sonata for Piano in D. Major, Op. 28*

First movement

We must be prepared for surprises when we seek out examples of what we call development. One of the first and most obvious places in which to look is, of course, the middle or development section of movements in sonata form: not only sonatas, of course, but in various sorts of classical (or neo-classical) movements or works having this form, e.g., overtures.

If we suppose that development is, as we have said, a kind of growing or growth, we may readily expect to encounter an expansion or enlargement of the materials used. But we find that Beethoven has done just the opposite in the development section of the Piano Sonata in D Major, Op. 28. My analysis is indebted to the suggestions thrown out by Leichtentritt in his *Formenlehre*.

The middle or development section in this sonata confines its attention largely to the ten-bar phrase or clause with which the movement opens. It is restated at the outset of this section in the key of G but closes in G minor (bars 167 to 186). After the principal theme reappears, Beethoven begins to confine his attention to it in an unusual manner. Instead of breaking up themes and motifs as he often does in order to transform, reconstitute, and recombine them, he here simply devotes an ever more careful attention to smaller and smaller parts of the theme. It is true, as Debussy said in his essay on the symphony, that second sections often seem "to take place in an experimental laboratory." In the present movement we have a motif which is being ever more closely viewed as if it were being put under a magnifying glass. One should add that although Beethoven has progressively divided the original theme, he has really not maimed it but only turned an ever brighter light upon it.

Beginning in bar 183, the final four bars of the theme read:

There immediately follow three further versions of this motif: first in the treble, then twice in the bass (bars 187 to 198). This is accompanied by a ceaseless running figure in eighths in the hand opposite the theme.

Beethoven has now abbreviated the first phrase (10 bars) of the main theme to four bars; "abbreviated" here means that he has confined attention to four bars only. Now he confines our attention to an even smaller aspect of it. The first two bars of the four fall away and we hear

and thereupon the same figure an octave lower in the left hand. After a variant of this in the same rhythm is heard three times, with accompanying running eighths knitting everything together, a further condensation is undertaken. Now the figure loses in effect the second bar. The result is a one-bar figure resembling bar 199 in rhythm that runs for some ten bars variously transformed in the treble, then in the bass for another ten with a variant of the figure in a higher voice, and then in a yet deeper bass for still another ten. Thereupon the entire figure is as it were reduced to a single chord, the tonic F# major, arrayed in a colonnade of chords running for nearly a score of bars, ending in a *fermata*. From this point, Beethoven extricates himself deftly from F# major via B major and B minor with brief and passing reference to the motif of the episode in the exposition. In a dozen bars we are on the dominant A, prepared for the recapitulation in the tonic D, the standard procedure in sonata form.

We may now seek to relate the techniques of this section to the types of unification we have had under general consideration. Here our interest must concentrate on certain smaller motifs. Beethoven's genius with such miniature motifs should be familiar to anyone who has ever heard the Fifth Symphony. The figure reappears in the Development Section about forty times, and these are prominant and not at all hidden mentions of it. Thus the unifying device in this section is principally repetition varied by a progressive apocopation:

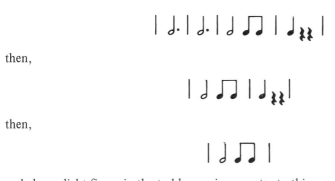

then,

then,

and also a slight figure in the treble running counter to this:

finally, in the bass

 etc.

Given the general limits and scope of what counts in the earlier Beethoven as a *sonata*, certain things are generally to be expected in the middle portion of a first movement since, in fact, Beethoven generally takes some trouble to observe (but also to break!) the "canons." What is expected in mid-movement is development. But what counts as development? Generally, this runs to a kind of musical "deduction" from the phrases and clauses of the exposition. The exposited material appears in new keys, combined in ways the composer did not permit himself in the exposition: detachment of parts or of themes or of motifs to "observe" or to exhibit them more closely, juxtaposition of main subject with secondary subjects or other detail, even the introduction of what is in effect new material.

None of these is exactly what is offered in the present movement. To be sure, there is repetition of exposition material to the extent that the main theme is immediately quoted almost verbatim except for a difference of key. Further, the development as it proceeds again takes off from the virtually *ipsissima verba* of the exposition. No essentially new rhythms are introduced. The motif that Beethoven develops most clearly is that which appeared in bars 9 and 10 of the exposition. He develops it by reflecting ever more deeply on its essence.

Referring to other categories of analysis developed earlier in our study, we may recall that the comparative, contextual, and tendentive relations of parts of elements in music are inherent in them; the composer cannot endow his materials with them any more than he can somehow create the *quality* green, by mixing blue and yellow *pigments*. All of these are, of course, present here. The *comparative* relations are illustrated by differences of pitch when motifs or themes are shifted from key to key, differences of *intensity* occur when the performer is asked to shift from p to pp or from f to ff, etc., of *duration* when the comparative time of a motif is spaced out or shortened. The contextual relations are exhibited in the different auditory look or feel that motifs have depending upon whether they appear in original or other keys, or in the treble or bass, and so on. Their *tendentive* powers are revealed in this instance largely in the movement set up by key modulation, by what we feel as we are led towards a key or hear it being established: for example, the scale passage beginning in bars 157–162 (at the end of the Exposition) points definitely toward the key in which the Development Section begins, G. Other expectations depend upon momentums such as those generated by rhythms.

What we now find that the composer has done, and not the materials themselves, is to elect to repeat certain things shown in the exposition, and to develop them either in accordance with a plan he has or in any way the spirit moves him to act, when he addresses himself to the task of developing.

Beethoven seeks to maintain a grand design in this section and to suit every part of the section to every other part. It is he who has elected to draw out of these themes and motives their consequence, their meanings, and the consequences are limitless. It is romantic nonsense to say, as has so often been done, that great composers like Beethoven always devise the "only conceivable solution" to their problems. The most we can ask is that the solutions they did offer are in fact convincing, that they are not trivial, but pregnant with power and with food for reflection.

In the light of this, Beethoven's solution is thoroughly apt, convincing, and powerful. We are invited to focus attention first on the whole main theme at the beginning of the development, then on four measures of it, then on two, then on one, and we are finally left musing on a single, and for this context, rich, if not exotic chord. It is as if we had somehow made our way to the heart or brain that animates a living body.

We must, at the same time, consider Beethoven's procedure also in another light, lest we fall to thinking that he has here shifted the focus on ever more confined and perhaps trivial detail. The power of "doing something with" these materials in the Development Section must not only defeat boredom (other hands might have offered a mere re-hash of them), but reach a peak of tension and expectancy when we are presented once again with the main theme in its primary form in the Recapitulation that follows the quoted passage. In this, I think we must say that the composer succeeds. We can understand it a little better when we telescope the motions and rhythms of the development section:

Beginning with the line of the main theme as it appears at the beginning of the Development (bar 168 et seq.) and confining ourselves solely to the rhythmic aspect, which is here most prominent we find the development section to consist of a theme that is progressively being reduced in size.

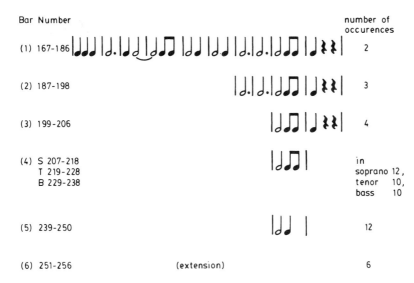

Bar Number		number of occurences
(1) 167-186		2
(2) 187-198		3
(3) 199-206		4
(4) S 207-218 T 219-228 B 229-238		in soprano 12, tenor 10, bass 10
(5) 239-250		12
(6) 251-256	(extension)	6

In (4) the syncopation that appeared first in bar 3 of (1) is reintroduced collaterally in two different forms, |♩♩|, and |𝄽♩♪|, and played against |♩♩|. In (5), |♩♪| subsides to |♩♩| which, of course, appeared in bar 5 of (1). The syncopation continues and the two motifs together produced a rocking motion that subsides gently to a *fermata* (a conclusion, here chordal, either relative or final).

One should also be aware of the apparent acceleration in the motion from the diminution in the phrase length, which seems calculated precisely to stay ahead of our inclination to weary of the repetition. At the same time dynamics are allowed to rise from p to ff after (4). Remaining for some time on this climactic peak there is a descent to pp at the end of (5) in 256. In this way interest is easily maintained.

This, then, is one way in which what we have singled out as continuity and development may be maintained. Repetition is incorporated in this particular device, but since by definition repetition is not development, we must think of it as simply an incidental support for it. The thematic material and its repeated fragments have the largest share in sustaining the unity of the section. The factors that make for development, that is, growth, are the direction provided by the progressive definition of the motif, the rise and fall of the dynamic development, the harmonic evolution toward the fermata, and the culmination in pitch at bars 216, 217, 218 from which there is a long somewhat undulant descent to the close of the Development Section in bar 268.

To praise this masterful work is not so much to add to Beethoven's repute, as to congratulate oneself for grasping some of its secrets.

(3) *Beethoven: Concerto for Piano in E♭ Major, Op. 73 (The "Emperor")*

Beethoven's fifth and last piano concerto is evidently a work of the most durable fabric to survive its almost ceaseless reappearances on concert and radio programs. Even if it should prove to be wise to lay it aside for a few years this might say little about its inherent musical value. Not the least reason for singling it out for the present discussion is the remarkable freshness with which the principal theme of the final movement, especially the opening motif, renews itself in its every repetition. We can also see displayed many procedures that composers can command to realize their thoughts. Since in fact there is far more than I can here bring to the surface, I shall forego any effort at a complete analysis.

The last movement is a brilliant echo of the first and a steep contrast to the middle movement. Both first and last movements are in E♭ major, a key that Beethoven also selected for his Eroica Symphony. For the intervening *adagio* he selects the distant key of B major and a complete change of mood: what precedes and follows is to be played with the greatest bravura. At the end of the *adagio* he proceeds to the *rondo* without pause and without elaborate modulation out of B major, or in fact any modulation at all. The middle movement comes to rest on B, played pianissimo in unison by about half the instruments. When the bassoons, which are here sustaining this B softly for a bar, drop to B♭, joined by the strings *pizzicato* and the horns, the last movement in effect begins. The organ point on B♭ in the horns keeps us poised for the surprise that is to follow and is held well into the next movement. B♭ is, of course course, the dominant that will lead us inevitably to the tonic E♭ of the last movement. The solo instrument enters softly, sketching out a few breaths of the approaching theme with the greatest restraint, and hovers on the dominant B♭ for some moments longer.

The theme of the final movement then begins with an explosive suddenness and force that is concentrated in a singular jagged rhythmic motif that ascends instantly with an air of triumph. The touch of syncopation in it must be rendered with complete ease and an exact sense of the tempo. Its inimitable quality is unique even among Beethoven's characteristic short meaningful motifs.

The strategy of the movement is not complex, but the principal theme is unusual in appearing in the middle of the movement five times running before the second theme is permitted to reappear. The frequent recurrences of the principal theme underline the *rondo* quality of the movement, but it is not at all a typical *rondo*, as we can see from the following outline.

A Main theme: E-flat major – Piano. Followed by orchestra (first violins and woodwinds carrying the theme). (Beginning in bar 83. Numbering begins with the first bar of the Second Movement, which leads uninterruptedly to the Third.)

B Second theme (or set of themes): E-flat major – Piano. Moving to B-flat major in closing episode. (131ff.)

A Main theme: E-flat major – Piano. The development that leads out of this key proceeds first to the relative minor (C minor) then to the dominant (G) of this key, which leads just as readily to C major (176ff.)

A Main Theme: C major – Piano. Here, as often elsewhere, the theme is stated only in part. This episode is brief but brilliant, as explained below. Modulation to the next key A♭ is effected by the horns sounding an E♭ octave softly. This

E♭ is both normal and surprising here. It is the hallmark of the key of C minor, which appeared briefly a few moments back. It is also the dominant of the next key in which the piano now states the main theme. (220ff.)

A Main theme: A-flat major – Piano. This is again a brief version of the theme. It is followed by an abrupt change to the next key, a surprising E major! This is effected by the second violins, which sound A-flat, or enharmonically G♯, the all-important third degree of E major. Thereupon, the oboe and bassoon suddenly shift up a minor third to B natural, the dominant of the next key, E major. (This exactly parallels the previous shift of key where the viola sounded a C natural and the horn answered a minor third higher on E♭, the dominant of the following key, A-flat.) (244ff.)

A Main theme: E major – Piano. Statement in this distant key offers still another version of the theme. It proves to be just as effective played *pianissimo* as it did *fortissimo* in other keys. Chromatic scales, trills, and broad arpeggios are heard. A complex modulation leads within three bars to the dominant of the home key. (271ff.)

A Main theme: E-flat major – Piano. We now hear the main theme in the original key. It has appeared uninterruptedly in four distinct keys. This return is now beginning what is in effect a recapitulation section. It repeats very closely the short introduction that preceded the opening of the movement (this time in the strings). A long trill some ten or twelve bars then ushers in the theme. Once again only the horn is sounded against the soloist. Thus the movement, although it is marked *Rondo*, has something of sonata form in it, where the development section is devoted to working over the theme in five different keys. (328ff.)

B Second theme: E-flat major – Piano. The second theme appears in the original key but the closing episode in bar 314 now appears in B-flat instead of F. (376ff.)

A Main theme: A-flat major – Piano. The principal theme makes yet another appearance, this time in A-flat major. Since this is the subdominant of the main key, we expect a modulation to be effected for the return. Instead, after some chromatic passages the subdominant in effect simply vanishes, E♭ is strongly affirmed and the movement continues with further interesting development particularly of the closing fragments of the main theme in the rhythm (423ff.)

A A colonnade of some eight bars of subtly shaded chords leads to a final cadenza-like passage and still another recollection of the theme in the strings at the end. (507ff.)

It would be difficult to pick out particular passages from this movement as being more splendid in structure and in sheer power than others. I would, however, draw attention to the effect made by the shifting of keys in the middle of the movement. After the principal theme or motif has been thoroughly expounded, it seems evident that it is of so unique if not idiosyncratic a character that development of it, even in Beethoven's manner, is out of the question. What could one *do* with such a motif, one may ask, that would not ruin it? Of course, since this is nominally a *rondo*, the kind of development appropriate to sonata form is not really "obligatory." Transformation, however, has certainly occurred, as we have seen, and the ingenious wide-ranging key structure (from E♭ to E and return!) must in our general sense of the term be regarded as *development*. The unique motif of the movement has the effect of *closure*, in a relative sense. The judicious use of *repetition*, carefully varied, is of course evident everywhere.

We seem to need to coin a mixed category of "transformed repetition" to account for this movement. One can count some eight "official" recurrences of the theme that appears at the outset and some dozens of appearances of the motif of its opening bars.

It etches itself upon the mind almost as if it were a mere "tune," even on minds of those who can scarcely whistle a tune. Considering the numerous reappearances of the motif one sees that only its strength and durability prevent our tiring of it. This, however, is not left to chance by the composer. After we have the theme clearly in mind the composer undertakes to exhibit it to us in several different "lights," that is, keys. These should be unmistakable to anyone who attends carefully. Thus Beethoven, as if he were mindful of the difficulty most persons have in hearing a shift in key, changes the keys in the development section with some rapidity — the more abrupt the better, in order to underscore the change, make it more noticeable. We cannot fail to catch the effect of shifting the key from E♭ to C: where the motif in the first key begins on B♭ and then rises through E♭, G, and B♭ to E♭, in the second it begins a huge major sixth higher, rising from G through C, E, G to C, high in the leger lines, and gains a kind of luminous quality with this transposition.

In order to derive the maximum effect from a shift in key, discrimination will be improved greatly if the shifts are not timed so far apart that the ear loses the recollection of what was previously present. Thus the last statement of the theme in E♭ occurred forty measures prior to the shift to C major, but after only twenty-four measures in C it appears in A♭. An almost equal time is then allotted to the statement in A♭ whereupon the E major version of it begins. After a similar length of time in E major the transition to what we have called the "recapitulation" begins. Some twenty-four measures are then devoted to effecting the reintroduction of the theme in E♭. The whole cycle is E♭-C-A♭-E-E♭. The appearance of the theme in these exotic keys is a perfect example of what we have called a contextual alteration. We see the motif and theme turned now this way, now that, in this light and in another. After some four or five contexts have been provided we have gained a new insight into the theme.

The concerto enables us to illustrate virtually all of the types of relation and artistic procedure we have discussed. Figure and ground are illustrated in virtually any kind of homophonic music such as this. The figure of the main theme or motif and the figure of the subordinate themes as well, emerge most commonly because they form the upper profile of the tonal mass. Elaborate grounds are provided for the figural appearance of theme or motif, the middle and lower registers usually serving as accompaniments. A glance at the left-hand part of the solo at the opening of the rondo shows a persistent and essentially monotonous accompaniment to the theme, consisting of two deep bass notes (E♭ for the tonic, B♭ for the dominant), each followed by harmonically significant chords. This structure is altogether supportive. It provides a fixed rhythm, an unambiguous harmony, and also a contrasting tonal mass as a ground for the figure. It should, however, be noted that when the figure is, as it were, offstages, there is little in the way of pounding rhythm, and far more or soaring fantasy — scale passages, octaves, arpeggios, but without cessation of the relentless rhythm.

We have seen elsewhere that grounds permit, tolerate, and even encourage monotony since their pulsations may maintain a kind of life for the figure even though they would be tedious if presented figurally themselves. In this concerto, the first figure of the bass occurs fourteen times over:

thereafter, the contour or rhythm, but not the harmony remains the same for another seven bars.

If we look next to the immediately following statement of the theme in the orchestra, we see even more emphatic examples of monotony in the vertical ground or recedent. The second violin part is given over to mere support of the harmony while the first violin is according the privilege of sounding the theme along with the woodwinds. The second violin is asked to play a double stop, B♭–G, a monotonous twelve times in each bar. The monotony is broken, but only slightly, by the alteration of this to B♭–A♭ and B♭–F occasionally. A glance at the page shows many examples of monotony that even a musically unschooled person can readily locate. It is safe to say that no single page of this concerto is free of dull chores such as this for some part of the orchestra. Without them the finished "picture" as we know it would not exist at all.

Turning back to the principal voice, usually the soloist, or the first violin (or one of the higher woodwinds, or more rarely the bassoon, cello, or trumpet), we must now observe another type of recedence besides the "vertical" monotony supplied by the supporting accompanists. This is recedence in the "horizontal" sense and what it means is that the prime figure is not permitted to display itself ceaselessly. Periods of silence for this figure are absolutely essential to its emergence at all. Thus after the soloist here has spoken for more than a dozen bars, he falls silent and a very brief and unobtrusive passage of two bars is heard in the lower strings. This is not intended to hold our attention, but to give it a rest. It is a very tiny version of what is called a bridge-passage. The name explains itself. Upon this there follows a statement of the principal theme in which all the voices participate except the soloist, who is given a rest for nearly thirty bars (until bar 124). Thus, from the accompanist's standpoint, the whole orchestra, or at least the woodwinds and the first violins, are now accorded the privilege of presenting the emergent, the figure. The privilege extends only until the solo instrument appears again. Hence, from the standpoint of the solo voice, as the concerted or emergent voice, the performance of the full orchestra without this voice has itself and a groundal function.

A hierarchy of emergent figures with their respective grounds is provided for to insure that the most momentous utterances shall be heard in a context, and with a suitable ground to perform the tasks of providing rhythm and harmony which the prime figure cannot itself provide. A hierarchic principle is sedulously observed by capable and experienced composers. For obviously if they think they have something worth saying they also wish it to be heard to the best advantage. Not all of even those whom we regard as competent composers are equally adept at orchestration or in agreement about distributing appropriate tasks to the various choirs or divisions of the orchestra.

We may observe the division or labor even in the (multiple) voice which has here been assigned to the soloist. On this occasion the composer seems to delay starting the second theme of the movement as if waiting to gain everyone's attention for it. The piano is assigned some seven bars that serve mainly to heighten our expectancy. The piano runs up and down the scale of E♭ major, on each run rising a bit higher to a peak three octaves above middle C (bar 130). After a brief descent, precisely calculated in its length or duration we are prepared for something more interesting than the scale of E♭ major.

The subordinate theme now enters (bar 131). It is not at all as momentous as the first nor is it intended to be. A certain rank generally prevails among themes where several appear in a single movement. Just as some material, brief or more extended, serves merely as a bridge from one theme to another, so themes themselves assume positions as figures and grounds in relation to one another. This is the "horizontal" application of the figure ground principle. The second theme of this movement serves in the capacity of a ground in relation to the massively dominant theme around which the movement is built.

We have even another theme, or an extension or episode of the second theme, that is introduced by the solo voice, beginning at bar 149. This introduces important material that is heard again later on but its significance is not so evident at first. It gives way to a passage of some ten bars that is of rather more pyrotechnical brilliance than one would expect in a mere transition to thematic material. In fact, however, the principle theme when it appears easily outdoes the brilliance of this and all such passages through the greater authenticity of its splendor. The opening theme is the message the composer wishes to leave with us and he now proceeds to drive it home with every resource at his command; changes of key, changes of register, changes of context and accompaniment, changes of dynamics, contrasts of thematic episodes, alternate presentation of materials in different choirs of the orchestra, escalations to climaxes, and more. Finally, before the end there are a few subdued moments that promote reflection on our part before the overwhelming final cadence. Even here the orchestra declaims the message once more. From all of it we learn how masters like Beethoven prove to us that they have deserved a half hour or more of our time.

It is now evident that Beethoven uses and chooses this musical material because in fact it is inherently endowed with certain powers, capacities, properties, and effects. In our discussion earlier we distinguished between the comparative, contextual, and tendentive powers of the materials of art on the one hand, and on the other, the disposition of these materials by the artist who orders them in complexes of his own devising and lends them whatever order or disorder he wishes. His creativity extends only to the latter. He can use or avoid the use of materials, he can break them, re-order them, and place them in various relations to one another. But he is powerless to endow them with even a single quality that they do not inherently possess. He is therefore a kind of steward looking to the best uses of his materials that he can imagine. This is the extent of his creativity.

Nothing illustrates this better than the works of Beethoven. Others may avoid the use of materials that suited Beethoven or they may neglect properties of these materials that interested him and attend to others. In our century composers have tried to ignore the properties that tones have by virtue of their overtones, properties which were treated as the sole source of the tendentive powers of musical tones, particularly harmonic connections, by the classical harmonists and the composers of the great tradition from 1600 to 1900. Tones have these powers as much today as ever they had, but they have for complex reasons lost their interest for composers, or at least a very different interest is taken in them. Their response of course must be to *discover* sources of tendence elsewhere, since this is clearly the kind of power that no one can conceivably *invent*, but above all since time compositions must have inner bonds, connections, or tendences. The new composers must therefore hope to uncover hitherto unknown properties that will serve this purpose in tones or content themselves with those that three centuries of practice proved them to have. It would be simply too self-destructive to deny oneself the use of them simply because one wants to differentiate oneself from his forbears. At the same time, those who have rigorously practiced this kind of "harmonic self-denial" have revealed some genuine new possibilities in the twelve classical intervals and tones. We shall next attend to a composer who has elected to follow the latter course.

(4) *Arnold Schoenberg, Klavierstück, Op. 33a*

This Klavierstück dates from 1929 when Schoenberg was well along in the development of the twelve-tone technique. Op. 33b is also a piano composition but did not appear until 1932. Our discussion does not undertake to show how 33a fits into Schoenberg's development as a composer, but rather to see how a composer who abandons tonality (key) manages to maintain unity and coherence.

Schoenberg's technique of serial composition calls for the use of a kind of theme constructed in accord with a self-imposed rule. In general, such a theme, or tone row, must contain all the twelve tones of the octave and none should appear in a given row more than one. After such a row or series is presented it may be inverted, reversed (or both), and subjected to various other transformations in the process of composition. Very often serial compositions are linear and contrapuntal in character.

The present composition employs the twelve tones but is rather less contrapuntal than many others in this idiom. It uses chords and arpeggios in a conspicuous way, the initial statement of the twelve-tone figure being made with a sequence of three chords of four tones each in which a tone row is implicit. This is followed immediately by a second sequence of three chords, constructed in the reverse and inverse order of the first sequence. For our purposes, the analysis in terms of the row is of less importance than the recurrence of the original chords. Although these chords sound somewhat unfamiliar the classic dominant seventh chord appears among them, being the chord number 5 in the first sequence. It is not, however, easy to hear it as a dominant in this context since, of course, Schoenberg does not use it as part of a cadence, which elsewhere would be one of its standard functions.

KLAVIERSTÜCK

ARNOLD SCHOENBERG, Op. 33a

KLAVIERSTÜCK

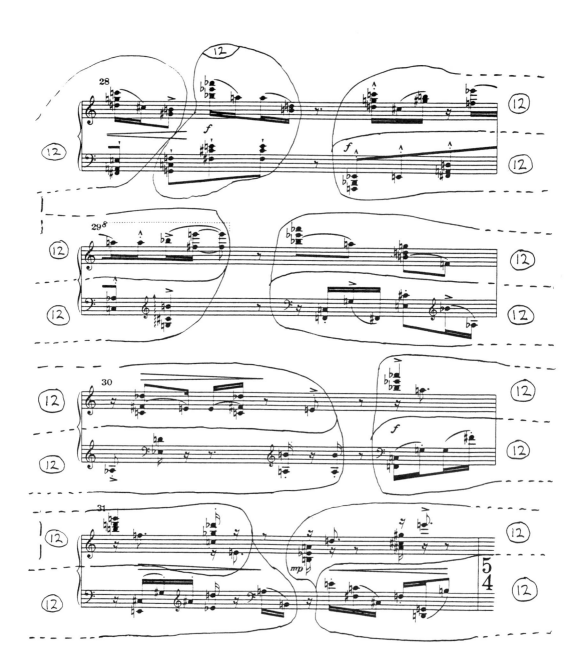

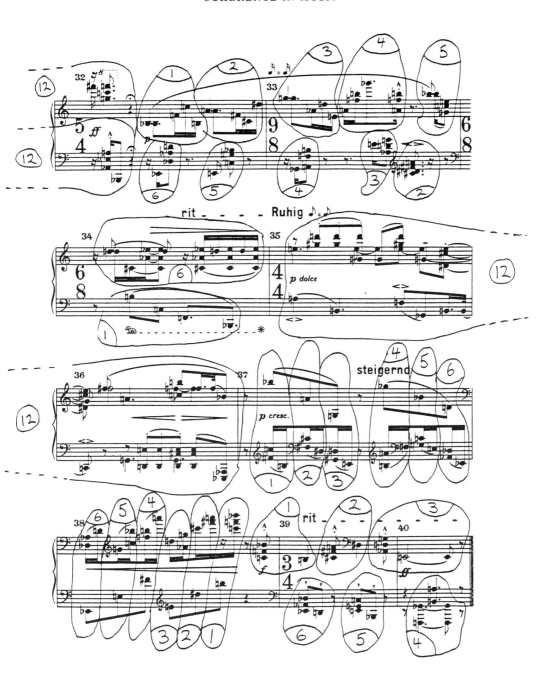

When we observe the construction of the chords closely, a mirror symmetry comes to light. The intervals stratified in the chords are these:

1	2	3	4	5	6
perfect 4	minor 3	minor 3	tritone	major 3	minor 2
perfect 4	major 2	major 2	major 2	major 2	perfect 4
minor 2	major 3	tritone	minor 3	minor 3	perfect 4

Thus, the superposition of intervals in the second three chords is the reverse of that in the first three (6 reverses 1, 5 reverses 2, etc.). I have marked the recurrences of all the six chords throughout; one can also identify other occurrences of them on other degrees of the scale. For example, chord 1 appears prominently not only in the (ascending) order B, C, F, B♭, but rising from C♯ and from A in bars 27 to 30 with the appropriate intervals.

From our system of marking we see that the chords reappear literally only once: in bar 10 and 11 they stand in the order 1, 6, 2, 5, 3, 4, and then in the reverse order 4, 3, 5, 2, 6, 1. But even when they appear in freer form their order is anything but random. In bars 3, 4, and 5, we hear chord 4 against 3, 5 against 2, 6 against 1. (For convenience we may represent these like a numerator and a denominator: 4/3, 5/2, 6/1.) The first group runs 4, 5, 6, the second 3, 2, 1. The next two bars present the same chordal material seriatim: 1, 2, 3, 4, 5, 6. The page ends in 1/6, 1/6, 2/5, 3/4. For melodic and perhaps other reasons, Schoenberg takes the liberty to repeat individual notes but only in close succession or reiteration. There are no closely adjacent notes in these first nine bars that do not belong to one of the six chord systems.

Bars 12 to 15, harmonically, already construe the initial chordal scheme rather more liberally in the sense that components of the chords lie somewhat scattered. In bars 12 and 13, chords 6, 5, and 4 appear in the soprano voice, and 1, 2, and 3 in the lower register. In bars 14 and 15, chord 1 occurs four times in the soprano and in parts of the intermediate (alto?) voice. In these bars, chord 4 seems to be tucked away twice in the alto. In the bass, chord 6 is stretched over the two bars.

Beginning in bar 16, the basic chords reappear only occasionally, or at other degrees of the scale, or do not appear at all, until we reach bar 32, where a kind of reprise sets in. We see them fairly explicitly in bars 16, 17, 18, and elsewhere at other degrees than the original. In general, the procedure from bar 13, or even 12, to 31, is not based on the specific chords, but is something else. Schoenberg now works in larger units, which for want of a better term I shall call "twelves," determined by the 12 chromatic tones as a whole. Thus bars 19 and 20 use every one of the 12 tones, but the order in which they appear is not that of the first six chords. In order for the chords to be truly repeated or to recur, the tones must lie together or in each other's very near vicinity.

Our lines of division of the twelves seem to be in a certain sense arbitrary. In fact, however, if we draw them in conformity to the phrasing, we find one distinct group of twelves after another: when all of the 12 tones have appeared the phrase also comes to a fairly natural end or break, and a new 12 begins. We may separate the notes for the player's two hands as if they were two voices; there is little or none of the interlocking of upper, middle, and lower registers such as appeared in bars 12 through 18. Where, however, there are strong chord statements, the "vertical" prevails over the "horizontal" organization. This occurs in bar 27: in a span of fewer than four beats two 12's appear, since the two hands strike as many as six tones at a time. (These chords are not drawn from the original six.) In bars 28 to 31 chords appear more as parts of voices than of colonnades as in 27.

After a major climax is reached at bar 32, we revert to ideas similar to those presented at the beginning and a reprise begins. The 12 chords reappear in strict order, although there seems to be a slight anomaly in the bass of bar 36. We begin in 32 with a progression from one to six in the right hand and a retrograde order in the left: 1/6, 2/5, 3/4, 4/3, 5/2, 6/1. Two bars are then slightly irregular. In 37 the most explicit order obtains: 1, 2, 3, 4, 5, 6, followed by 6, 5, 4, 3, 2, 1. The last two bars read 1/6, 2/5, 3/4.

Thus the components are ordered in a very strict fashion. The counterpoint is strictly adapted to the powers of the piano, often as a kind of percussion instrument. The unique capacity for chords on a keyboard instrument is exploited thoroughly. The instrument is also asked to play legato, to hold tones in a "singing" manner (in the *cantabiles*), and to exhibit the basic chords cohesively even when they are broken into parts.

We may next consider the broader formal organization and also the general character the work appears to have and the impression it makes. Using such guides as the tempo markings, the phrasing, and the inner contrasts, we may observe the following organization:

Bar	Marking	Features
1–9	*Mässig: cantabile*	First subject: Colonnade of chords and the articulation of their tones.
10–11	*A tempo*	Double statement of the first subject: chords in order 1, 6, 2, 5, 3, 4, and the reverse.
12–13	*Poco rit., molto rit.*	As in the later instances a *ritardando* precedes a short *cantabile* section.
14–18	*A tempo, cantabile*	A single line here brings in a second subject. Cool and detached.
19–20	*Heftiger, martellato*	The foregoing cantabile leads to a more animated episode, ending abruptly.
21–24	*Ruhiger, cantabile, ritardando* at end	This is reminiscent of the first cantabile in spirit. The section draws on the entire 12-tone range but without reference to the 6 basic chords.
25–31	*A tempo, energisch; dolce,* and *scherzando* give way to *steigernd* (escalating). Bars 27–31 are mostly *forte*.	This is a developmental section in which the animation mounts fairly steadily. Basic chords are not employed, but each phrase has a 12-tone range.
32	*Fortissimo*	The foregoing subsection reaches a very high climax, a kind of "dominant." Fermata.

Bar	Marking	Features
32–40	*Piano, ritardando, Ruhig, dolce*, toward the end *steigernd* to a *fortissimo* close.	Opens with a 3/8 rhythm that for a moment is reminiscent of a 19th-century *concert-* or *salon-valse*. Then a quiet third third section *dolce* suggesting the two previous cantabiles.
37–38	*Steigernd*	A rapidly mounting tension with rising pitch.
39–40	*Ritardando*, f to ff.	A close that simulates a firm cadence.

Looking back we see some three or four important developments. After the opening subject is worked out there are two *cantabiles* that are brief and similar in character (there is a rather similar *dolce* in 35). Each of these is preceded by a *ritardando* and in fact all the *ritardandos* (except the final "cadence") are followed by such singing episodes. The *ritardandos* and the *dolce-cantabiles* provide a full contrast to passages that reaffirm the basic chords, which are emphatic or even percussive: *martellato*, that is, hammering. The bars preceding 32 are developmental and a recapitulation of a sort begins there.

Concerning the basic devices of unification nothing is more obvious than the repeated affirmation of the chords in various forms. They are colorful and unique, in no sense hackneyed. Repetition is inherent in the very fabric of the 12-tone system, and most-used device for unification. Its use in the present instance is, however, most prominent in the opening and the closing pages. The repetition in the latter is thus an instance of recurrence, and is, of course, most effectively placed at the end, supposing that we have not been wearied by it in the intervening time. Very roughly this suggests an ABA order, but with such different procedures that we must be careful not to confuse it with classical uses of this order.

Since there is no melodic theme or even motif, unification must be present, if at all in rhythmic or harmonic form. Since there is little in the way of rhythmic repetition, unity must principally be effected by harmonic means ("harmonic" is, of course, to be construed in a 12-tone sense). This is amply provided for, but the ear must at first diligently seek it out. (Schoenberg's music has sometimes been accused of "chaotic rhythm.")

Is there evidence of the use of the third family of devices open to the composer: continuity and development? This is a difficult question to answer and may, in any event, be passed on to the music theorist. We shall content ourselves with a few suggestions.

Certainly, the statement or use of the basic chords shows important changes. At first the chords are boldly presented in an interesting rise and descent. They are immediately developed through the device of displaying their components in arpeggios or broken chords. When they reappear in bars 10 and 11, their order has changed, each chord appears twice, and more is made of their rise and descent. As we proceed, there is a gradual dissolution of the clustering of the chord families.

The inner parts of the Klavierstück are rhythmic and vigorous, with characteristic large leaps. Some of the basic chords reappear momentarily but at other degree levels. Taken together with the free organization of the groups of twelves they contribute to the development of the subject. A contrast to earlier and later sections is thus effected. Certainly, one of the most salient aspects of development here is the single-minded thrust from about bar 25 or 27 that heads toward the climactic chord in 32. Excitement and "vocal" brilliance increase. This motion is handled in a masterly fashion.

The composer seems certainly to have succeeded in uniting this material, but the devices are, to the ear, extremely complex. The justification of the connections is often so tenuous, recondite, or erudite that it tends to elude the listener. Certainly, the composer does not pamper the audience. If I have taken so much trouble, you can take at least half as much, he seems to say.

Looking to the composition as a whole, after all of these seeming "mere technicalities" have been explored, we must ask, what of it? What is the sum of its being? The exterior appears as if it will remain forbidding indefinitely. It is not easy for anything of such complexity to receive the aid of the imagination to keep alive at the end what we heard at the beginning. Without its aid we are reduced to *having* the composition only when and while it is being played. I do not say this must be the outcome for all listeners, but it may well be so even for those who do have a significant amount of musical imagination. Being reduced to *having* a family of perceptual data only when they are realized in the organs of sense is exactly the situation we are in with respect to the extraaesthetic senses (as explained earlier). Schoenberg's idiom exposes itself to the danger of alienation from the imagination.

But there is no doubt of the composer's conviction that he was producing musical art. When he was asked why he did not write in a more familiar idiom, he is said to have replied, "I have been listening to something else." Since the justifications were clear in *his* mind there is no doubt that musicians can acquire the kind of familiarity with this music that enables it to be harbored by the imagination. But it is a musician's music and this is not at all true of Beethoven or Berlioz. All this is to be understood in a factual rather than an evaluative sense.

Although all kinds of difficulties present themselves with such music they scarcely demonstrate the state of chaos it is often charged with. There is scarcely any other musical idiom in which the composer takes greater care that his music be unified and coherent, that he be intelligible to all who will take the trouble to heed innumerable clues and cues. But the difficulties of it are created by the composer not by the listener. The composer chooses to forego a large part of the *tendentive* resources that are an intrinsic aspect of tones, while he retains other properties: rhythm, pitch, dynamics, timbre, contextually determined quality, and the organizational devices of isolation, repetition, and development. He denies himself the use of much of the natural powers of motion in tones and in fact his musical ideology dictates that he do everything he can to nullify them, as if they were mere conventions. If we have been correct in our study, such *tendences* are indefeasible aspects of tones. If so, then the inherent tendence of most tones in 12-tone music is likely to be opposed to the direction in which the *composer* (not the tones themselves) may be moving. This cannot but result in tension. This does not mean that every composer ought to return forthwith to a tonal medium but that he ought to be constantly and totally aware of the sources of tension because it now becomes in a sense a new part of the medium or a part of a new medium.

Of course, composers like Schoenberg were aware of this inner conflict or tension, and it is just because they are so aware of it that they took pains to compensate for the neglect or defiance of tonal tendence and sought other ways to maintain the life of their music and to assure its growth and development. If is safe to say that no composer has ever spoken more emphatically than Schoenberg in favor of unity, coherence, and formal vitality in music. It is precisely because he has sought to gain what we have called *justification* through the ear of one tonal entity in and through another entity that he has taken so many steps to try to ensure that the *ear* be satisfied in such a justification. The charge of "cerebralism" against such music is valid only if the *ear* never comes to a conviction of such justification.

As we saw at the very beginning of our study, the appeal in artworks is necessarily to be found either in elements or in forms or relations. Atonalism, even after sixty years, seems to many to defy both of these, offering us little that gratifies the ear either in the sheer richness and emotional magnetism of its tonal, intervallic, or chordal elements or in the gravitational movement in them. It espouses a more Spartan creed. It must, nevertheless, reckon with these same two appeals, for there are no others, and it must direct its effort to showing that they may be provided by other than the traditional means. It must waken in us the desire "to listen to something else."

I shall leave to critics and musicians themselves the decision whether the ear does or does not generally obtain satisfaction and justification in such music. It is not part of the philosophy of art to decide what shall be the medium or a part of the medium of any of the arts. If composers wish to dispense with the tendence of tones that derives from the overtone series they are free to do so. What they are not free to do, in my opinion, is to let their art speak incoherently and without appeal.

NOTES

[1] P. E. Vernon: 1934–35, 'Auditory Perception', *British Journal of Psychology* **25**, Parts 2 and 3, 123–129, 265–283.

[2] Robert U. Nelson: 1948, *The Technique of Variation*, University of California Press.

[3] J. A. Smith: 1984, 'The Ancient Synagogue, the Early Church and Singing', *Music and Letters*, p. 1ff.

[4] See Bibliography.

[5] One may also mention in this connection the appearance of Gloria VIII in Respighi's *Church Windows*. Its use, or misuse, there is scarcely anything more than decorative. The same needs to be said of his use of the opening phrases of the *Dies Irae* in his *Brazilian Impressions*.

[6] Diether de la Motte: 1968, *Musikalische Analyse*, Bärenreiter, Kassel.

[7] Tchaikovsky and Brahms are sometimes contrasted in this respect. The intervals in Brahms's melodies are generally those of chords. In Tchaikovsky's they are characteristically derived from scales.

CHAPTER 17

CONCLUSION: THE USES OF FORM

We may draw a few lessons from the range of examples, particularly those from the music of Europe of the past thousand years, cautioning ourselves with the reminder that we have lifted only a few drops from a great sea. We ask what our examples, when set alongside one another for comparison, teach us about the devices music employs to choose its elements and to knit them together.

We may first observe a rather profound difference between our examples of liturgical music and all the others. Beginning with the Bach example, we have something that is made to be represented and presented, to be borne before an audience. Although modern concerts do have something ritualistic about them this is not true of the music that is generally played at them. The performers are concerned to produce a result which must be thought of first of all from the standpoint of listeners, but communicants. The Mass and the Dies Irae, on the other hand, are meant not to be heard so much as overheard.[1] In them, the singer is first of all a suppliant of penitent. He is not creating a tableau for an audience, not even for a religious congregation. The religious song is an invocation of emotion (13.0), and since it is not a performance for an audience it is not made to evoke a particular emotion directed towards itself as a "work of art." It is meant to include everyone who is within earshot as himself a participant.

This bears directly on the manner in which ritual music is internally organized. It is, in general, necessary with musical works to increase the potency of climaxes as time elapses (not, of course, that they must get increasingly louder) in order to counteract any possible incipient *ennui* of the audience. But in a ritual, one does not count on feelings of this sort at all. If one is truly involved in the rite, one is bound to suppress them. One must participate fully in the rite, invoking and realizing its values and emotions: all else is, for the time being, an irrelevance or even an impiety. Escalating theatrical climaxes are not needed in order to justify the length of time the rite occupies. In fact, a certain monotony and repetition may well be in order if it will enforce a proper state of feeling in the participant, as may be seen in the Dies Irae and in the Kyrie and other movements of the Mass. Such procedure would almost certainly be thought inexcusable in the music of theater and entertainment. One need only look carefully at Verdi's characteristic and masterly treatment of the traditional movements of the *Missa pro Defunctis* to see how the sense of theater controls the course of the composition. Although in its own manner the religious feeling of his Requiem is altogether genuine, it evokes feelings towards itself as something being presented or played. Even the medieval morality play or Bach *Passion* has something of this character, but of course neither of these is an explicit part of a rite. The *thought* (in the sense used by Aristotle in the *Poetics*) of the rite is serious, dread, and awesome: it is an *action* not a theatrical *act*. The purpose of the Dies Irae is to have the soul here and now realize its grief and resignation, the only attitudes that befit it in the circumstance that is being celebrated. It is too serious a matter for a mere "work of art."

Of course, we here raise some aesthetic questions to which no solution is likely to be

233

propounded that will satisfy everyone. What should we say in answer to the question how noncommunicants can enter into and "appreciate" (to lean on this miserable but necessary term) complexes which invoke thoughts and feelings they cannot share at all? They seem to be driven to seeing or hearing them as "works of art," which, as we have said, in an important sense they are not. How shall a devout Jew or Moslem hear the Dies Irae? Or a Christian the Kaddish? In an ecumenical age, everyone tries to "appreciate" everything. But is or is not the aesthetic "use" of many of these things an inevitable misuse of them? Or must we now invoke a moral criterion of art and value everything for the sincerity and depth of its feeling? Or is there no really proper way to appreciate them, so that we simply go through certain histrionic motions and make-believe? If the ecumenism is indeed profound enough, the problem seems to solve itself, but only because we can and do enter into the spirit of many modes. This still does not help the earnest unbeliever and the nonbeliever, nor will it satisfy the committed believer.

What we ought to think of here is whether, in the end, the devotion to pure art, which has been idealized ever since the Renaissance (though not unfailingly) is the only way in which our "aesthetic instincts" should be realized. Should we return to that earlier circumstance where all art is the handmaiden of other pursuits? We do not need to wait for Marxists to prompt us to ask ourselves whether the only banner art may fly must read "art for art's sake."

We reach a further extreme from music such as that of the Christian liturgy the closer we approach to our own time. The "objectification" of the musical instrument is approached in Berlioz, Liszt, and Wagner, and then more emphatically in Debussy, Ravel, Richard Strauss, the Russian and other national schools, until it culminates in the earlier Stravinsky. Between the two extremes lies a "subjective" tradition which even now forms the musical center, even if it is no longer the mode in artistic practice. This tradition has been largely German, but prior to the nineteenth century it was international, in a European sense. Especially in the German context such music is subjective in the sense that it is mainly directed toward a kind of clarification or illumination of the soul. The "intimacy" so characteristic of most German musicial thought remains from Bach through Brahms, Mahler, and even Schoenberg, lending a quality of chamber music, even when large orchestras are employed.

We may thus distinguish three large traditions or orientations in music, and each determines a particular use of form. *Liturgical* music is directed toward the realization of God or some unseen value, the great *subjective* tradition is directed toward humanity, and the *objective* tradition looks toward the outer world, a world of things. ("Serious" composers, among our contemporaries, are still extending this objective grasp. On the other hand, "popular" music, as always, is largely oracular, lyric, expressive, subjective.) We may now extend our glance somewhat further at the last two of these orientations.

Music of the intimate and subjective stripe seems first of all intended for those who perform it or sing it. It, therefore, performs a function which was served earlier by the liturgy. Unlike this, however, it is a communion of subjects, listening persons, or of composer and respondent. It is an intensely personal rite and does not lend itself to use for the purposes of the theatre, which is closer to the third extreme. The Bach Courante (Chapter 16 §2(1)) has this personal character. Bach also deliberately undertook works more in the spirit of the Italian and French schools, but even here he imbued them with his own subjectivity. Handel, of course, significantly advanced the objective style, or what in our day we might call "show business," if this were said not to evaluate but only to characterize one side of him.

Bach and the German voice generally sing as the soul wishes it could sing, and in it we feel ourselves to be singing. No one suffers from such an illusion in hearing many works of the great Latin tradition, for this is theatre, object, tableau. And while these works undulate in and out of fashion, those of the German tradition have never lost their appeal even temporarily, despite the danger of being played to death. In them, the heart has felt its own beat. Of course, each of those two great traditions is subject to its own pathology and must not be judged by its failures. No partisan of the one can any longer desire the extinction of the other. (Schoenberg, however, speaking of himself and his colleagues Berg and Webern, remarked that either what they or what the French were writing was music: it could not be both!)

It is thoughts of this sort that must form the background of our assessment of the order inherent in the selections we have made from the German-Romantic repertoire. It is evident that music of the objective tradition is more hospitable to literary and theatrical influence and draws its cues for form from that source. More subjective music must draw upon abstract sources of organization, especially repetition or recurrence and inner development. It is, therefore, not surprising that Debussy professed to be weary of endless Germanic sonata reprises recurring like the cow's cud. He was, of course, a master of form in this sense, too, but he may have been at his best when he was creating a freer and more novel imaginative structure. Berlioz had already stuck this note early in the century. Except for deeply introspective personalities like Fauré or the versatile Saint-Saens, and a few others, French composers were more explicitly and often exclusively devoted to the "objective" world of opera or to that of the tone-poem. Examples are to be found in La Mer, The Afternoon of a Faun, La Peri, Daphnis and Chloe, and so on. Many other works in this spirit also appeared, became in fact the rule rather than the exception early in the century: Falla, El Amor Brujo, The Three-Cornered Hat; Rimsky-Korsakov, Scheherezade; Respighi, The Pines of Rome; Griffes, The White Peacock; above all, Stravinsky, Fire-Bird, Rite of Spring, L'histoire du Soldat, and many recent works.

We have presented several samples of the use of formal devices in the German tradition, but we must be careful not to identify these devices with that tradition. Debussy, as we have said, resorts to them as often as he follows a freer fancy. Our point is rather that music which elects to realize emotion itself, but in no form that the standard vocabulary identifies (recall the Schubert-C-Major-Symphony-emotion mentioned earlier), is rather compelled to order itself by "abstract" devices. When these devices are strongly tonal, as they were for some three consecutive centuries, a perfect medium is brought into being for a music of unique intimacy and subjectivity.

On the other hand, freer forms are open to the composer when the listener is preoccupied with an "object" — whether it is an opera plot or a girl with flaxen hair. The form, as it were, takes care of itself, and an appropriate form suggests itself for every such "object." We have leaned toward the subjective in our choice of examples, but only because the forms on the objective side are so limitless: each must be studied for itself alone. But the purely artistic devices of organization are still the same, unless the composer chooses to rely wholly on the direction and development inherent in connotation or content, in plot, in fact and myth, and to content himself with making the music the handmaiden to this master.

The use of form, then, is no mere causal fashion. Liturgy freely employs repetition in what may seem to the noncommunicant an excessive degree, simply because it is a useful thing, a *Heilsmittel*, a means to salvation, a way to concentrate thought and feeling on some transcendent objective. Instrumental or chamber music, including most of the great symphonies, employs form to induce, order, and clarify feelings, which for the most part are not classifiable "objectively" under familiar names (anger, love, hatred, desire) or identifiable as occurrences in familiar situations in which men pursue their favorite purposes: money, power, satisfaction, renown. A quite different kind of form is involved when the artwork serves neither a ritual nor a subjective purpose but simply stands "there" as an object to afford its own kind of satisfaction, such as entertainment, enchantment, amusement. The respondent becomes a voyeur, art becomes a spectator sport.

Our examples of the first type of music are drawn from liturgy but we could as well reach outside music for arts in which the same values are celebrated, for example, the dance, whenever it is entered into it as a kind of communion and not as a performance for spectators. The second, the subjective tradition is eminently typified in instrumental music of the eighteenth and nineteenth centuries, especially German but is in no sense confined to this. The third, the objective, reflects a greater preoccupation and fascination with a world of affairs and of things so that music itself becomes an auditory *object*.

The subjective and objective differ as poetry from prose, the *aria* from the *recitative*. Subjective music is eminently a part of ourselves. It is lived and lived through. Not so the other. We cannot become "objects": they can only belong *to* us, be *ours*. Whatever is so ob-jected to us is nothing *we* can in-form, on which we can impose forms: we follow it wherever *it* leads us, and it has its own form. Aleatory aesthetic objects are but the logical outcome of this development in the present. We do not now know where it will lead us and its trends and tendency may be determined by causes that are wholly nonaesthetic.

Although we may suppose that liberation from the constraints of self-imposed forms particularly those of repetition and recurrence moves in the direction of a freer, more "poetic" response, the result is inevitably the opposite, a movement that is essentially toward "prose." It is in prose that we learn about our world, tell ourselves about it, and in the end subject ourselves to it. Poetic forms on the other hand are ways in which we succeed in humanizing the world, and domesticating it to our purposes, asserting ourselves in it. Poetry, however "free" it is, cannot dispense with formalism, and indeed *is* form. Form is the poet's liberation from the constraints of prose.

All of this merely suggests two or three directions in which music may at times move. It appears to have been moving toward the third mode for more than century. The *arioso* mode has been recessive in opera throughout our century and has largely been replaced by the *recitative*. This has arisen either from a diminished confidence in the power of poetry or simply from what may, frankly, be a weakening of poetic powers. Whenever it is thought that art *must* be "relevant" and realistic, it simply moves farther toward prose, away from poetry.

The foregoing offers at least a clue to the decline of poetry for many decades as the dominant literary mode, although it has recently appeared to undergo a considerable revival. The nineteenth century was eminently the age of the novel as we see from the masterworks in the English, Slavic, Scandinavian, and other languages.

Our two literary examples are somewhat atypical of literature; they are in poetic form. But in poetry the several genera of the compositional order are highly noticeable and normal: repetition (in rhyme, rhythm, stanzaic form), closure (from the comparative brevity and concentration of poetic form), as well as development, whereas prose fiction in the novel largely denies itself the first two orders and makes the best and the most of the third. It has, of course, not only concentrated its effort on this order, but has brought it to a high degree of perfection.

The greatest loss sustained by the approach to art through prose is, of course, the dispensing with repetitive devices which are invariably effective in poetry. That that they may lead to surfeit and ennui only proves their immense power in uniting elements. Of course, the novel is the natural (or unnatural?) heir of the epic. But the shift to prose has entailed the virtual abandonment of the compositional forms in the purely verbal medium. In consequence, the prerequisites for order must be fulfilled almost entirely within the connotational dimension. Satisfying the imperious demand for what is thought to be "truth to nature" weakens if it does not eventually extinguish the poetic instinct. Prose is first of all the language of conceptual thought which, with the sole exception of mathematics (since speculative philosophy is extinct), has been placed wholly at the service of the comprehension of nature, in a fairly narrow sense of this phrase. For this the language of poetry is unsuited. We have, as Bacon says, "submitted our minds to things," and our submission is uttered in prose. One might suppose that we are too self-conscious for the *arioso* mode of expression, but it is not self-consciousness so much as being-in-the-world, other-consciousness, that prevents it. We tend to accept the myth that the world is "there," "in itself," "ready-made," and that knowledge consists in humbly conforming the mind to it.

The hope for a restoration of a more poetic interpretation of life can come only with a realization that the "ready-made" world is not only a myth but intellectually pernicious. Our world is the result of art and artifice — it is what is made of it. We either forget or never come to realize that it is by means of imagination and art that we fashion even theories, that it is by means of such artful constructs that we apprehend the world, possess it. And not only is the world of "objects" we were speaking of a few moments ago so grasped. Rather, all three, the world, the self, and God are constructions of art. Equally as pernicious as the ready-made world is the effort to exalt science by making art something less than knowledge. This is a misinterpretation of both art and science. The success of art is the increase of knowledge, particularly of ourselves.

NOTE

[1] Appropriating a phrase from John Stuart Mill's 1867 'Thoughts on Poetry and its Varieties', *Dissertations and Discussions*, Longmans, Green, Reader and Dyer, London, I, 71: "Eloquence is *heard*, poetry is *over*heard."

To Rest, To Rest

To rest, to rest, o weary members,
And press each drooping eyelid tight;
I am alone, the earth is fallen:
That I may see, let there be night!

O lead me upward, inward powers,
Where darkness glows: so I depart
From earthly pain, through night and dream
To cradle on a mother's heart!

Justinus Kerner

BIBLIOGRAPHY

Aristotle: 4th century, B. C., *Poetics*, translated by Ingram Bywater, 1967.

Aschenbrenner, K.: 1959, 90–108, *Journal of Aesthetics and Art Criticism*.

Aschenbrenner, K.: 1963, 149–151, *Journal of Aesthetics and Art Criticism*.

Aschenbrenner, K.: 1974, *The Concepts of Criticism*, D. Reidel, Dordrecht.

Aschenbrenner, K.: 1971, *The Concepts of Value*, D. Reidel, Dordrecht.

Beardsley, Monroe: 1958, *Aesthetics: Problems in the Philosophy of Criticism*, Harcourt, Brace, Jovanovich, New York.

Berkeley, George: 1914, *New Theory of Vision*, J. M. Dent and Sons, London.

Broad, C. D.: 1952, *Philosophy, The Journal of the Royal Institute of Philosophy* 27.

Browning, Robert: 1895, *The Complete Poetic and Dramatic Works*, Houghton, Mifflin and Co., The Riverside Press, Boston and New York.

de la Motte, Diether: 1968, *Musikalische Analyse*, Bärenreiter, Kassel.

Dickey, James: *Poems 1957–1967*, Collier Books, New York.

Ehrenzweig, Anton: *The Hidden Order of Art*, University of California Press, Berkeley and Los Angeles.

Eliot, T. S.: 1919, 'Hamlet and His Problems', *The Sacred Wood*, Knopf, New York.

Graduale Romanum, Missae Ordinarium: 1908, Romae, Typis Vaticanus, (pp. 1–54, 18 Masses).

Gwynn, Frederick L. *et al.*: 1954, *The Case for Poetry*, Prentice Hall, New York.

James, William: 1890, *Principles of Psychology*, Henry Holt, New York.

Kant, Immanuel: 1781, *Critique of Pure Reason*, tr. N. K. Smith, Macmillan, London.

Křenek, Ernst: 1940, *Studies in Counterpoint*, G. Schirmer, New York.

Kyriale, seu Ordinarium Missae: 1927, J. Fischer and Bro., New York.

Landwehr-Melnicki, Margaretha: 1955, *Das Einstimmige Kyrie des Lateinischen Mittelatters*, Gustav-Bosse Verlag.

Meyer, Leonard B.: 1959, 486–500, Vol. 2. *Journal of Aesthetics and Art Criticism*.

Mill, John Stuart: 1867, *Dissertations and Discussions*, Longmans, Green Reader and Dyer, London.

Nelson, Robert V.: 1948, *The Technique of Variation*, University of California Press.

Ogden, R. M.: 1938, *The Psychology of Art*, Scribner's, New York.

Pepper, Stephen C. 1938, *Principles of Art Appreciation*, Harcourt, Brace, New York.

Santayana, George: 1896, *The Sense of Beauty*, Scribner's, New York.

Schalz, Nicolaus: 1980, *Studien aur Komposition des Gloria*, Verlegt bei Hans Schneider, Tutzing.

Schildbach, Regensburg, Martin: 1967, *Das Einstimmige Agnus Dei und seine handschriftliche Überlieferung vom 10. bis zum 16. Jahrhundert*, Inaugural Dissertation der Universität zu Erlangen-Nürnberg.

Schoen, Max: 1940, *The Psychology of Music*, Ronald Press, New York.

Smith, J. A.: 1984, 'The Ancient Synagogue, the Early Church and Singing,' *Music and Letters*, p. 1ff.

Stephens, James, *et al.*: 1934, *Victorian and Later English Poetry*, (Thomas Hardy), American Book Company, New York.

Thannabaum, Peter Josef: 1962, *Das Einstimmige Sanctus der Römischen Messe in der handschriftlichen Überlieferung des 11. bis 16. Jahrhunderts*. Verlegt bei Walter Ricke, München.

Vernon, P. E.: 1934–1935, *British Journal of Psychology* 25.

Winters, Yvor: 1943, *The Anatomy of Nonsense*, New Directions, Norfolk, Conn.

Woodworth, Robert S.: 1946, *Experimental Psychology*, Henry Holt, New York.

Yeats, William Butler: 1962, *Selected Poems and Two Plays*, M. L. Rosenthal, ed., The Macmillan Company, New York.

INDEX OF NAMES

'Adoration of the Shepherds' (Giorgione) 135
Amiens Cathedral 129
'Apostles' (Dürer) 136
Aristotle: size of an aesthetic complex 25, 112
Aschenbrenner, John ix

Bach, C. P. E. 191
Bach, J. S. 30, 158, 161, 162, 191, 197ff. (Courante), 233, 234
Beethoven, L. van 30, 59, 154ff., 157, 161, 191, 202 (Sonata Op. 28), 210 (Concerto V, op. 73), 231
Berg, Alban 197, 235
Berkeley, George, *New Theory of Vision* 75
Berlioz, Hector 101, 181, 231
Boulez, Pierre 97
Brahms, Johannes 161, 194, 234
Broad, C. D., leap (saltus) from the body 77
Browning, Robert ('Abt Vogler'), ('The Confessional') 32, 112ff.
Bruckner, Anton 194

Cage, John 97
Chartres cathedral 129
Chopin, Frederic 99, 100, 191
Clementi, Muzio 191
Constable, John 132
Corot, Jean-Baptiste 132
Couperin, François 68
'Crucifixion' (Perugino) 135

Debussy, Claude 98
de La Motte, Diether 197, 199
de Pres, Joaquin 197
Diabelli, Antonio 161
Dickey, James ('The Shark's Parlor') 123
Duchamp, Marcel 67, 136
Dürer, Albrecht 17, 136
Durham Cathedral 129

Ehrenzweig, Anton 29, 34
Eliot, T. S. 69
Emerson, John: University of California, Berkeley, Library of ix
Emerson, Ralph Waldo 66

Falla, Manuel de 235
Fauré, Gabriel 194, 235

Fra Angelico 130
Fragonard, Jean-Honoré 132
Franck, Cesar 162

Gattamelata, equestrian statue (Donato Donatello) 128, 133
Giorgione da Castelfranco 95, 135
Gluck, Christoff W. 101
Griffes, Charles T. 235
Guggenheim Fellowship, award of ix

Handel, G. F. 234
Hardy, Thomas ('The Sacrilege') 115
Harnett, William 129
Haydn, Joseph 101
Helmholtz, H. L. F. von 154
Hesbert, Dom René J. 169
Hofmann, Hans 67
Homes, Oliver Wendell, the elder 66, 71
Horse of Selene, Elgin Marbles 128, 132

James, William 19, 154
Joyce, James 66

Kant, Immanuel 16, 73, 87
Kandinsky, V. V. 154
Kerner, Justinus 192ff
Kienholz, Edward 132
de Kooning: Lithograph 137
Krebs, Johann Ludwig: Fugue 27, 28
Krenek, Ernst; atonalism 60, 97

Leonardo da Vinci 87
Liszt, Ferenc 68, 181, 194
Locke, John 11
Lorrain, Claude le (Gellée) 132

Madeleine, the (Paris) 128
Mahler, Gustav 194, 197, 234
Margareta Theresa, Infanta (Velazquez) 129, 134
Master of the St. Lucy Legend 130
Mathieu, Georges 67
Mendelssohn, Felix 7, 46, 194
Meyer, Prof. Leonard B. 3
Michelangelo Buonarroti 72, 181
Mill, J. S. 237
Monteverdi, Claudio 100

Moore, Henry 133
Mörike, Eduard 194
Mozart, W. A. 13, 72, 91, 101, 191
Müller, Wilhelm 185–190

Nelson, Robert U. 161
Notre Dame de Paris 129
'Nude Descending a Staircase, No. 2' (Duchamp)
    131, 136

Ogden, Robert M. 32, 39, 47

Paestum, Temple of "Neptune" 132
Palestrina, Giovanno da 30
Parthenon (Athens) 132
Perugino, Pietro (Vannucci) 17, 130, 135
Pierce, Soli ix
Pius X, Pope 169
Pollock, Jackson 137
Pothier, Dom Joseph 169
Poussin, Nicolas 130

Raphael Sanzio 24, 129, 134
Ravel, Maurice 234
Read, Sir Herbert 137
Respighi, Ottorino 235
Rimsky-Korsakov, N. 235
Rothko, Mark 67
Rubens, Peter Paul 181
Rubin, Edgar 153

Sacré Coeur (Paris) 130
Saint-Saëns, Camille 194
Santayana, George 87

Schoen, Max 63
Schoenberg, Arnold 30, 161, 217ff., 234
'School of Athens' (Raphael) 130, 134
Schubert, Franz 104, 161, 162, 185ff., 196
Schumann, Robert 191
Shakespearean characters 42–44
Siena Cathedral 130
Solesmes, Monks of 169
Soulages, Pierre 67
'Stilt Race' (Marc Haeger) 136
Stablein, Bruno 169
Stockhausen, Karlheinz (Klavierstück III) 31,
    32, 97
Strauss, Richard 68, 94, 194, 196
Stravinsky, Igor 235
Suñol, Dom Gregorio 169

Tchaikovsky, Peter I. 196
Thomas of Celano 181
Trollope, Anthony 70
Twin Rocks (Oregon) 133

van Eyck, Jan 130
Velazquez, Diego Rodriguez 129, 134
Vernon, P. E. 153ff.

Wagner, Richard 101, 194, 195, 234
Watteau, Antoine 132
Webern, Anton von 235
Whistler, James Abbott M. 68
Wolf, Hugo 63, 191ff.

York Cathedral 129
Yeats, William Butler 131

INDEX OF SUBJECTS

Accommodation 18
Aesthetic complex: its elements 9
Agnus Dei 169, 170
Alberti bass 98, 200
Aleatory or chance creativeness 65
Algedonic sensation (pain), no aesthetic possibility 73
Anti-Form, form, *Urform* 5
Apparent distance, as a dimension of elements 36
Apparent temperature, as a dimension of elements 36
Ascending and descending motion of tones 58
Asymmetrical accommodation 129

Beauty, defined 87
Body localization, organo-centricity 76

C-C, and S-S order 17, 18, 19, 27
Cadence, its effect 52, 53
Causal and motivational interaction 42
Centralized figure 130
Closure, isolation, centralization in art 6, 93, 159
Characterization and description 36
Chinese and Scottish scales 39
Chord 31, 33
Chord of nature 55
Classic symmetry 128
Coherence in art ix, 7, 64
Coherence in music 153
Coherence in narrative art 112ff
Coherence in visual art 128
Color cone 40
Collocations 17
Compositional order of art 6, 89, 91
Conflict: its place in art 7, 18
Connotation; or expression 64ff., 71, 131
Consonance; dissonance 7, 52, 63
Content, only another set of relations in art 71
Context of relevance 19
Contextual differentiation, supreme importance for art elements 11ff.
Contextual effect in colors 47
Contextual interaction 29
Contextual relation of elements 45
Counterpoint 27, 29, 33

Credo 169, 170

Decoration, art as 71
Development in art 6, 92, 95, 161
Dies Irae 172
Dimensions of elements: their comparative relations 35ff., 83
Diminished seventh chord, its effect, its resolution 54, 55
Dominant seventh chord, its effect 53, 54

Electric shock, sensations 76
Elements and intervals 27ff.
Elements: its unique sense for art 9, 10
Emotion: invocation, evocation, provocation 103
Employment of artistic resources 91
Embodiment, in art; vehicle, in art 70
Enharmonic change 30
Envelopment 131, 132
Erotic sensations, no unique quality of 80, 81
Expression: "Instant Coherence" 64ff.
Extensity and intensity distinguished 84
Extensity, vocality 36

Feelings, emotions: classification 104
Figure and ground, emergence and recedence 10, 14, 18, 21, 22, 99, 159
Flanking symmetry 130
Focal and non-focal, as applied to elements 12
Formal appeal; elemental appeal 61, 96

Gestalt, importance of 13, 154
Gloria 164, 166, 169, 171
Golden Section 35
"Gravitational system": attraction of tones 57
Greek scales 39, 40

Hedonic potentiality of elements 84
"Hidden order of art" (v. Ehrenzweig) 29
Hue, brightness, saturation 36

Illusion of motion; illusion of rest 97
Imagination, revivability, necessary for art 76, 78
Intentional in art, the 66
Interpretation of form 110ff

Interval: the true structural unit 29
Intervals and blends 29
Identifying by illustrating difference of an
    element 11, 12
Intrinsic order of art 6, 30, 89ff.
Isolation, closure 128, 159

Javanese and Siamese scales 39
Justifying: its place in art 7

Kinaesthetic sensations 75
Kyrie 163, 164, 169

Limit of vision, indefinite; possibly eight
    98
Literary and dramatic applications 42
"Lower senses", not to be neglected 88

Magnitude, size, of figures 21ff
Mass, The Ordinary of the 163
Monotony, tolerable and intolerable 18, 98,
    200, 215
Multi-modalism, bimodalism 18, 19
Musical compared to visual complexes 24

Names: their effect on artworks 66

Objectification 87
Objective character, objects of art 80
Objective correlative 69
Objectivity or subjectivity of tendentive powers
    of elements 51
Octave, a unique cyclic phenomenon in music
    37
Olfactory sensations 77
Ordination, number, of elements 17
Organo-centricity 80
Organum 46
Overdominance, underdominance 23
Overtones, the series of partials 55

ris, map of 22, 133

Pythagorean tonal system 52
Perfection of vision, audition 7
Pervasive development to climax 130
Philosophical idealism 11
Pitch, intensity, timbre, duration 36, 37
Pitch series, origin of scales 38ff
Plagal cadence; Amen cadence 60
Plainsong 30
Polyptych 17
Predominance, Subdominance, Superdominance
    21, 22, 23, 24

Repetition, recurrence in art 6, 92, 97, 160

Sanctus 169
Savor and ingestion, sensations 76
Scalar system of relations 35
Semitone series 38
Seven Classes of relations 17ff
Smell prisms, odor squares 79
Soprano: usually dominates a complex 27
Steps and skips, in the gamut of pitches 38
Surfeit, absence in vision and audition 80
Surround; importance of in placement of
    sculpture 23, 93
Symmetry 7
Symmetrical accommodation 129
Symptom: its application to art 69
Synoptic vision and audition 13

Tactile or haptic sensation 75
Tendentive powers of elements 51ff
Thermal sensation 74
Tobacco addiction 78
Tonic trend; tonic tendence 57
Tritone, its effect 52, 58, 63
Truth in art: its limited place 9

Unorder, disorder in art 5

Vision and audition, preeminence of in art
    73